TELEVISION
AND THE
AFGHAN
CULTURE WARS

BROUGHT TO YOU BY
FOREIGNERS, WARLORDS,
AND ACTIVISTS

Wazhmah Osman

UNIVERSITY OF ILLINOIS PRESS
Urbana, Chicago, and Springfield

© 2020 by the Board of Trustees
of the University of Illinois
All rights reserved
1 2 3 4 5 C P 5 4 3 2 1
∞ This book is printed on acid-free paper.

Library of Congress Cataloging-in-Publication Data
Names: Osman, Wazhmah, 1974– author.
Title: Television and the Afghan culture wars: brought to you by
     foreigners, warlords, and activists / Wazhmah Osman.
Description: Urbana: University of Illinois Press, 2020. | Series: The
     geopolitics of information | Includes bibliographical references and
     index.
Identifiers: LCCN 2020038269 (print) | LCCN 2020038270 (ebook) |
     ISBN 9780252052439 (ebook) | ISBN 9780252043550 (cloth) | ISBN
     9780252085451 (paperback)
Subjects: LCSH: Television broadcasting—Social aspects—Afghanistan.
     | Television and politics—Afghanistan. | Television programs—
     Afghanistan—History—21st century. | Afghanistan—Social
     conditions—21st century—Press coverage.
Classification: LCC PN1992.3.A27 (ebook) | LCC PN1992.3.A27 086 2020
     (print) | DDC 791.45/658581047—dc23
LC record available at https://lccn.loc.gov/2020038269

Contents

Acknowledgments

WHILE MUCH HAS CHANGED across the research trajectory that informs this book, I am grateful that a few key people in my life remain constant. I thank my advisor and mentor Faye Ginsburg and committee member Bruce Grant who have continued to be there, providing me invaluable insights and feedback at every junction and crossroad of this book and academia more generally. Faye's rigorous scholarship, dedication to intensive fieldwork, extensive research, and activist spirit have guided my academic path throughout the world and infused every word I have written. Bruce's regional expertise in the former Soviet Caucasus extended my regional perspective and helped me to see Afghanistan in a broader cultural framework.

Other mentors and colleagues from the New York University community to whom I am indebted include Ella Shohat, Robert Stam, Deborah Kapchan, Charlton McIlwain, Radha Hegde, Arvind Rajagopal, Craig Calhoun, and Helga Tawil-Souri. I am especially thankful to Paula Chakravartty, Bilge Yesil, and Susan Murray who helped me think through and develop key concepts.

This book would not have been published without the incredible team at the University of Illinois Press who guided me through every stage of the process with professionalism and patience: the editors Danny Nasset and Jennifer Argo; the art designers and marketers Roberta J. Sparenberg, Kevin Roger Cunningham, Dustin Hubbart, and Hsin-Ya Liu; as well as the anonymous reviewers, copyeditor Julie Bush, indexer Anna Corrigan, proofreader Tess Rankin, and book coach Craig Willse. I thank the editors of the Geopolitics of Information series, Dan Schiller and Yuezhi Zhao, for supporting critical topics in global media studies with a focus on questions of political economy.

I especially thank the Afghanistan studies scholars who helped me navigate the contentious terrain of Afghan history and the Afghan present with academic rigor and nuance: Nancy Dupree, David Edwards, Vartan Gregorian, Hasan Kakar, Senzil Nawid, Timothy Nunan, Nazif Shahrani, and a special shout-out to Robert Crews, my coauthor of *Afghanistan: A Very Short Introduction* (Oxford University Press). Afghanistan studies and, by extension, this book has benefited from the work of the postcolonial, global media, and cultural studies powerhouses Lila Abu-Lughod, Timothy Mitchell, Charles Hirschkind, Saba Mahmood, Purnima Bose, Zeynep Gürsel, Matt Sienkiewicz, and Karin Wilkins.

I thank the following people and institutions for providing me with a much needed interdisciplinary space and resources to conduct fieldwork trips or workshop various parts of the book: Petra Goedde and Peter M. Logan at the Center for the Humanities at Temple University; James English and Chi-ming Yang at the Wolf Humanities Center; and Seteney Shami and Holly Danzeisen the Social Science Research Council, along with the International Dissertation Research and Transregional Research Fellowships. They join Karen Redrobe, Rahul Mukherjee, and Nicola M. Gentili at the Penn Cinema and Media Studies Program; Marwan M. Kraidy and Marina Krikorian at the Center for Advanced Research in Global Communication; Briar Smith and Monroe Price at the Center for Global Communication Studies; Ania Loomba and Suvir Kaul at the South Asia Center; Deborah Thomas and John Jackson at the Center for Experimental Ethnography; James Ryan and Greta Scharnweber at the Hagop Kevorkian Center for Near Eastern Studies; Cheryl Furjanic and Pegi Vail at the NYU Center for Media, Culture, and History; Ellen McLarney at the Duke Middle East Studies Center; Jude Browne and Veronique Mottier at the University of Cambridge Centre for Gender Studies; Bhavna Dave and Ruth Mandel at the SOAS Centre of Contemporary Central Asia and the Caucasus. Thank you all for your collegiality and generosity of spirit and for making me feel at home. Also, although none of the chapters in this book have been published in their entirety elsewhere, parts of some chapters have been presented at conferences, the institutions mentioned above, and in the following publications, which can be found in the References: Osman (2011, 2012/2013, 2014, 2018, 2019b). For all transliterations, I have followed the International Journal of Middle East Studies (IJMES) guidelines, the Middle Eastern Studies Association (MESA) standard.

To protect the many who aided me in Afghanistan, I cannot thank all the individuals and organizations who kindly opened their doors to me and generously shared resources and information. However, I can thank the following people for their fierce dedication to freedom of speech: Najiba Ayubi, Sanjar Sohail, Charmaine Anderson, Elise Jordan, Heidi Vogt, Nabila Alibhai, Danish Karokhel, Abdurahim Danesh, Masood Farivar, Ian MacWilliam, Sima Samar, Habiba Sarabi, Azizullah Ludin, Azam Dadfar, Dominic Medley, Elizabeth Mathias, Roya Sadat, Zahra Sadat, Rahimullah Samandar, Diana Saqeb, Royce Wiles, Paula Kantor, Reza Kateb, Omar Sharifi, Thomas Barfield, Margaret Mills, Renee Montagne, Mir Aziz Ahmad Fanoos, Abdul Mujeeb Khelwatgar, Wadan Farahi, Mohammad Zia Bumia, and Barry Salaam. I am grateful to the following Kabul-based organizations for fostering independent research and exchange in a war zone: the Kabul University Faculty of Journalism, Afghanistan Journalists' Federation, Afghanistan National Journalists Union, Afghan Independent Journalists Association, the US Embassy, the Afghanistan Research and Evaluation Unit, the American Institute of Afghanistan Studies, Internews/ NAI, the Press Office of the United Nations Assistance Mission in Afghanistan (UNAMA), the French Cultural Center, the BBC World Service and Media Action, the Asia Foundation, the Voice of America, the Turquoise Mountain Foundation, the Aga Khan Development Network, and the German Society for International Cooperation. I also nod to Razia Jan, Fauzia S. Assifi, and Tahira Homayun for letting me join them on their noble humanitarian work and travel to parts of Afghanistan I would not have otherwise experienced. I am lucky to have had the chance to meet and venture off the beaten path in and around Kabul with Asiyah, Serwat, Taran, Marzia, Homa, Aman, Frank, Marie, Nina, Mia, Jonathan, Salima, David, Halima, Mary, Penelope, Tom, and Sara.

My heartfelt thanks to the following people for their invaluable and fastidious research assistance: Morgan L. Bartz, Alexandra Budz, Natasha Cohen-Carroll, Sophia Hameed, Basir Bita, Ali Karimi, and Malek Shafi'i. I also want to thank the following people for their administrative and IT support: Danielle Martinez, Rob Velez, and Sammip Parikh.

Last but not least, I am grateful to my friends and family who showed up to mark the passing of time for occasions big and small: Shirly, Velina, Jen, Ray, Susanne, Sary, Tiff, Eva, Krissy, Tima, Hatim, Scott, Nadja, Tara, Jeannine, Munira, Emily, Vanessa, Emilie, Anna, Cassie, Kat, Katie, Fischer, Kasturi, Kartik, Naomi, Stephanie, Brooke, Sharon, Amy, Heather, Leslie, Nobuko, Sunita, Chris, Damien, Christina, Helena, Leila, Zohra, Sahar, Marjan, Seelai, Gazelle, Rachelle, Alice, Marco, Carlin, David, Nova, Kelly, Molly, Jenna, Beth, Ezra, Narges, Rowena, Durba, Manan, Kadji, Zeb, Sima, Zohar, Laimah, Candace, Mar, Fatima, Nathan, and Juno.

I am especially thankful to my roshan fikr (progressive) parents Mina and Abdullah. I dedicate this book to them and all the other Afghan reformers and activists, past and present, who have worked to build a better Afghanistan.

Introduction

ONE OF MY FONDEST MEMORIES as a child growing up in Kabul in the 1970s was gathering with my extended family to watch television at my grandparents' house. I was awed by the modern visions of Afghanistan that the state broadcasting station, Radio Television Afghanistan (RTA), projected to the Afghan public. As a city kid, I was dazzled seeing the incredibly rich diversity of traditional cultural practices of Afghan people in the countryside alongside urbanized women and men cheerfully working together in modern, technologically advanced settings and children attending modern schools. In news, cultural programs, and public service announcements, RTA showed the camel caravans of nomadic tribes, the latest fleet of the national airline Ariana, and everything in between, such as the traditional dance, attan, and the electrical light shows on the Kabul River on Friday nights. The urban scenes I was familiar with as they reflected my own family's life, with both of my parents working for the city of Kabul and me in the first grade. Little did I know that decades later, in an Afghanistan subsumed by both war and culture wars, the international development community via UN mandates would be deploying television for similar modernizing and "nation-building" purposes, and I would return as an expatriate to study its complex media worlds.

My work on this topic began with my interest in Western discourses of Afghan women as early as the mid-1990s, when the Taliban first rose to power in Afghanistan. With their extreme brand of Islam and draconian laws, the Taliban had effectively enforced extreme gender codes of marriage, education, and work on Afghan society. What was equally troubling for me was that post-9/11 Afghan people were stereotyped in the mainstream Western media and popular culture. In order to justify the American military assault on the Taliban and Afghanistan, all Afghan women became extreme victims of backward, misogynist Afghan men. Afghan culture was interpellated as static, unchanging, and bound by archaic, problematic traditions. Anyone who is familiar with Afghan history knows that the long struggle for women's rights and sexuality has been an ongoing battle between modernist state policies and the more restrictive and repressive interpretations of Islamic and tribal laws. I knew this history not only through my graduate training but also through experiential knowledge and stories passed on by my family. I witnessed my parents, aunts, and uncles engaging in progressive social movements through meetings, demonstrations, and protests.

The image of Afghan society in Western discourse as a hopeless landscape of powerless people at the mercy of ruthless and backward traditions stuck in another time is not only inaccurate but also disempowering. This dominant narrative erases the dynamic culture wars of the last century and present-day developments that are currently unfolding via an internationally supported media infrastructure in Afghanistan. Thus my goal with my book research became to redirect the global dialogue about Afghanistan to local Afghans themselves.

Based on over 100 interviews and wide-ranging fieldwork I conducted, this book examines the role of media in the development of the public sphere in Afghanistan, the cultural contestations that the media is inspiring, and the political economies that sustain it. Via production and reception studies as well as content analysis of the most popular genres on Afghan television, I assess the everyday influence of new media forms. I argue that despite operating in a dangerous arena—facing a range of constraints, threats, violence, and regimes of censorship—Afghan media producers are supported by the popularity of their work and provide a platform for local reform, activism, and indigenous modernities to challenge both local conservative groups and the international community that has Afghanistan in its sights.

In post-9/11 Afghanistan, debates about women's rights, democracy, modernity, and Islam are part of the fabric of local and international development efforts to "nation-build." The medium at the heart of the most public and politically charged of these debates, instigating often-violent cultural contestations and clashes, is television. My research into the current televisual mediascape in Afghanistan grew out of this initial interest in women's rights and local cultural contestations. However, I quickly learned that *quowm*, or ethnicity and race, plays an equally critical role in the current Afghan culture wars. While Afghans have always been sensitive about gender and ethnic sectarian issues, over forty years of successive wars and warlordism, including a divisive civil war in the wake of the Soviet withdrawal from Afghanistan, have made these issues highly politicized and volatile. In fact I soon learned that most international development "Calls for Projects," including in the media sector, have women's rights and national unity as two of their main goals.

Because gender, sexuality, and *quowm* have played and continue to play such a fundamental role in the mediation of Afghanistan to the world, I address these concerns here as critical background to this study. Additionally, because imperial projects of the past, namely during the Great Game and the Cold War, are ever-present in negotiating present-day relationships with the international development community and in the US-led international military campaigns that have Afghanistan as their focus, I highlight key historical moments. I simultaneously situate my own family's history and positionality within this complex array of factors, past and present, in the interplay between internal and external dynamics that make up the Afghan culture wars. Here I also elucidate the details of my methodology and issues of access, which were partially contingent on my family's position and standing within these broader social structures.

Television—more specifically the televisual representations of women and women's rights, along with other national and cultural signifiers such as ethnic, racial, and religious difference and the role of foreign powers—has instigated a series of escalating battles among Islamists, moderates, and others. Without a doubt, television is at the center of violence in Afghanistan—generating it and also being targeted by it. Yet at the same time, after decades of ethnic, racial, tribal, gender, and class violence, television is providing a semblance of justice, debate, and healing. I argue that the media in Afghanistan, particularly television, has the potential to underwrite democracy, national integration, and peace.

Saving "Afghan Women": Gender and the Global World Order

Since the events of 9/11 and the start of the War on Terror, Afghan women have come under the Western spotlight in popular culture and the academy, evident in the proliferation of media such as feature films, television programs, documentaries, books, and news reports that focus on their plight under repressive Islamic regimes. These media forms have been embraced by some scholars and

PHOTO 0.1. **Women and girls at a bazaar in Kabul buying chadors/headscarves.**

critiqued by others from a variety of disciplines (Abu-Lughod 2002; Hirschkind and Mahmood 2002; Maley 1996) concerned with the overwhelming portrayal of women as victims, without accounting for their actual or potential agency. Building on the work of these scholars, I have argued that by a complex process of "spectacling," Afghan women have become "Afghan Women"—a singular passive entity conforming to stereotypes of women under Islam that have gained new currency since 9/11 (Osman 2005).

Calling on an old but powerful lexicon of imagery from the era of colonialism, the saving of Afghan women was used in part as a justification to start a military assault on the Taliban specifically and on Afghanistan more generally. In line with the rhetoric of masculine protection (Young 2003), attacking the Taliban and Osama bin Laden without the pretext of saving Afghan women from their brethren would have been even less popular than it was, especially within intellectual and anti-war groups in the United States. One of the secret CIA reports that WikiLeaks published also revealed that the plight of Afghan women was used as a PR strategy by the Obama administration to persuade Western European countries to increase their troop contributions to the International Security Assistance Force and continue their involvement in the war (WikiLeaks 2010).[1] It is important to note that prior to 9/11, the iconography of Osama and Al Qaeda with the accompanying "smoke them out of their caves" rhetoric was virtually nonexistent. In fact, if you had asked most Americans, and even most Afghans, they would not have heard of Al Qaeda prior to this point.

The plight of Afghan women, with its foundations harkening back to earlier iconographies, was the most efficient route to first launching "Operation Anaconda," then "Operation Enduring Freedom," enabling all the subsequent bombings of an already war-ravaged country, thus beginning the War on Terror and the United States' longest war. Instead of giving Afghan women the podium from which to speak, as one would presume, this double-crossing discourse actually took what was left of Afghan women's agency in order to aggrandize the power of so-called expert individuals and organizations, both governmental and nongovernmental. So while "Afghan Women" as a body of imagery proliferated and circulated widely, this imagery made its subject matter a hollowed-out, empty signifier at best. Their silent overexposure actually made Afghan women a joke, a caricature that was mocked and ridiculed in satirical exposés in magazines and videos, in genres ranging from comedy to pornography (Mendrinos and Santopadre 2004).

While such discourses pertaining to gender in Afghanistan and other Islamic countries have been reverberating globally at unprecedented volume and on an unprecedented scale, little attention has been given to the cultural productions that constitute gender subjectivities in the daily lives of Afghans.

Beyond Critique: Constituting Subjectivity and Locating Agency

After writing on the question of Afghan women's portrayals in the West (Osman 2005), I knew that I had reached the limits of criticism as an effective tool to challenge problematic and inaccurate representations (Latour 2004). Instead of continuing to privilege a disconnected discourse, I realized it was time to do a feminist/postcolonial/subaltern intervention by going to the source and learning from local media practices, using an ethnographic approach that would allow me to see how gender was being shaped in an emerging Afghanistan media world. After all, in order to understand how local agents and actors within diverse groups use the media to assert their political claims, we have to observe the local cultural contestations that open up a space for collective action, social movements, or self-representation.

In general, Afghanistan has been neglected as a serious site of ethnographic research, with a few notable exceptions (Barfield 2010; Crews 2015; L. Dupree 1973; N. Dupree 1988, 2002; Gregorian [1969] 2014; M. Mills 1991; Shahrani 2018; Shahrani and Canfield 1984; N. Tapper 1991; Tapper and Tapper 1982). The media industry in particular has had almost no scholarly attention, apart from a few influential scholars (Edwards 1993, 1995, 2002; Skuse 2002; Skuse, Gillespie, and Power 2011).

I went in with many questions. How are charged issues such as gender/ sexuality, human rights, democracy, and religion contested, framed, and negotiated by local cultural producers? How do local Afghan institutions "talk back" to the global circulation of images of Afghan women? Why is television particularly catalytic in fueling public debates and dissent? In terms of gender, why is the tele-presence of women, as compared with their circulation in other mediums, particularly problematic to the religious sector?

Going into fieldwork, I was afraid that I was imposing my own gender lens. I was quickly surprised by how central a role gender and sexuality actually play in the culture wars. As we shall see, gender issues permeate this study because, culturally speaking, Afghans are very sensitive to expressions of gender and sexuality. However, I had to account for the complex "intersectionality" that shapes everyday life in Afghanistan as other cultural/national signifiers and socioeconomic factors—such as racial, ethnic, tribal, and religious affiliations along with class—were also central to the cultural contestations.

Race, Ethnicity, and Tribe within the Framework of the Nation-State

Quowm, or ethnicity/tribe, which also connotes race, permeates every aspect of Afghan society and every social engagement. Contrary to popular understanding, Afghanistan is a very multiethnic, multiracial, and multireligious society. While Afghans have always been sensitive to sectarian issues in their quest for equal rights, representation, and resources, the forty years of war have exacerbated ethnic/religious tensions. In the power vacuum left by the Soviet withdrawal from Afghanistan in 1988 and 1989, most of the Soviet-era mujahideen commanders and leaders vying for control and a place at the table for their ethnic groups took part in the ethnically divisive and violent civil war (1992–94). The line between protecting their own people, retaliation, and hate-motivated attacks and mass killings became blurry.

PHOTO 0.2. **Police officers at the Blue Mosque in Mazar-i Sharif.**

My own family's social standing and *quowm* were key factors to gaining access or being denied entry to my sites of study. In Afghanistan, a person's last name is virtually irrelevant for identification purposes; rather, one's ethnic/tribal names are what matter. In a society where kinship structures have been an integral part of the culture, genealogical information about the various tribes/ethnicities is passed down orally at a young age, though not always accurately. Thus most Afghans have an incredible aptitude for knowing by memory vast amounts of information related to their own and often other tribal/ethnic genealogies. They can immediately identify, locate, and map lengthy tribal/familial trees or roots of anyone.

Every *quowm* has a specific region or regions of the country that it presides over and is affiliated with. For example, the Uzbeks and Tajiks are from the north of Afghanistan, and their regions border Uzbekistan and Tajikistan, respectively. The Pashtuns are more spread out, affiliated with the south, Iran to the west, and the Northwest Frontier, which borders Pakistan.[2] The Hazaras are from central Afghanistan; their region known as Hazarajat encompasses about seven different provinces, the capital of which is the ancient and historic Buddhist city of Bamiyan. Large cities, such as Kabul, Mazar-i Sharif, Jalalabad, and Herat, tend to be multiethnic due to decades of migration and intermixing.

To a degree, *quowms* were semiautonomous and partially self-govern their areas of the country. The leaders of every *quowm* maintain sovereignty over their designated regions and protect their people from incursions from the central government as well as from other *quowms*. This has involved negotiating with other *quowms* as well as government mandates to institute national modernizing projects such as a national educational system. The government, in exchange for *quowms* not revolting, has compromised in allowing them to maintain to a degree their own traditional tribal practices, crafts, languages, and educational systems. In a tacit agreement, there existed a precarious equilibrium of peace, established over the years between various Afghan governments and different *quowms*, as well as among *quowms*, with occasional ruptures and violence. However, while this insularity and kinship-based order has been instrumental to protecting the incredible traditions, cultural practices, and wealth of knowledge of the different ethnic groups, it has also bred distrust, tension, and misunderstanding of one another. In the power vacuum that was left in the wake of the Soviet withdrawal from Afghanistan, this underlying xenophobia erupted into a violent civil war among the various ethnic groups.

Similar to the caste system in India, which is also based on birth and hereditary lineage, ethnic minorities in Afghanistan have been historically discriminated against.[3] However, other intersecting factors such as gender and socioeconomic standing and class play a role equal to if not more significant than *quowm* in Afghan society. For example, men and people who come from wealth or high-status families or sub-tribes tend to have more privileges and opportunities than women and people with less means, regardless of their ethnicity.

Reformers of previous generations and today see the *quowm* system as a relic of a problematic social order of the past. There is a growing sentiment among progressive-minded people from all *quowms* who share a nationalist and pluralistic vision of Afghanistan to curtail what is commonly referred to as *quowm baazi*, literally meaning "tribe games," or "playing the ethnic card" in the vernacular. More broadly, *quowm baazi* is defined as tribal parochialism, in particular the ways in which *quowm* is used in the political arena by elites to establish and set racist hierarchies that serve the interests of their own *quowm* but often only serve the personal interests of elites. A prime example of *quowm baazi* can be found in the heated, multiyear parliamentary debates over what identification information should be included on new electronic identity cards, or *tazkiras*, which the government planned to issue to all Afghan citizens as a way of curbing election fraud as well as for many other reasons related to statecraft. Ethnic-minded MPs wanted to include ethnicity as a category, while nationally minded MPs were in favor of only stating nationality. A compromise agreement to disclose both sets of information was reached and signed into law in 2018.

As a strategy, in order to de-emphasize the significance of *quowm* and avoid answering the *quowm* question, post-9/11 reformers began to give the name of the city closest to their hometown or village or simply their nationality, Afghan. However, as a result of years of war and ethnic violence inflicted by all groups on one another, despite such efforts by reformers, *quowm baazi* has become even more entrenched in the social order. Hence, stating to potential research contacts that I am a Kabuli, born and partially raised in the capital, which implies both a sense of multiethnic cosmopolitanism and a belief in the irrelevance of ethnic identity, was never enough or acceptable for sectarian-minded people. The questions would persist and become more direct in nature. I soon learned that for parochially oriented people and organizations, *quowm* markers are not optional but a requirement for entrance in their arenas. However, in most situations and social circles, I believe the questions related to my background were motived by nothing more than a universalist sense of human curiosity as a way to start a conversation and connect.

Although I am in agreement with the reformers, in the interest of transparency and reflexivity, and because it was central to my research, I am disclosing and discussing my family's ethnic background and how I negotiated that identity within the complicated social structures of Afghanistan. My family's ethnic makeup is mixed, mostly Pashtun but with a significant amount of Tajik, and to a lesser extent Hazara in my great-grandparental generation. Using Lila Abu-Lughod's term "halfie" (2006, 153) which she defines as being of mixed national or cultural identity due migration, overseas education, or parentage, would be only partially correct because my inquiries into my family's genealogy revealed many other ethnicities/races/nationalities that I was surprised to discover. It is difficult to scientifically ascertain the contradictory oral accounts various family members shared with me. What little DNA evidence exists in the region suggests that Pashtuns, Tajiks, and north and western Indian populations have genetic affinity and shared ancestry. More importantly, though, the first genetic study of Afghan ethnic groups reveals that all Afghans originate from a common ancestral population (Haber et al. 2012).

By virtue of being at the crossroads of Central and South Asia, Afghans—long before the current era of globalization—have had regular cultural exchange in the region through circuits of trade, travel, and war-related displacement. Thus, it is not unusual that most Afghans are of mixed race/ethnicity, which in Dari (a dialect of Persian) is termed *dou raga* or "two-veined." Yet due to racist notions of racial/ethnic purity that uphold hierarchal structures of power, being of mixed race is stigmatized, seen as a blemish to conceal, within all groups. This is changing to some extent as politicians such as Dr. Abdullah Abdullah, Afghanistan's second-in-command to President Ashraf Ghani, tried to use the fact that he is half Pashtun and half Tajik in his multiple campaigns for the presidency. Yet most people perceived him as Tajik because of his close ties to the Northern Alliance. Abdullah came in second place to Hamid Karzai in 2009 and Ashraf Ghani in 2014, both ethnic Pashtuns.

In fact, intermarriage between tribes is quite common in the major cities. By virtue of being from the diverse and multiethnic capital of Afghanistan, I have aunts and uncles from many ethnic groups. In order to gain entry to my sites of research—twenty-six television stations of the fifty television stations that currently broadcast actively and regularly and other media, governmental, and nongovernmental institutions, as well as people's homes—I had to emphasize one or another side of my family's ethnicity by mentioning well-known male relatives from a specific ethnic group. For example, my father's half brother Dr. Akram Osman, who is half Hazara, is a famous novelist, poet, and journalist in Afghanistan. Prior to the years of war, he taught literature at Kabul University and had his own very popular literary radio show on RTA, the national broadcasting station. He is well known and revered not only by the marginalized Hazara community but also among all Afghans because in his prose and commentary he advocated for a nationalist vision of Afghanistan, which was egalitarian and inclusive of all ethnic groups. That he is almost unanimously beloved and remembered also speaks to his talents and abilities as a writer and presenter to reach people across different segments and ethnic groups of Afghanistan. The fact that he is my uncle was indispensable to gaining access not just to Hazara stations but to almost every television station. Likewise, another of my uncles is the prominent mixed Tajik and Uzbek archeologist Dr. Chaibai Mustamandy. A prolific and well-respected scholar and archeologist in the 1960s and 1970s, Mustamandy discovered many of Afghanistan's most prized archeological sites and directed their excavations. As refugees in the United States, he and his wife, Mehria Rafiq Mustamandy, became staunch advocates for the preservation and return of Afghanistan's historical artifacts, many of which were looted and sold on the black market to major Western museums.

Another equally important aspect of my identity that helped me gain access to the Afghan media world is my immediate family's history. During the ten-year Soviet-Afghan War, my father, Dr. Abdullah Osman, a physician, was actively involved in helping different sectors of Afghan society in exile. During the Soviet invasion, the Soviet-backed government imprisoned my father, and my family fled Kabul to take refuge in neighboring Pakistan. While most of our extended family and other Afghans moved from the refugee camps of Pakistan to other countries, when my father was released after serving a year and a half as a prisoner of war he stayed in the camps to help with efforts to assist an estimated three million Afghan refugees of all *quowms*. He set up multiple free health clinics and medical training workshops. He along with my mother, Mina Osman, a teacher also established the first girls school in the refugee camps, Nahid-i Shahid (Nahid the Martyred) School, which my sisters and I attended.[4] With the help of the Inter-Aid Committee he also started the collective Union of Mujahid Doctors and became its director. He is well known and respected as a humanitarian and human rights advocate for all Afghans.

My family's diverse lineage and matrimonial ties, along with our pluralistic and multiethnic ethos and work, became crucial to opening doors for my research. For ethnically minded people and organizations, I was granted entry only once it was established that I had connections to their ethnic group. For the television stations and other organizations that were nationally oriented, ethnicity was a nonissue and therefore not a precursor for entry. Being Afghan American, having spent most of my life in the United States, further complicated how I was perceived and received. Depending on the context and situation, I would either highlight my Americanness or my Afghan-ness.

Why TV? Media Forms in a Cross-Regional Context

Often, at conferences and other venues, I am asked, Why study television? Why not study the Afghan film industry, Afghan radio, or the internet or print-based media in Afghanistan? They all seem valuable media to study. I am also frequently reminded that in the Iranian Green Movement and the Arab Spring, social media and the internet played a determining role in energizing and uniting the public into massive social movements (Sreberny and Khiabany 2010). Yet in Afghanistan, due to the slow development of broadband internet infrastructure, the high cost of high-speed mobile technologies, and high illiteracy, television and radio are the dominant mediums. During my fieldwork, depending on where I was in the country and what year it was, I could watch anywhere from thirty to a hundred television channels for free. Currently, out of this large

PHOTO 0.3. Since 9/11, this mountain, which is part of the historic Asamayi mountain range in Kabul, has been colloquially called Television Mountain, renamed due to all the telecommunication towers that have been raised on its peak. Its original name is in reference to the Hindu and Zoroastrian goddess Asa/Asha, who is believed to be present on the hilltop, merging the ghosts of today's communication technology with the spirits of the past. Photo credit: Adam Levin, Center for Global Communication Studies.

selection of channels, only about fifty stations broadcast actively and regularly. The rest are intermittent in their broadcasting.[5] Yet by global comparison this is still a remarkably large number of television channels for a population to have free access to.[6] In fact the historic Asamayi Mountain has had so many telecommunication towers raised on its peak that it is now colloquially called Television Mountain. Internationally too, Television Mountain has become emblematic of post-9/11 development in Afghanistan.

Since one of the main goals of this book is to redirect the global dialogue about Afghanistan to local Afghans themselves, television became a natural choice of study to answer my thesis questions: How do modern Afghans conceptualize and measure signifiers of cultural progress and regression outside of the developmental models? What do terms like *conservative* or *progressive* mean in contemporary Afghanistan? How are diverse belief systems, sensibilities, and understandings of themselves constituted and expressed on a daily basis? How are charged issues such as gender and sexuality, human rights, democracy, and religion contested, framed, and negotiated by local cultural producers?

As I have argued elsewhere (Osman 2014a), technological determinism and the fetishism of digital and new media have precluded more nuanced understandings of social activism in the region and beyond. By focusing exclusively on the transformative or liberating aspects of new media, such studies erase the socioeconomic and political digital disparities that exist between and within nations. While social media played a pivotal role in the Arab Spring and Green Movements, this is not the case everywhere. In Afghanistan and many of the former Soviet republics, internet diffusion is low due to issues of state surveillance and barriers to access. Television is still the dominant media form in many parts of the world and therefore one of the best means to study national politics, popular movements, and social activism across the Middle East, the Caucasus, and South and Central Asia (see Abu-Lughod 2004; Kraidy and Khalil 2009; Mandel 2002; Mankekar 1999; Oren 2004; Rajagopal 2001; and Rollberg 2014).

In order to understand how local agents and actors within diverse groups use the media to assert their political claims, we have to observe the on-the-ground cultural contestations that open up a space for collective action, social movements, and self-representation. Early and contemporary media scholars have been exploring the potential and problems of communication technologies in establishing the conditions for democracy in large-scale societies (Dewey 1927; Lippmann 1925; McLuhan 1962; Schudson 1999). The role of media in the formation of identity and subjectivity, both in the individual and collective sense, has been a central concern of media theorists. An integral part of this research is scholarship on the formation of publics, counterpublics, and split publics (Calhoun 1992; Dornfeld 1998; Rajagopal 2001; Robbins 1993).

Television has become the medium that is both a mirror and an amplifier of Afghanistan, enabling Afghans to see themselves and speak to their own images and projections. Because television is broadcast nationally and simultaneously, viewed together within large household structures, and relatively accessible and popular, it is an important nationwide institution in Afghanistan—perhaps the medium that best provides a sense of Afghanistan as an "imagined community" (Anderson 2006)—as well as a site of social contestation. For example, the battles over censoring women's bodies are carried out only in the context of terrestrial television. This is due to the fact that the owners of terrestrial television stations, constrained by technology, are obliged to heed government regulations regarding what is acceptable to broadcast in order to maintain or secure a limited frequency band. Paradoxically, pornography and pornographic imagery is readily available and accessible on satellite television. In addition, such content is also downloadable on cell phones even in remote provinces and available for sale in the form of cheap videodiscs behind the counter in every media kiosk in shopping bazaars.

Thus, television is a national barometer of the state of the nation, its heartbeat and pulse, the venue that is inciting and inspiring the most cultural contestations. It is the only medium in Afghanistan that reaches the masses and enables large-scale dialogue, even though that dialogue sometimes takes violent forms as well. It also has the subversive and counter-hegemonic potential to help support broad reform and change. The larger question as to whether television is elevating debate and creating a public sphere or refeudalizing the country by inciting sensationalism and polarizing public opinion is central to this book.

Although it is slowly gaining traction, digital media access and usage is still limited in Eurasia and the Central Asian republics compared with the rest of Asia. Within the region that is considered to be one of the least internet-connected in the world, Afghanistan and Tajikistan rank in the bottom. According to the 2020 Internet World Stats, Afghanistan measures at a mere 18 percent internet penetration.[7] According to my research, usage is limited primarily to urban elites and some university students for two main reasons: high illiteracy rates and the relatively slow development of broadband and cable infrastructure. Some 28 percent of the Afghan population is literate, with a gender breakdown of 43 percent of men and 12 percent of women (UNDP 2009). These high illiteracy rates are in part due to over forty years of constant war. Most people have had their education interrupted repeatedly or have been denied an education entirely. Due to the rise of extremism and Islamism, education and literacy have been particularly difficult for Afghan girls and women to attain.

Thus, print media and the internet are accessible only to a select portion of the population who can read. Additionally, while newspapers and magazines are very affordable, the infrastructure for a widely accessible digital environment is far from reality. While broadband cable infrastructure is slowly being extended to non-elite neighborhoods, most people have access only to dial-up Wi-Fi internet that is offered by Chinese companies through satellite. Yet gaining access to even this unreliable and slow internet form is difficult due to the barrier of its high cost, which averages anywhere between a quarter to half of an

PHOTO 0.4. A Fortec Star Digital System Antenna on the roof of the village khan's house in a village in Andkhoy on the border with Turkmenistan.

average person's monthly salary. College students do have access to the internet through Kabul University and other large provincial universities; however, due to high demand and poor funding, the service is intermittent. Mobile phones are one of the few digital technologies that have become prevalent, but data plans are similarly costly, so people are limited in their use of mobile devices. Ultimately, internet with decent speed is available only to wealthy businesses and organizations that can tap into high-speed internet through satellite or cable infrastructure.

By contrast, the broadcast media of television and radio have grown exponentially and reach large segments of the population in the region. It is important to note that this is not the case with all television forms but only with broadcast or terrestrial television, because the signal can be picked up for free with indoor and outdoor antennas so long as a person owns a television. In other words, satellite and cable television, like digital media, are exclusive and accessible to certain segments of society that can afford them. Due to their high cost, I would estimate that less than a quarter of urban populations have access to satellite and cable. In rural areas even fewer people have access to paid television platforms.[8]

In Afghanistan, owning a television set means having access to over four dozen active television stations for free. Of course, the chronic nature of electricity problems makes television viewing difficult. Unless one owns a large generator, which international or transnational organizations and some government offices can afford, regular and consistent electricity is not available to most households and businesses during the day. In fact, some weeks there were complete electric blackouts for as long as three or four days in Kabul. People have kerosene lamps, gas stove ranges, and candles on hand for such times. However, in Kabul and other major cities, electricity was more constant and regular in the evenings.

Yet despite the poor infrastructure, Afghans I met all over Afghanistan were quite inventive, tapping into sources of electricity and watching TV. Peaceworks, a project of the US Institute of Peace, estimates that close to 89 percent of those living in urban areas of Afghanistan own a television and watch broadcast television on average four hours a day. In rural areas, 26 percent own a television, making it the second most common form of media after radio (Fraenkel, Shoemaker, and Himelfarb 2010). Chinese imported television sets that run on car batteries are relatively inexpensive. They also can be easily bought secondhand or rented. Additionally, the government and the private sector have increased television ownership by providing loans to Afghans who would not be able to afford them otherwise.

Even in little villages in remote parts of Afghanistan I found people watching television. For example, in a small village on the outskirts of the historic Buddhist city of Bamiyan, families were watching television using solar power they had salvaged from a defunct international NGO. In another small village outside of the capital Maymana, in the Faryab Province, the local villagers had created their own makeshift hydroelectric dam on a nearby river; though the contraption looked very precarious, it managed to generate electricity to over a dozen homes.

For these reasons having to do with poverty and lack of electricity, radio tends to dominate in rural areas, although most households have a television set. Across the nation, wind-up radio sets are cheaper and therefore more accessible to most Afghans. In most regions, radio signals are transmitted locally and not nationally. In this respect radio plays an important role in serving niche/ethnic groups, remote regions, and local communities.

Additionally, due to the less expensive cost of laying the infrastructure of radio transmission technologies, radio was the dominant medium in Afghanistan long before Radio Television Afghanistan launched television broadcasting. However, due to the propagandistic use of radio by the Soviet-backed regimes of the 1980s and by the Taliban regime, state radio lost much of its popularity and credibility. During these media blackouts, in the void of information and news, the BBC World Service Dari and Pashto stepped in to regain the trust of people with their consistent programming and reporting (Skuse 2002). The BBC has built and continues to build an extensive network of FM shortwave relay stations throughout Afghanistan. Currently the BBC World Service operates almost two dozen relay stations that are fed programming through satellite transmission, making radio broadcasting a reality and in many ways an equally powerful medium in Afghanistan.

Terrestrial television viewing happens mainly in the context of extended family groupings. Most families cannot afford to own more than one television set, so the American model of families with multiple television sets and personal mobile devices watching different programs individually in different rooms is not a reality for most Afghan households. Often, extended families gather to watch television programs together on one television set that is owned either communally or by one family. When I was growing up, my middle-class Afghan family did not own a television set; like many others, we would gather with the rest of the extended family at my grandparents' house to watch the nightly programs. In these ways the conditions for television ownership and viewing have not changed much from the first wave of television in Afghanistan.

Due to the precarious present-day situation in Afghanistan, in the evenings the majority of people stay indoors and consume media at home. While men, and especially young single men, will watch television in cafés, *chai khanas* (tea houses), restaurants, ice-cream shops, and other public places, women generally do not watch television in public places. Although they are not forced to stay indoors, as they were during the Taliban regime, women still are captive audiences because they are affected disproportionately by the violence and instability of public life in present-day Afghanistan. In this respect, terrestrial television is also an egalitarian and democratizing medium that enables women's engagement with the public sphere.

Additionally, the technology's electro-visual mass appeal, sensory integration, simultaneity of exposure, and broadcasting potential, which imbue it with an illusory sense of communal live-ness, have always made television a source of social power and cultural imaginings, both dystopic and utopic. As television scholars have theorized, television has the eerie ability of conjuring face-to-face community gatherings but with the power of reaching large-scale audiences (McCarthy 2010; McLuhan 1962, 1989; Ong 1982; Parks 2005; Williams [1974] 2003).

Thus, in a country where the vast majority of the population is illiterate and access to computers and the internet is limited, it is not surprising that television has become an especially powerful form. No wonder then that the hopes and fears about the future of Afghanistan, on the part of TV executives, government officials, religious leaders, and international governmental and nongovernmental consultants, are being funneled into the medium. The popularity of television and its intrinsic qualities also are recognized by elites interested in Afghanistan. They are well aware of television's power, especially in a country like Afghanistan, and have come to the same conclusions about the medium's inherent possibilities. Television also has the potential of reaching people across Afghanistan's harsh mountainous terrain and impasses, uniting the country and perhaps creating the conditions for peace.

Method

Television and the Afghan Culture Wars draws on a wide-ranging ethnographic study I conducted from 2008 to 2014 of television in Afghanistan, analyzing the programming itself while also looking "outside the box" at the complex social relations, cultural and religious frameworks, power structures, and financial streams that make Afghan television so distinctive and controversial. My research is the first in-depth ethnography of the Afghan mediascape.

Since leaving the region in 1984, I have made many trips to Afghanistan as a journalist, filmmaker, NGO humanitarian volunteer, activist, and academic. One of my most significant trips to the Afghanistan-Pakistan region took place in January 1999. During the height of the Taliban regime, I was sent by the US-based Feminist Majority Foundation to secretly film the violence of the Taliban against women. The footage that I shot launched the foundation's "Stop Gender Apartheid" campaign video. In the summer of 2004, I returned to Afghanistan to produce the critically acclaimed documentary feature *Postcards from Tora Bora* (2007) with filmmaker Kelly Dolak.[9] Finishing the film in 2007 led to my most serendipitous trip, which was in the summer of 2008. *Postcards from Tora Bora* was selected by the Kassel Documentary Film and Video Festival as part of its special program Second Take: Gender and Society in Cinema. This was a transnational film festival that traveled to different destinations across Europe and Asia. The *Postcards'* film crew was invited to attend the Kabul screening that was billed as "the first post-conflict film festival in Afghanistan."[10] It was during this trip that I had the privilege of meeting key figures in the Afghan media world and discovered the exciting public discourse that they have generated. These are surprisingly cosmopolitan circuits and networks of local and transnational media in Afghanistan. The contacts I made include fellow filmmakers and directors, television and cinema celebrities, and journalists and reporters, as well as other media makers and producers.

These earlier trips, along with my media production experience and my multiethnic background, laid the groundwork for my academic research trips. I conducted a total of eighteen months of fieldwork in Afghanistan and in the region. With the support of the Social Science Research Council's International Dissertation Research Fellowship I returned for a full consecutive year, from 2009 to 2010. In 2014 I was awarded a SSRC Transregional Inter-Asian Postdoctoral Fellowship, which enabled me to return again to the region to update my research in Afghanistan and expand it to Tajikistan, Pakistan, India, and Turkey. In total I have made four post-9/11 trips to Afghanistan, adding to my prior trips to the region for other types of work and to maintain cultural ties and connections.

My methods are largely ethnographic, drawing on studies that have inspired my own, including the work of Lila Abu-Lughod (2004); Faye Ginsburg (1998, 1999); Ginsburg, Abu-Lughod, and Brian Larkin (2002); Purnima Mankekar (1999); and Arvind Rajagopal (2001), among others. My book is primarily based on different types of ethnographic observation including participant observation and interviews in Afghanistan's televisual "media world." I conducted a total of 109, ranging in length between half an hour to three hours, interviews during my fieldwork trips in Afghanistan and to a lesser extent in the neighboring countries of Tajikistan and Pakistan, as well as in India. The majority of the interviews were formally structured and conducted in my primary language of Dari while some were in Pashto, the two official languages of Afghanistan.[11] Most of my face-to-face interviews were conducted in 2009-10 because it was my longest consecutive stay in Afghanistan since leaving my family home in Kabul as a child.[12]

While my research started as an ethnography of local and transnational television production in Afghanistan, given the absence of serious media scholarship on Afghanistan, I also had to engage with the reception of the media. In the absence of technologies that assess viewership, the interviews I conducted became crucial for gauging the popularity of programming—specifically, what audiences across different demographics value about television programs and if they see a reflection of the issues that are important to their daily lives.[13] On the production side, I interviewed high-level and low-level television employees, including television station owners at twenty-six of Afghanistan's fifty actively broadcasting television stations, to assess their own meaning-making processes. Additionally, I analyzed the political economy supporting their work by interviewing international consultants, embassy officials, and media producers and distributors in order to understand their motivations and goals for funding, marketing, and circulating their own cultural products as well as supporting "local" coproductions in Afghanistan. Thus, I carried out over 100 formal interviews with media producers and government officials as well as with a cross section of Afghans ranging from those living in slums to presidential candidates and religious leaders.[14] My interviews with audiences and prominent figures, both in their homes and in their offices, are also important for distinguishing between the way these issues are discussed publicly and privately.

While I visited and conducted research in almost all of the provinces and major cities of Afghanistan, I was primarily based in the capital of Kabul because most media production and development projects are located there. Likewise, although the majority of the television viewers I interviewed are from Kabuli households, I have also included data from other major cities such as Jalalabad, Pul-i Alam, Bamiyan, Andkhoy, Herat, Mazar-i Sharif, Khost, Maymana, Logar, Sorubi, Istalif, Kunduz, Faizabad, Asadabad, and Panjshir, among others.

The Kabuli television viewers in this study represent a cross section of Afghan society from a wide range of neighborhoods. To the north of the Kabul River are the wealthy neighborhoods of Wazir Akbar Khan and Shar-i Now that cater predominantly to international consultants and the old elites of Kabul. The north also includes the nouveau riche neighborhoods of Khair Khana, Sherpur, and Quallah Fatullah as well as the middle-class neighborhoods of Karte 3, Karte 4, Pul-i Sorkh and the Macroyans. On the south side of the Kabul River are the lower-income neighborhoods that encompass the historic Old City, including the cultural district of Kharabad. To the west are Kabul University Town and Dasht-i Barchi and to the east are Bagrami and the new neighborhood Golden City, among others. In addition to these recognized and demarcated neighborhoods, my analysis of reception in chapter 6 also includes data from households located in the ever-rising slums of Kabul. Officially known as "informal settlements," these houses are built higher and higher into the surrounding mountains of the city. The inhabitants of the "informal settlements" who currently do not pay taxes and do not own deeds to their homes are slowly coming under the purview of the government via new initiatives that aim to grant property rights and official recognition to them.

Synopsis of Chapters

In the current culture wars, for human rights and media rights activists as well as for other reformers and conservatives, the past is essential to the authentication and legitimizing of what constitutes a "true" Afghan culture and what is marked as "foreign." With this in mind, in chapter 1, "Legitimizing Modernization: Indigenous Modernities, Foreign Incursions, and Their Backlashes," I provide a brief history of the last century's reform and modernity projects by highlighting a few key moments and the repercussions of them. For reasons of transparency, I also situate my own family's standing and role within these complex social worlds and political movements. Using these case studies as examples, here I also distinguish between what I posit as the development gaze and the imperial gaze categories. I demonstrate how many of the interventions initiated by the British, Russians/Soviets, and Americans, from the colonial era through the Cold War, were designed with an imperial gaze that benefited those nations at the expense of Afghans.

In chapter 2, "Imperialism, Globalization, and Development: Overlaps and Disjunctures," I delve deeper into the dynamics of foreign involvement in order to assess its impact on the contemporary moment. Here I analyze development projects on a case-by-case basis to reveal a more complex and contradictory picture. The post-9/11 international development interventions in Afghanistan have yielded imperialistic and problematic projects but also some positive ones. Whereas the imperialistic projects are top-down, shortsighted, and duplicitous and consider only the interests of the sponsoring country, the beneficial development projects are well intentioned, well researched, collaborative, participatory, financially equitable, and ground-up.

Chapter 3, "Afghan Television Production: A Distinctive Political Economy," offers a roadmap of the various types of economies that shape the Afghan television industry and give it such a distinctive profile, along with a layout of the key political players—all with their own ethnic and foreign affiliations—who underpin it. I analyze the Afghan television stations I studied and categorize them into three groups: national, sectarian, and niche. The most commercially successful private stations such as Tolo TV, Ariana Television Network, and 1TV downplay their ethnic origins entirely. Here I also demonstrate how media laws, spaces for public protest, and other infrastructural conditions have fostered a vibrant media environment.

Chapter 4, "Producers and Production: The Development Gaze and the Imperial Gaze," begins by tracing relevant literature pertaining to television studies. I show how television has been imagined as a problem in the Western academic tradition and contrast that with how television has been conceptualized in non-Western nations. Using both of these discourses as a framework, I compare and contrast them with the case in Afghanistan. Building on Lila Abu-Lughod's concept of "development realism," I differentiate the category of the "development gaze" from its more problematic other half, the "imperial gaze." I argue that although both the development and imperial gazes are premised on the rhetoric of development, the key difference is that there is an inherent duplicity built into the imperial gaze.

Chapter 5, "Reaching Vulnerable and Dangerous Populations: Women and the Pashtuns," is a continuation of the previous chapter. Given the recent history of gender violence, civil war, and ethnic tension, two main targets of the Afghan and international development gaze are women in need of "uplift" or "saving" and ethnic Pashtuns, who by their association with the Taliban are considered a risk to the security of the nation. These two groups are also the objects of the imperial gaze of the past and present. In fact, many television Calls for Projects specifically focus on these groups. The differing ways in which they are interpellated by television programs, sometimes with dangerous consequences, also illuminate the differences between the development and imperial gazes.

Chapter 6, "Reception and Audiences: The Demands and Desires of Afghan People," explores the overlaps and disjunctures between what producers and other industry people imagine audiences want and need versus what they actually do and do not respond to. Building on my interviews with a wide spectrum of Afghan audiences, I show in what ways television is and is not meeting its potential of delivering to and representing the public at large as well as different ethnic groups and women. My research suggests that after experiencing over four decades of warfare and trauma, Afghan audiences have very high expectations of media and journalism in general, and television in particular. These audiences want television to bring justice and retribution to local and international warlords who have been sowing the seeds of war, gender violence, and sectarian strife for decades. With public service announcements, the news, and political satire, media makers uncover, investigate, and expose corruption, abuses of power, and violence by local and international warlords and government officials.

However, I show that the antidote to war and its atrocities is equal parts reflection and distraction/entertainment. With dramatic serials and reality television programs, Afghan media programmers are providing the avid and large viewership of these programs glimpses into the diverse lifestyles, cultures, and televisual representations of gender and sexual practices of people from around the world. This opens up space crucial for private and public discussion around sensitive cultural issues of national importance. This chapter demonstrates that

Afghan peoples' need for a higher spiritual order, justice, and entertainment are not mutually exclusive.

In the conclusion, "The Future of Afghan Media, the Future of Afghanistan," I recap the media needs and expectations of a traumatized Afghan public who has experienced over four decades of war. My conclusion is that Afghan media producers are delivering and meeting those high demands. Without a doubt the combined power of public space and broadcast media is a very effective social tool for collective action in Afghanistan. Yet there is a huge cost to this emergence and quick expansion of a public sphere. High-level media personnel and wealthy media owners who are often prominent public figures, such as politicians, warlords and drug lords, religious leaders, or businessmen, hire bodyguards and live behind gated fortress-mansions, while low-level television personalities and reporters are subjected to threats, physical attacks, and death for providing people with programming they want to watch. If violence against media makers continues to increase without any real consequences, it does not bode well for the future of Afghanistan. Currently, self-censorship is becoming more and more prevalent among media makers.

In addition to the dangers of domestic regimes of violence and censorship, here I also elucidate the problems with foreign intervention, namely military violence, election manipulation, and extraction of natural resources. I demonstrate that the imperial project with its imperial gaze is alive and well in Afghanistan.

Finally, with the attrition of international development aid, which is the foundation of Afghanistan's artificially inflated and robust media sector, media venues are closing; this further limits the potential of television in Afghanistan. The saving grace for Afghanistan is that the model of media development being implemented there is multilateral; resources and funding are dispersed from the international donor community, thus making it more akin to the public interest model. That is, there is a direct correlation between the amount and diversity of international resources that are being funneled into the Afghan media sector and the number and diversity of television outlets and programs made available there. The fact that Afghanistan is not unilaterally dependent on US aid is precisely why Afghanistan has not yet fallen down the slippery slope of commercialization, and its media world remains vibrant and viable, albeit fragile. For these reasons—increasing violence against media makers and attrition in international development aid in favor of military expenditures—the future of media and therefore the future of Afghanistan are uncertain. As the only counterbalance to the government, warlords, and foreign interests in Afghanistan, the media is the only hope for providing a semblance of justice, debate, and healing.

CHAPTER 1

Legitimizing Modernization

Indigenous Modernities, Foreign Incursions, and Their Backlashes

Western history has had an overriding importance—for good or ill—in the making of the modern world. The history of modern Western thought, for example, can be (and is) written on its own, but not so the history of contemporary Arab thought. One opposition between the West and the non-West (and so a mode of connection between them) is constructed historically by these asymmetrical desires and indifferences.

—Talal Asad, *Genealogies of Religion: Discipline and Reasons of Power in Christianity and Islam*

The bitter truth about our present is our subjection, our inability to be subjects in our own right. And yet, it is because we want to be modern that our desire to be independent and creative is transposed on to our past. It is superfluous to call this an imagined past, because pasts are always imagined.

—Partha Chatterjee, "Our Modernity"

The history of the "modernizing" world is often written as one of failed imitation of the West—failures of secular democracy, failures of nationalism, failures of enlightened modernity, failures due to the pull of tradition, travesties of modernity. But in recent years, a number of theorists of the postcolonial have been thinking more creatively about the encounter between West and East. They have pursued the analytical implications of the insight that modernity is a construct and an organizing trope, especially for the national developmentalist successors of colonial regimes. They have also suggested that translation, hybridization, and even dislocation might be more useful metaphors than imitation, assimilation (forced or attempted), or rejection for grasping what happened in the colonial encounter.

—Lila Abu-Lughod, *Remaking Women: Feminism and Modernity in the Middle East*

IN ORDER TO HAVE A HOLISTIC understanding of the present-day situation of Afghanistan, at least a preliminary understanding of Afghan history is necessary not only for contextualization purposes but also because the past is particularly present in today's Afghanistan. In a present plagued with constant reminders of war and its aftermath and fallout, such as lawlessness, corruption, violence, and the rise of conservatism, the past becomes a source of pride and hope, a reminder of a time of peace, moderation, and progress. Afghans enact their attachments to different historical periods daily to support their progressive and reformist ideas and make rights-based claims. In the current culture wars—for human rights and media rights activists as well as for other progressives and conservatives—the past is essential to the authentication and legitimizing of what constitutes a "true" Afghan culture.

This is because since the creation of the nation there has been a long history of foreign manipulation, control, and invasions, which has made Afghans extremely suspicious of foreign influence or involvement. During British colonial rule of the region, the British tried to build railroad tracks to stretch their empire. Fearing foreign invasion and influence, Afghans in tribal areas repeatedly destroyed their "iron horse." As a result, whereas India and Pakistan have intricate national railroad systems, Afghanistan did not have any to speak of until this last decade. (There are now two railway lines.)[1] But Afghans are equally dubious of national projects, which they deem transgressions against their local independence and autonomy. In the same manner, today the Taliban and other religio-tribal groups destroy the foreign-funded telecommunication satellite towers that transmit and broadcast signals for wireless telephones, radios, and televisions (Killid Group 2016).

Due to the many incursions and invasions from the West and Soviet north, Afghans are suspect of foreign interventions. The pejorative Persian word *gharbzadegi*, a term first coined by Iranian intellectuals, literally translates to being hit or struck by the West but is commonly translated as "Westoxification," referring to the negative influence of Western culture and values.

Mindful of this, media makers know they must demonstrate that their agendas, platforms, and programs are deeply rooted within Afghan culture and history. As agents of change on the forefront of the culture wars, television producers also try to buttress their work from government, tribal, and religious censors not only by appealing to their present-day popular support but also by calling on *mahaly* or "indigenous" modernity movements of the past.[2] Therefore in this chapter I highlight a few key historical movements of reform and modernity in Afghanistan, along with the backlash against them.

Of course, Afghan history is just as contentious as the Afghan culture wars; this is as true among Afghans themselves as it is between Afghans and non-Afghans. In fact a significant part of the media culture wars is over the interpretation of Afghan history. Here I offer one history of the last century organized around the theme of modernizing moments, drawing from academic research as well as from my lived experiences and oral traditions.

As postcolonial scholars from a variety of disciplines have shown, the history of the Global South and East has always been written as one of failure and Othering by the Global North and West (Abrahamian 2008; Abu-Lughod 1998; Asad 1993; Chatterjee 1997; Fahmy 2009; T. Mitchell 1991, 2002a, 2002b). Afghanistan is no exception. In order to justify Western colonial and neocolonial rule and violence, the vast majority of Afghanistan studies scholars conform to a view of Afghan history that is a narrative of failure and despotism. This ideologically problematic narrative presents Afghanistan as a static culture and Afghan people as bound by problematic, anti-modern, archaic traditions and tribalism. In popular culture and academia, the people are represented as fierce, militant, isolationist, and inherently against the forces of cultural exchange and international globalizing forces.

In *Afghan Modern: The History of a Global Nation* (2015), historian Robert Crews offers a refreshingly alternative view, one that focuses on historical change and global interconnections, and explains the insidiousness of this prevailing racist image: "The most enduring image of Afghanistan evokes a desolate, inward-looking, and isolated place. Numerous twentieth-century writers mythologized this 'hermit kingdom' over and over, claiming that its ostensibly primitive inhabitants have remained immobilized in time and space in a morass. . . . Ancient tribes reign supreme, undergirded by patriarchy and xenophobic religious authority. Ethnic chauvinism trumps ideas. And loyalty goes to the highest bidder. A French ethnologist sketched out most of this forbidding picture already in the late nineteenth century when he wrote, 'The Afghans do not have a history, because anarchy has none'" (3). Today in development circles and in international relations and political science terminology, Afghanistan is frequently described as a "failed," "broken," "fragmented," or "collapsed" nation (Ghani and Lockhart 2008; B. Rubin 2002; Coburn and Larson 2014), terms that have replaced the earlier classifications of "late state formation," "the rentier state," and "third world despotism" (B. Rubin 2002).

The pervasive colonial and neocolonial rhetoric of "failure" is frequently used as a teleological framework to prejudge Afghanistan and its people as dehumanizing caricatures. Modernity and democracy, with their indicators of human rights, economic/class parity, and social mobility, have been wielded to applaud the progress of the Global West and North and condemn the failures of the Global East and South. Modernity and its counterpart, progress, have become the ultimate litmus tests to judge countries and their leaders. Through the lens of modernization theory, progress is the variable factor on the linear path to modernity. The theory assumes that Western nations have achieved modernity and progressed in terms of providing rights for their subaltern populations such as women and religious and ethnic/racial minorities. Based on these already biased assumptions, "third world" nations are scrutinized to determine the degree of their progress or lack thereof. Questions are asked as to how much, how little, how fast, or how slow they have progressed. Western experts substantiate their deductive and inductive claims—such as the claim that third world nations rank poorly in comparison with first world nations—via theories and methods of measurement that abstract, generalize, and interchange MENASA[3] (Middle East, North Africa, and South Asia) countries without crucial in-depth analysis. Theories of the "rentier state," "third world despotism," and "game theory" may have useful applications in some contexts, but in the case of Afghanistan, they have been applied in ways that are simplistic and problematic.

Whether modernity and democracy have actually advanced or improved the lives of human beings has been explored in depth by poststructuralist, postcolonial, and feminist scholars. Such scholars situate colonialism, imperialism, and slavery as central to the projects of modernity and democracy. Michel Foucault analyzed the institutions of the modern state and how they constructed and normalized an individual's sense of self and sexuality by disciplining the body (Foucault 1988). Partha Chatterjee and other subaltern studies scholars have shown the duplicity of Western enlightenment theory, especially democracy, when applied by the British Empire to India (Chatterjee 1997). In addition to the institutions of the prison and hospital, the family was structured and normalized to perpetuate the status quo. Likewise, as Lila Abu-Lughod (2005) and Timothy Mitchell (1991) have demonstrated in the case of Egypt, the state's endorsements of the nuclear family, heterosexual marriage, and individualism extended its reach into the domestic and private spheres and weakened the power of traditional communal structures and ties. As they have effectively argued, the "premodern" society, lacking organized mechanisms of surveillance, policing, identification, and other modern apparatuses, can be a freer and more empowering society for subaltern people. While I agree with these apt criticisms of the apparent virtues of modernity and democracy and that some traditional practices are worthy of further exploration and preservation, my intent here is not to add to them, as I have done elsewhere. For the purposes of this book, I am taking modernity and democracy at face value and analyzing them on their own terms because, for better or worse, they have been used as an organizing trope and system of ordering and ranking countries and civilizations.

Social Movements, Indigenous Modernities, and Transcultural Hybridity

The dominant "failed state" paradigm thereby erases not only historical moments of achievements, such as periods of democratization and modernization, but also the fundamental agency, creativity, and intellect of the Afghan people. With this in mind, I have provided in this chapter a condensed history of the last century's reform and modernity projects by highlighting a few of the key movements and their repercussions. Here I rely on and build upon the work of a small but notable group of Afghanistan studies scholars (Adamec 1974, 2005; Crews 2015; Crews and Osman, forthcoming; L. Dupree 1973; N. Dupree 1984, 1988; Gregorian [1969] 2013; Nawid 2000; Shahrani and Canfield 1984) who have defied this trend in the Western academy by producing nuanced work. We situate our work within the broader fields of postcolonial studies, cultural studies, performance studies, and revisionist history and use approaches that demonstrate the complexity of cross-national and cross-cultural encounters. This approach goes beyond the dominant framework of failed imitation of the West and acquiescence to Western culture and values (forced or consensual), that is, the homogenization thesis. It also goes beyond complete rejection and resistance to all things Western. By taking into account factors such as alliances and divisions between hegemonic/democratic, elite/non-elite, and urban/rural vectors between countries, these scholars have demonstrated the inherent complexity and cultural hybridity of global phenomena (Kraidy 2005; García Canclini 1995; Appadurai 1996b). Even in cases of imperialism and subjugation of a weaker entity by a stronger one, these scholars have shown how cross-cultural and cross-national encounters are discursive processes that result in a degree of exchange and mixing that leave their imprint on both sides. Robert Crews explains, "It was as subjects of empire that residents of places such as Kabul and Kandahar came into contact with cosmopolitan court cultures in Isfahan, Delhi, Agra, Samarkand, and elsewhere. These imperial contexts proved fertile ground for state-building projects" (2015, 6). However, Crews continues that these empires also left their negative mark on Afghan history: "It was in this setting that the opponents of these Afghan political movements [for independence] began to circulate narratives about the supposedly 'wild,' 'unruly,' and 'warlike' Afghan, an idea that subsequent observers would take up and apply to very different contexts, even in the face of considerable evidence to the contrary" (6).

In best-case scenarios, global encounters can be mutually constitutive. Arjun Appadurai refers to this process as "indigenization," which is also the word that the Afghan reformers I spoke to use but in a different way. Afghan reformers use the Dari and Pashto word *mahaly*, meaning "of the people and land," to describe and defend their modernization projects that they believe have roots in Afghan culture and history. Appadurai argues that "the homogenization argument subspeciates into either an argument about Americanization or an argument about commoditization, and very often the two arguments are closely linked. What these arguments fail to consider is that at least as rapidly as forces from various metropolises are brought into new societies, they tend to become indigenized" (1996a, 32). However, Appadurai does not discuss that the reverse is also true, that weaker states affect stronger ones.[4]

Here it is also important to raise Marwan Kraidy's warning. Kraidy explains in his book *Hybridity, or the Cultural Logic of Globalization* that while hybridization is "a productive theoretical orientation" compared with its predecessors, it must be invoked critically, what he calls "critical transculturalism," since if applied without taking hegemony, power, and inequality into account, it can be used to strengthen the position of globalizationists: "Hybridity entails that traces of other cultures exist in every culture, thus offering foreign media and marketers transcultural wedges for forging affective links between their commodities and local communities . . . and hides its inherent contradictions as it mystifies globalization's material effects" (2005, 148). In other words, even though the cultural hybridity and homogenization theses challenge globalization theory, both have been subsequently used to justify globalization and hide the negative consequences and asymmetrical aspects of global encounters. For example, John Tomlinson argues that cultural diversity is not always worth defending and that in some cases homogenization or the influence and transmittance of Western values is a good thing, especially if it is replacing dangerous anti–human rights traditions (2002). This is similar to Ithiel de Sola Pool's claim that "the Americanization of the world so often commented on and often deplored might be better described as the discovery of what world cultural tastes actually are" (1979, 145). While these claims in support of human rights and the universal appeal of Western ideas, lifestyles, and products might sound innocuous and even agreeable, it is important to think through their underlying assumptions. Arguments in support of the Westernization of the world are embedded in dubious neoliberal "free market" logic and Western-centric assumptions that all Western values are inherently positive and that the West is the forebear of human rights and democracy.

Challenging Westernization- and homogenization-friendly arguments requires a deep dive into local cultural contestations and social movements. Only by paying close attention to how global encounters unfold on the ground and intersect with local cultures and history can we complicate the false binaries between Eastern religiosity/traditionalism versus Western modernity/secularism, which fuel simplistic and inaccurate discourses of Eastern despotism and failure against Western progress, development, and humanitarian/human rights interventions (Asad 1993, 2003; Chatterjee 1997; Göle and Ammann 2006; Mahmood 2005; Hirschkind and Mahmood 2002; T. Mitchell 2002a, 2002b; Wilkins 2010). For example, contrary to the stratified belief that the US government has been the bearer of democracy and human rights in MENASA countries, the postcolonial scholar Timothy Mitchell explains in his article "McJihad: Islam in the US Global Order" that American financial and military support for the ultra-religious Afghan and Pakistani groups was neither random nor coincidental. "When other governments moved closer to the United States—Egypt under Anwar Sadat in the 1970s, Pakistan under Zia ul-Haq in the 1980s—their political rhetoric and modes of legitimation became avowedly more Islamic" (2002a, 1).[5] Likewise during the Soviet invasion and occupation of Afghanistan, the CIA clandestinely funded some of the most conservative elements of the Afghan population. As many journalists and scholars have reported, the Bush administration, in conjunction with the US oil company UNOCAL, also actively wined and dined the Taliban regime at the start of their ascent to power in an attempt to negotiate building a $2 billion pipeline that would run through and tap into Afghanistan's vast oil reserves (Cloud 2006; Hirschkind and Mahmood 2002; T. Mitchell 2002a; Rashid 2001). These are the types of critical nuance that are often missing from the hegemonic American discourse and that I will direct readers' attention to in this chapter.

Early Culture Wars: Key Historical Moments

Instead of starting from the premise of these false mythologies, binaries, and tropes that present Afghans as anomalous prehistoric creatures outside of modern time and space, the revisionist postcolonial scholars I mentioned in the last section treat Afghans as just as creative and global as any other group of people. In the same vein, in our forthcoming book *Afghanistan: A Very Short Introduction*, Robert Crews and I aim to redress and rectify the dominant interpretation:

PHOTO 1.1. Darul Aman Palace, Kabul, built in the 1920s, stands in ruins. The palace is situated in what was supposed to be the new capital city of Darulaman, which King Amanullah initiated as part of his vast modernizing projects.

"Rather than view Afghanistan as a benighted land frozen in time, this book tells the story of the dramatic changes of the last five centuries that have transformed the lives of Afghans and how Afghans have transformed the forces around them too. We link Afghanistan to societies and cultures in South and Central Asia, the Middle East, and across the globe. Afghanistan is a product of modern globalizing forces. Like so many countries, Afghanistan today reflects the imprint of empires, nationalism, capitalism, communism, Islamism, global drugs trade, and so forth" (n.p.). This historical chapter aims to highlight a few of these sociopolitical movements and ruptures, with a focus on recurrent moments of experimentation with modernity. I will also highlight the impact of foreign interventions and the gap between the rhetoric of foreign governments and their actual policies. The key historical moments start chronologically from the early twentieth-century progressive movement of King Amanullah and his struggle to end British imperial interference and rule and proceed to its repercussions, the liberalization programs of King Zahir and Prime Minister Daoud Khan in the 1960s and 1970s, and the Soviet occupation of the 1980s, finally ending in the present day. In this chapter I also introduce my categories of the "development gaze" and the "imperial gaze" as a way of distinguishing between those Afghans and foreigners who genuinely strived for the betterment of Afghanistan and those who did not. I further explicate these concepts in chapters 2 and 5.

Amanullah and Soraya, the Modernizers

During his tenure, King Amanullah and his entourage, known as the Young Afghans (modeled after the Young Turks), implemented many modernist ventures such as building roads, railways, and telegraph lines and funding archaeological excavations, museums, and newspapers. Yet historically he is remembered for his gender/sexuality reforms, which rallied his opponents and brought his downfall.

In 1924, the Mangal tribe led by local mullahs (religious leaders) from the Khost region of Afghanistan started an uprising against Amanullah Khan. They were incensed by Amanullah's new laws and policies that placed issues concerning women's lives under the jurisdiction of the state and not the village elders. With his Family Code of 1921, which required registry of marriages, Amanullah attempted to curtail polygamy, regulate marriage age and dowry, and curb unjust marital practices such as forced marriages and spousal abandonment/neglect. Also during his tenure, Queen Soraya, along with Amanullah's sisters, spearheaded the enrollment of an estimated 5,000 girls in primary schools.[6] According to British officers stationed there at the time, "This legislation has already been used effectively as propaganda by mullahs in southern Afghanistan who during the 1924 Khost Rebellion went about the tribal areas brandishing in one hand the Quran and in the other the Nizamnamah [constitution], inviting true Muslims to choose between them" (Poullada 1973, 85).

Known as the Khost Rebellion by Western academics and as the Jung-i Mullah Lang (War of the Lame Mullah) by Afghans, the fighting lasted for almost one year, until Amanullah Khan was forced to revoke some of his laws and modify others. For example, education for women was no longer mandatory and was limited to girls between the ages of six and eleven. Though Amanullah Khan had successfully defeated the British in the Third Anglo-Afghan War in 1919, also known as the War of Independence, his popular support could not save him from the next conservative blow five years later in 1929, which was also led by outraged mullahs.

Thus began and briefly ended one of Afghanistan's first experiments with modernity, state media, and women's rights. Orientalist scholars and some Afghan scholars generally attribute the failure to the overall ignorance of the majority of the Afghan population. A British general who was stationed in Afghanistan during this time wrote, "Amanullah's flamboyant personality and his attempt to modernize so backward a country . . . made it inevitable that the foreign press should take an unusual amount of interest in the Revolt" (Mac-Munn 1977, 175). Scholars well versed in the language, culture, and history of Afghanistan tend to explain the events of the era with greater nuance and complexity. Historian Vartan Gregorian writes, "Whereas their [the government's] Pan-Islamic and nationalistic teachings and clamor for complete independence of Afghanistan appealed to the masses and most political and religious leaders, their modernist views, however, in the absence of a cohesive social force, lacked similar support" (1967, 367). Notice how Gregorian does not automatically attribute the rebellions against Amanullah and his modernist reforms to the "backward" nature of Afghans but to more complex phenomena. Nor does he entirely dismiss them as a failure.

Prior to the rebellions and revolts, which ultimately deposed his government, Amanullah Khan and his father-in-law, Mahmud Tarzi, known as the "father of Afghan media," along with the Young Afghans, launched a series of newspapers such as *Siraj al-Akhbar* (The torch of the news), *Bidar* (Awake), *Shams al-Nahar* (Bright day), and *Irshad-i Niswan* (The guide for women).[7] They all addressed the role and contribution of women in a modern society. The ranks of these Afghan intellectual reformers and journalists consisted of both men and women. The newspapers also clamored for nationalism and modernity by highlighting the achievements of Japan and Turkey. They were fanning the sparks of a new kind of secular pan-Islamism and pan-Asianism, one that was grounded in modernity, thereby reclaiming modernity as a non-Western venture. Simultaneously, the modernist reformers stirred anti-colonial sentiment toward the British and Russian colonizers. In this latter case, their rhetoric briefly overlapped with the traditional base. Yet overall, Amanullah's new initiatives and policies, which were encapsulated in the new constitution and reiterated in the newspapers, brought the modernist reformers into direct confrontation with the religious establishment and the tribal leaders. According to Gregorian, "The importance of the new penal code lay in the fact that it represented a major attempt to increase the power of the secular authority at the expense of the religious establishment" ([1969] 2013, 250).

The general consensus surrounding these and similar historical moments leads us toward the classic dichotomous struggle between the agents of secular modernity and the agents of regressive and repressive religion. While there is certainly some truth in this oppositional binary, by critically rereading history and revisiting the archive, I questioned how the events of these time periods have too neatly fallen into a simplistic binary, that of the classic dysfunctional tribal society in conflict with its modernizing elements (Osman 2005). Besides the "backward" masses who were apparently misled by fanatical clerics and the elitist modernist reformers, British colonial agents who were threatened by the rise of nationalism on its Indian border from neighboring Afghanistan played a key role in instigating the Islamist revolts against the nationalist and secular government. The impact of this intervening factor on the culture wars and events of that time period is rarely taken into account in official histories but often discussed in oral traditions and popular culture.

However, there is limited but notable scholarship that does reveal British interference and subterfuge in the affairs of Amanullah's government (Emadi 2005; Gregorian [1969] 2013; Nawid 2000; Sims-Williams 1980). For example, the archivist Ursula Sims-Williams in her article "The Afghan Newspaper *Siraj al-Akhbar*" presents several key pieces of evidence of imperial British duplicity that aimed to thwart Amanullah's nation-building projects. In 1919, the British viceroy wrote this panicked telegram to the British secretary of state in regard to the nationalist fervor of the newspaper *Siraj al-Akhbar* and the addition of Indian nationalists to the paper's staff: "Notwithstanding Amir's promise, the paper after slight improvement continued dangerously anti-British. Barkatullah seditionist acted as editor during deputation of Turkish Editor Mahmud Tarzi with German Mission. Mahendra Pratab contributed signed article. Last May tone so objectionable that we arranged for quiet interception of copies sent by post specially exempting those addresses to Amir's Agents so as to avoid publicity" (1980, 120). The British were clearly threatened by the prospects of a modern Afghanistan since it bred nationalism in bordering British India. An independent nation was also less accessible in terms of economic exploitation.

Furthermore, even though as part of their "civilizing mission" agents of the British Empire were actively promoting women's liberation and modernity throughout their colonies, they were simultaneously undermining those same principles. Feminist scholar Leila Ahmed calls this duplicitous sort of feminist invocation and activity "colonial feminism" (1992, 244). Her work has revealed many instances of how in colonized Egypt British viceroys and lords used women's rights merely as a rhetorical device to further their colonial domination. Examples of colonial feminism in its original context as well as in its new neocolonial or neoimperial forms are plentiful in Afghanistan too. For example, the Afghan scholar Hafizullah Emadi has shown how British agents

PHOTO 1.2. The exterior of the main Radio Television Afghanistan (RTA) building located in the Wazir Akbar Khan neighborhood of Kabul, which was built in the 1960s by Prime Minister Daoud Khan.

spread anti-Amanullah fervor within the religious sector by disseminating pictures of his wife, Queen Soraya, in European clothes from her tour of Europe. Thus riling the religious Mojaddedi clan and driving them to declare a fatwa (decree) and jihad (holy war) against Amanullah Khan for being un-Islamic (2005, 33). This in turn instigated other conservative tribes, first the Shinwaris and then the Kalakanis, to fight Amanullah Khan, leading to his disposition. Thus any analysis of the "failures" of Amanullah's modernist reforms must take into consideration the role of British imperial agents in throwing a wrench into the internal affairs of Afghanistan.

Finally, as Robert Crews reminds us, a rereading of this era requires an understanding that the deposition of Amanullah in 1929 did not entirely end all reforms, as scholars often state. Certainly the British and Islamist opposition slowed the pace of change. However, in the 1930s and 1940s some of the progressive steps initiated by Amanullah's government in the areas of education and media were restarted. By the 1950s, the Afghan government began to seek and welcome international development aid. International development staff from the United States, the USSR, and Europe landed in droves in Afghanistan and initiated many aid projects, ranging from large-scale affordable housing and transportation to new farming methods, mining, industrialization, and many others. Thus, social mobility and state capacity and presence increased.

The Public Works Programs of the 1960s and 1970s

The next wave of modernist revisions was launched in 1964 with the ratification of an equal rights amendment to the constitution or quanun-i issaasi of Afghanistan. The amendment stated that all Afghans, "without discrimination or preference, have equal rights and obligations before the law" and "women have the right to dignity, compulsory education, and freedom to work" (N. Dupree 1984, 309). Shortly thereafter, Prime Minister Daoud Khan ended obligatory veiling and purdah (the separation of men and women). During Zahir Shah and Daoud Khan's tenure, primary education for the first time became compulsory for all children in Afghanistan. As for higher education, men and women were encouraged with stipends to continue their education, and the University of Kabul was tuition-free. According to my interviews, in order to support students who completed high school to attend college, the government offered a stipend of 300 afghanis every two months. As one woman explained, "At the time that was a decent amount of money to buy school supplies and dress properly. The stipend was much appreciated by all students but especially needed by poor village kids not familiar with city styles" (Osman 2005, 67).

In an effort to boost the educated class and foster cultural exchange, the government also formed educational alliances with many countries to offer promising Afghan students the opportunity to study abroad. In fact, every valedictorian in every high school in Kabul was offered a scholarship to study abroad. While today competition for Fulbrights to American colleges and other foreign scholarships is extremely fierce, for a variety of reasons people were reluctant to take scholarships at this time. However, a number of my family members accepted foreign scholarships. Some of my uncles, who were Pashtun, Tajik, Hazara, and Uzbek, accepted scholarships to American, Iranian, and French universities, while others were sent to the former Soviet Union to study or for military training. Though contentious, the government's scholarship programs encouraged women to apply as well. My mother, Mina Osman, and her sister Dr. Tahira Homayun were among the women who went abroad for college in the early 1970s, to France and the United States respectively. These were broad-based programs that reached across ethnic and class lines, although city students definitely had significant advantages over students from the provinces. Some prominent Afghan Americans who were recipients of such scholarships in the 1950s through the 1970s include President Dr. Ashraf Ghani; Dr. M. Ishaq Nadiri, professor and economic adviser to former president Karzai; author and columnist Tamim Ansary; professor Dr. M. Nazif Shahrani; and US ambassador Zalmay Khalilzad.

My parents were a manifestation of Zahir Shah and Daoud Khan's modernization projects as well as Amanullah Khan and Mahmud Tarzi's earlier projects. For young people aspiring to reach the middle class, the state offered social mobility through access to education, travel, and jobs, with the condition of being open to and accepting of its progressive secular worldview over tribal or religious ties. Ever since I can remember, I knew we were a *roshan fikr* family. *Roshan fikr* literally translates as "enlightened thinking," but the connotation is open-minded, progressive, and secular. Whereas my grandparents on both sides had arranged marriages, my parents met at Kabul University. And while my father's father had multiple wives, my father's generation frowned upon polygamy. When my parents married, they chose to go against tradition and not live with my grandparents. Instead, my parents moved to a subsidized apartment building in a new part of Kabul called Shar-i Now, or New City, designed to encourage nuclear families, which could more easily be put under the purview of the state. The state also subsidized my parents' education, and upon graduation my father began working at Kabul University Hospital as a doctor and my mother became a French teacher at Lycee Malalai, a K–12 public girls school that I attended. My parents embodied the state's vision of ideal citizens. By working in the service of the state and not for kin or tribal/religious networks, they were also benefactors of the state. Another Afghan American who also came of age during this time period in Kabul, Dr. Ahmad Ansari, of no relation to Tamim Ansary, tells a similar story of his happy childhood in his memoir, Tragedy and Triumph: An Afghan Immigrant's Journey to America (2020). Of Tajik, Pashtun, and Kashmiri ancestry, Ansari writes,

> During the 1960s, Kabul, not a very modern city by western standards, still offered relative 'modernity' compared to the rest of the country. As a constitutional monarchy, the then King and his administration created a moderate Islamic country based on the concept of non-alliance, freedom of religion, and relative freedom of speech. A country the size of France, it had about 14 million habitants then. . . . The majority were Muslims; however, about two million Hindus and Sikhs lived there, who had the same rights as any other Afghans and were free to practice their faiths freely. We

also had a very small Jewish community with a synagogue not too far from where we lived (2020, 8).

The Afghan American author Tamim Ansary, who is of mixed Hazara-Pashtun ancestry, tells a very similar story in his award-winning memoir, *West of Kabul, East of New York: An Afghan American Story*, of how his family achieved social and economic mobility by abandoning their provincial kinship ties, moving to Kabul, going abroad for higher education, and returning to work in the service of the state.

Likewise, the late academic husband-and-wife team Louis and Nancy Dupree, who lived in Afghanistan for many years, recalled how it was impossible to walk into either a governmental or a private office without seeing women working in both administrative and civil servant areas. In fact, during this time four women were elected to the Parliament. By these accounts it seems that the residents of cities were ready to accept the entrance of women in the public sphere (Osman 2005, 533).[8]

Simultaneously, in the late 1960s and 1970s, the state sponsored the establishment of many media institutions and training facilities in the mass communication technologies of radio, television, and cinema. During this time the state broadcasting station Radio Kabul, which was launched by Amanullah Khan in 1925, began to broadcast television and became Radio Television Afghanistan (RTA). The state film production company Afghan Film was also launched. These state-run production and broadcasting organizations developed programs that advocated women's active participation in the public sphere. These programs included serials of a variety of genres and public service announcements (PSAs) and public information campaigns (PICs). One of my fondest childhood memories is of watching television at my grandparents' house and seeing highly stylized PICs showing women working cheerfully in a variety of posts such as flight attendants for the national airlines and telephone operators for the state telephone company. The PIC that encouraged women to travel on the national bus fleet was especially entertaining because it included women dancing and singing.

In response to these new policy changes and the media assault, the Islamic Law Faculty of Kabul University, representing a more conservative position, organized a series of protests and rallies against the government. On July 22, 1968, several conservative members of the Parliament attempted to undermine the new constitution by proposing a prohibition that would prevent Afghan women from studying abroad. Immediately following the proposal, hundreds of women students organized a demonstration outside the Parliament. My parents and aunts and uncles were among the demonstrators. Faced with the demonstrations and public opinion, the conservative members quickly withdrew the proposal before it could go to a vote. During this wave of feminist activism, there were numerous cases of acid being thrown at the faces of female college students who did not veil. One of the key suspects, Gulbuddin Hekmatyar, was later sponsored and funded by the CIA to lead the mujahideen resistance against the Soviet invaders. Kabuli schoolgirls such as myself and educators like my mother lived in fear of Hekmatyar and his movement. Commonly referred to as the "Acid Monster of Kabul," Hekmatyar was the ultimate bogeyman. In response to such acts, women organized in much larger numbers at protests on the streets of Kabul. An awareness of women's rights and human rights had grown into a collective social consciousness.

With the exception of some notable scholarship (Adamec 1974, 2005; Crews 2015; L. Dupree 1973; N. Dupree 1984, 2002; Gregorian [1969] 2013; Nawid 2000; Crews and Osman, forthcoming; Shahrani and Canfield 1984; Shahrani 2018), in Western discourse this historical time period of social agitation and contestation in Afghanistan is also glossed over and couched in the pervasive narrative of failure. In its more recent incarnation, the discourse has been reframed in terms of a different set of theories such as late state formation, the rentier state, third world despotism, and more failure (Ghani and Lockhart 2008; B. Rubin 2002; Coburn and Larson 2014) that once again make it difficult to see the complexities on the ground.

For example, the political scientist Barnett Rubin, who is considered a leading expert on Afghanistan, in his book *The Fragmentation of Afghanistan: State Formation and Collapse in the International System* (2002) describes all the leaders of twentieth-century Afghanistan, including the ones I have discussed, as Westernized elite sycophants who were despotic, classist, tribally stratified and hierarchal, out of touch, and inept at democratic governing. He does not cite any achievements and dismisses the social movements and modernizing moments that I have presented here as a combination of insufficient and insignificant. For example, Rubin dismisses two pillars of Afghan representational politics—the traditional *loya jirga* (grand council in Pashto) and the modern Parliament that was established by Zahir Shah in 1949 and then expanded in 1963—as ceremonial and patrimonial. This is not surprising given that he has a tendency to paint with wide brushstrokes. In fact, in his book he characterizes the entirety of modern Afghan history, from Abdul Rahman to Najibullah, as "pre-modern" and "undemocratic": "Abdul Rahman Khan used these coercive resources (weapons and cash provided by the British) to establish the basic state structure that endured until the fall of Najibullah in 1992: a Pashtun ruler using external resources to reign over an ethnically heterogeneous society while manipulating that social segmentation to weaken society's resistance" (2002, 19). This sweeping generalization is akin to stating that in the United States white Anglo-Saxon Christian men have ruled for more than two centuries over an ethnically heterogeneous society—and on that basis to discredit all Americans within and outside the government who led social justice and civil rights movements for and by women and minorities like African Americans, Native Americans, and immigrants. It is similar to entirely negating all the progressive achievements of US history such as FDR's New Deal programs; the Supreme Court's decisions that reversed previously racist, sexist, classist, and queerphobic or anti-LGBTQ decisions; and all the movements for the rights of the subaltern and disenfranchised. The dominant image of Afghanistan as forever static and unchanging is so ingrained and rigidly fixed in the minds, policies, and theories of Western technocrats that there is no room for deviance or stretch of the imagination from these perceived notions. Thus, the history and present of Afghanistan cannot be seen on a continuum of change or swinging pendulum of culture wars like Western countries are afforded, even during brutally extreme repressive governments.

This is not to say that the *loya jirga* and the Parliament were problem-free and fully representative. Afghanistan's traditional system of representational governance, the *loya jirga*, is a centuries-old institution. The grand assembly of elected representatives convened both on the provincial and national levels. Some *loya jirgas* met regularly, while others were considered emergency *loya jirgas* to discuss urgent situations, such as the first and second British invasions. Depending on the kind of *loya jirga*, the people of every village, town, province, or region sent a designated number of men to represent their area of interest. By most accounts, the chosen people were usually men of power or respect within their respective communities, such as tribal elders and khans. The same is true of the upper and lower houses of the Parliament that Zahir Shah and Daoud Khan created during their tenure. With the exception of four elected women, all the other members of Parliament—MPs—tended to be elite men from their respective provinces. While Daoud Khan implemented many progressive programs including those aimed at democratization, he also had an autocratic and authoritarian streak, whereby he persecuted anyone whom he perceived to be a threat to his modernizing plans for Afghanistan. While the religious sector bore the brunt of his antipathy, they were not his only targets. Likewise, Zahir Shah was reluctant to give away the power of the monarchy, but he initiated the Parliament and representative government as a way of increasing the power and legitimacy of the central government. Whereas the *loya jirga* could be summoned and conducted entirely without official government input, the new Parliament was a part of the national government. In this respect, as a representative body, the *loya jirga* and Parliament were just as effective or ineffective as the congress or parliament in "modern" Western nation-states where powerful politicians, usually white men, manage to bypass campaign reform laws, gerrymander, and use their influence and wealth to get elected into government offices. The United States has a long history and active practice of engaging legal and illegal mechanisms of voter suppression in order to prevent minority and working-class citizens from voting.

Furthermore, two pillars of Western democratic thought, John Dewey's town hall meetings of the American pioneers (1927) and Jurgen Habermas's idyllic café culture of mid-eighteenth-century Europe ([1962] 1991), on which many foundational theories of democracy across different disciplines rest and which I use as a framework throughout this book, were both exclusionary, racist, and bourgeois. And yet we continue to extol the virtues of those traditions and the theories by extracting the aspects that were democratizing, like the public sphere and deliberative democracy. By contrast, similar traditions in the MENASA region are held to a different and much higher standard as a means of discrediting them. Yet Eastern traditions and institutions such as the *loya jirga* also contain the seeds of democracy and also have the ability to transform and become more democratic. With the creation of socialist and royalist all-women assemblies, from the 1960s onward, we see examples of *loya jirgas* becoming more inclusive. Participation in the 2003 *loya jirgas* held to ratify the new post-9/11 constitution of Afghanistan, for example, was contingent on electing delegates from all the provinces and including many female elected delegates. Likewise, Dr. Habiba Sarabi, an ethnic Hazara, who was appointed as the first woman governor by Hamid Karzai during his presidency, held all-female *loya jirgas* in her province of Bamiyan; I had the privilege of attending one.

The Soviet Invasion and Occupation of the 1980s

The decade-long Soviet occupation of Afghanistan is as complex in its interplay between internal and foreign forces as the other time periods discussed thus far. On the one hand, many of the progressive achievements of the previous era came to a sudden halt with the Soviet-backed Communist coup and then invasion. On the other hand, Afghan Communists and their Soviet benefactors launched many new socialist, modernizing projects. The historian Timothy Nunan, in his book *Humanitarian Invasion: Global Development in Cold War Afghanistan* (2016), based on vast Soviet and Afghan archives and interviews

PHOTO 1.3. The Ghaazi family from the Farah Province visit Kabul for medical treatment in 2014. Mr. Ghaazi lost his leg as a teenager in a battle with the Soviets in 1987.

with Soviet officials and development workers, sheds light on this polarizing time. He writes, "The intervention led to disaster: of the perhaps fifteen million souls inhabiting Afghanistan in 1979, one third would become refugees outside the country, while another third would end up wounded or internally displaced. Over a million Afghans would be killed. Parallel to this carnage, however, thousands of Soviet nation-builders . . . and tens of thousands of Afghan Communists would seek to turn Afghanistan into a test site for the construction of socialism at the scale of the nation-state" (4).

On April 27, 1978, in a bloody coup d'état, Daoud Khan, his extended family, and the presidential guard were all killed. The Communist People's Democratic Party of Afghanistan (PDPA) took power. Three months after the coup, the two branches of the PDPA, the Khalq ("people") and the Parcham ("flag"), became more adversarial, and the Khalqis (members of the Khalq Party) took control of the government. On Christmas Eve 1979, thousands of Soviet troops invaded Afghanistan by land and air. After another round of killing, the Soviets intervened directly and installed the Parcham Party into power. The Parchamis (members of the Parcham Party) imprisoned and killed most of the former Khalqi government officials. In less than two years the PDPA had three regime changes due to popular revolt, internal differences, ambitious leaders, and Soviet involvement. Thus, the Soviet-Afghan War was launched.

The ten-year Soviet occupation of Afghanistan was marked by violence, torture, and the disappearance of many Afghans across class, gender, and ethnicity lines. The Khalqis imprisoned my father, Dr. Abdullah Osman, in the infamous Soviet-built Pul-i Charkhi (Spinning bridge) prison for thirteen months, subjecting him to torture and solitary confinement. Two of my uncles also disappeared during this time, never to be found again. In the post-9/11 era, many large mass graves have been discovered. The International Criminal Court has launched multiple investigations to bring the torturers and executioners to justice but have convicted only one person so far (Arbabzadah 2013; Loyn 2013; Nordland 2013).

In the midst of all this political repression, the PDPA launched a series of ambitious modernizing reforms. Nunan explains how thousands of Soviet nation-builders came to Afghanistan with a Communist utopian vision to modernize and secularize the country, modeled on their work in the Central Asian republics, which were part of the then USSR. Over time their vision and tactics shifted because they had to confront the opposition and realities in Afghanistan. The PDPA's rhetoric regarding women's rights, education, and class disparities was very progressive, and the statistics the party published showing the success of its programs in empowering women, the poor, and ethnic minorities were also quite impressive.

Yet upon closer inspection of the PDPA's policies, many of its projects fell short. The Khalq Party instituted an ambitious literacy program. According to Nancy Dupree, "By September the remarkable and improbable figure of 926,141 men and women enrolled in literacy courses was announced" (1984, 321). For the Khalqis to initiate a large-scale literacy project with incredible results of almost a million students enrolled in a matter of a few months was unrealistic. Students enrolled in one of the Kabul-based offices also complained that the courses consisted of political ideology training in the guise of literacy training and that practical teaching materials that had been used during Daoud Khan's time were discarded (321).

In her article "Afghan Women between Marxism and Islamic Fundamentalism," Afghan scholar Parwin Ali Majrooh concurs that the PDPA statistics on its own education and literacy programs were highly suspect. Majrooh illuminates how the Communist coup of 1978 was damaging to the progress achieved thus far, particularly in the field of education for all. Due to the PDPA's forced literacy program in Soviet ideology, active recruitment of students in the army and intelligence services, and imprisonment of students who did not comply, many students stopped attending school. With their loss of control in the rural areas, many schools outside of Kabul became nonoperational and shut down. By 1984, 78 percent of the schools that had operated during Zahir Shah and Daoud Khan's administrations were shut down (Majrooh 1989, 89).

Given the public backlash, especially outside of cities, to any government-instituted programs deemed as incursions on provincial and village sovereignty, all governments after Amanullah Khan's proceeded with caution when instituting national projects. According to Majrooh, "Regarding women's reforms, King Amanullah's successors, Nadershah (1929–1933) and Zahershah (1933–1973), followed a moderate course. More high schools were eventually established. In the academic year 1973–1974, there were 16,027 girls registered in 229 village schools, 73,304 in 174 primary schools, 13,044 in 51 middle schools, 6,020 in 30 high schools, and 733 in one vocational school. Prior to 1964 separate classes within Kabul University were opened for girls. In 1963 there were faculties of Medicine, Literature, and Natural Sciences for women" (1989, 88). In Majrooh's words, the policies of Nadir and Zahir Shah enabled women's rights to "follow a moderate course" to progress. During Daoud Khan's ten-year term as prime minister, though, his reforms as described before, including ending obligatory veiling, passing the equal rights amendment, and giving scholarships to women for higher education in Afghanistan and abroad, were considered daring reforms on the scale of Amanullah Khan. And where Daoud Khan had enshrined human rights into law, the new PDPA constitution of 1978 stripped many of his progressive codes. For example, Decree 7, titled "Dowry [*mahr*] and Marriage Expenses," despite its rhetoric, favored only men. Article 3, the *mahr*, which protected women in cases of divorce or neglect, was dissolved. "Principles crucial to true emancipation, such as the equal rights of women to demand a divorce, work opportunities, and inheritance—all guaranteed by Daoud's Civil Law—were not considered" (N. Dupree 1984, 324).

Within the Afghan community, from the perspective of the religious Right, the monarchs and prime ministers followed a radical path to secular modernity by challenging their extremist interpretations of Islam. From the perspective of the Afghan Socialist and Communist Parties, the monarchy and prime ministers were conservative with their reforms and did not do enough to promote class and ethnic equality and elevate the position of women.

During this time the media, the arts, and culture continued to flourish and thrive under Soviet sponsorship. Radio Television Afghanistan, the state television station, remained prolific and produced news and cultural programming. Afghan Film, the state film ministry, continued to produce many fiction and documentary films. Furthermore, numerous new Socialist and Communist magazines and newspapers began to spring up. So long as Afghan television makers, filmmakers, and musicians stayed within the proscribed Soviet line, the Soviets provided many opportunities for them. Media makers who opposed the Soviet Communist project or invasion, on the other hand, were persecuted and killed. The media production of this time corresponds to Soviet press norms, which meant that all content was subjected to the editorial gaze of Soviet advisers. As Soviet media scholars have written, the Soviets carried over their statist mechanisms of media censorship and control to the countries that they occupied but also allowed a degree of artistic creativity (Evans 2016; Kalinovsky 2018; Roth-Ey 2011; Stronski 2010). The media projects that the USSR sponsored in its satellite Caucasus and Central Asian republics, including occupied Afghanistan, were embedded in the Cold War politics of the time. The USSR-sponsored media in its colonies offered an alternative vision of third world modernity that was meant to serve as a bulwark against Western visions of third world modernity that were broadcast on the BBC, Voice of America, Radio Free Europe/Radio Liberty, Radio Free Afghanistan, and other media organizations that the West sponsored.

In the Cold War media propaganda battle, both sides used their state-sanctioned media outlets across Eurasia to portray their own countries' values and the exportation of those values via militarization to Afghanistan in a positive light while slandering the other side. Additionally, they sponsored and helped produce media for their respective proxy armies, namely the Afghan National Army under the PDPA and the mujahideen, representing them as freedom fighters and liberators against the oppressive forces of the other side. The Soviets produced many promotional PDPA films including public information campaigns that showed a progressive and thriving Afghanistan during the Soviet occupation. Similar to the dominant Western discourse, these public relations films and newsreels made absolutely no reference to the fact that many of the featured signs and images of reform and human rights advancement were actually initiated in the previous era. Of course, these Soviet and PDPA coproductions didn't reveal the fact that most of the rest of the country outside the bubble of the capital had taken up arms and was actively battling the Soviet occupation. To counter Soviet propaganda, the US government launched the Afghan Media Resource Center (AMRC) in 1987 in order to train Afghans to document the Soviet-Afghan War from the frontline perspective of the mujahideen and feed this narrative to news agencies internationally. Unlike the highly stylized

Soviet PR films the more than one thousand hours of raw, unedited audiovisual footage that the AMRC trainees captured was not propagandistic. On the contrary, they served then and now as a veritable archive of the Soviet-Afghan War, which nonetheless does not preclude their use in similarly propagandistic ways. Additionally, as media scholars have shown, competing propaganda or viewpoints create a marketplace of ideas and therefore reduce the dangers of a one-sided monopoly on representation and the disseminations of information. During this time, according to the anthropologist David Edwards, "the only independent Afghan source of news" and the most prolific was the French funded Afghan Information Centre (AIC), which was started by the Afghan intellectual Sayyid Bahauddin Majrooh in 1980 and ran until his assassination in 1988 (2002, 279).

As the Soviet occupation continued, some Afghans continued to believe in the socialist project and worked for the state and its media, army, and educational system; others became disillusioned and defected, escaping Afghanistan to join the refugees or resistance abroad. My uncle Akram Osman was among the defectors. He was an active PDPA member who worked with the pro-Soviet regime before going into exile in Sweden and becoming a staunch critic. As state violence, propaganda, and repression intensified, so did the opposition to the Soviet/PDPA rule. Defectors lost hope in the socialist dream as they realized the PDPA's social justice movements were becoming more ideological and rhetorical, a sentiment that is echoed in the academic writing of scholars who experienced that era (Kakar 1995; Majrooh 1989; Nawid 2007). In 1980 a female staff writer for the *Kabul Times* wrote, "There is nothing more ridiculous than granting privileges on paper without pushing them practically." Shortly thereafter the women's pages were replaced with features dedicated to Moscow (N. Dupree 1984, 332).

In the Wake of the Soviet-Afghan War and the Cold War

With the final withdrawal of the USSR from Afghanistan in 1989, the Soviet-Afghan War, which had become the centerpiece of the long-standing Cold War between the United States and Russia, culminated in the collapse of the USSR, the end of the Cold War, and the emergence of the United States as the victor and sole world superpower. These events of global proportions led to a series of other events that threw Afghanistan into a series of endless wars stretching now into its fifth decade. It has subsumed the country into the chaos, violence, and disorder of war.

During this time the US and Saudi governments, via Pakistan's ISI (Inter-Services Intelligence), secretly funded the Afghan resistance, the mujahideen "freedom fighters." The bulk of the financial and military weapons were funneled into the hands of the most conservative elements of Afghan society. Out of the seven mujahideen resistance groups that were officially recognized by the United States and funded by the CIA and Congress, most of the leaders were Islamists who had been exiled or imprisoned by the prewar Afghan governments for their extremist views and attempts at overthrowing the government. Yet in the mainstream US corporate media and in the dominant Western discourse, about half of the religious clerics are categorized as "moderate."

A prime example is the financial support from the Zia al-Haq and Ronald Reagan administrations of people like Gulbuddin Hekmatyar, who received the largesse of CIA funding. Among Kabulis, Hekmatyar has the notorious reputation as the misogynistic extremist who threw acid on schoolgirls and college women's faces during Daoud Khan's tenure. The efforts of generations of Afghan leaders to marginalize these groups were squashed. Most of the mujahideen leaders did not necessarily have popular support or constituencies. They became powerful warlords as a result of billions of dollars of weapons and funding they received from the ISI via the United States and Saudi Arabia, thus enabling the rise of conservative forces that have turned women's bodies and sectarian ethnic markers into a battleground.

All the jihadi leaders used their newfound war clout and largesse to increase the ranks of their foot soldiers and their influence by funding the creation of many madrassas, or religious schools. For many impoverished and orphaned Afghan refugee boys, attending these madrassas was their only way to receive a meal. During the four years we were refugees in Pakistan and on my subsequent trips, I witnessed firsthand how the jihadi madrassas were turning the boys and young men, including relatives, who we lived with in various refugee compounds into extremists who began to oppose women's rights and other modernist ideas that they previously did not. In the power vacuum that was left in the wake of the Soviet withdrawal, the United States funded warlords who had vast paramilitary forces and caches of weapons unleashed their extreme interpretations of Islam, ethnocentrisms, and xenophobia on the people of Afghanistan in a series of bloody civil wars, resulting in mass tribal ethnocides and femicides and the further destruction of Afghanistan's national and cultural institutions. Gulbuddin Hekmatyar, with his antipathy toward the people of the capital city for their progressive inclinations and lifestyles, killed an estimated 50,000 Kabuli civilians alone, hence gaining the new title the "Butcher of Kabul" to add to his former title, the "Acid Monster of Kabul" (Myre 2017). The former mujahideen-cum-warlords continue to wreak havoc on the people of

PHOTO 1.4. **A US soldier stands guard by a USAID-built telecommunication** tower, Kabul, US embassy.

Afghanistan, nation-building, and democratic processes. Their reign of terror is not over in Afghanistan. Instead of being tried and prosecuted, many of them were invited, post-9/11, by the United Nations and the US-led international community to join the Afghan government, thus legitimizing them by giving them positions within the government.

Western accounts of this recent history tend to be ahistorical, assuming that Afghan culture has always been a hotbed of misogyny, sectarian xenophobia, lawlessness, militancy, and other extreme patriarchal practices. Within this narrative, among policy makers and academics two camps have emerged: the interventionists, who aim to save Afghans from themselves via education and the media or bombing and other military campaigns, and the nonintervention- ists, who argue that any action is futile in a culture that is static, unchanging, and bound by archaic problematic traditions.

Considering America's large financial investment in arming a proxy army, the mujahideen, to fight the Cold War and the heavy price of modern war- fare paid by the Afghan people, it is a strategic and moral disaster that the American government did not aid the rebuilding of the war-torn country and its war-torn people. In the wake of the Soviet withdrawal, America lost inter- est, and Afghanistan fell into years of civil wars and sectarian violence as the seven mujahideen factions vied for control of the country until the Taliban came to power in 1994 to put an end to civil war with their punitive system of justice and draconian interpretations of Islam. Similar to the Khost Rebellion of 1925, which tried to depose Amanullah Khan, the Taliban—also from the south of Afghanistan—marched along the same path into the capital, Kabul, and battled the government for control of the nation. After a brief and bloody struggle, the Taliban publicly castrated and hung the Soviet-backed president Najibullah. Although, after years of war, women dominated Kabul's workforce, the Taliban prohibited women from venturing outside the domestic sphere for work or education.

Purnima Bose in her book *Intervention Narratives: Afghanistan, the United States, and the Global War on Terror* (2020) offers an alternative reading of this narrative, that the United States abandoned Afghanistan after its Cold War agendas were served. She writes, "Instead of positing the problem of Afghani- stan to be the premature disengagement of the US from the region . . . what if we consider that the problem in the first place was in itself the result of US covert operations during the 1980s? And that we mull the possibility that the decision to render aid to the Mujahideen did not correspond to any verifiable threat to US interests by the Soviet Union, but rather emanated from the delu- sions of Cold Warriors . . . ?" (87). I would add that aiding the most regressive and conservative elements of Afghan society to create the mujahideen in the first place was a grave mistake.

An understanding and rereading of Afghan history allows us to move beyond the language of failure and retell the story as one that includes agency. Many Afghan reformers from all sectors of society throughout the last century have worked tirelessly to lay the foundations of a modern, progressive, democratic, and inclusive Afghanistan. They fought and challenged conservative elements within and outside of Afghanistan to build institutions and infrastructures that foster a public sphere and functioning civil society. Dismissing their countless nation-building projects undermines the reforms that have taken shape throughout the decades.

Of course, the omission of historic progressive movements of the Global East and South is not random but in accordance with colonial and neocolonial discourse. If modernity is the litmus test of progress, then contrary to the hegemonic Western narrative, prior to the Soviet invasion, in Afghanistan human rights and equality were progressing and advancing forward. Though Afghan society continued to be patriarchal and women did not occupy an equal position in society, and of course class and ethnic disparities exacerbated gender inequalities, a feminist consciousness had developed and the women's movement was mobilized to ensure women's continued active membership in society. Yet the forces of Saudi, Pakistani, and Afghan Islamic extremism in conjunction with American and Soviet imperialism thwarted the achievements gained over the course of the last century.

To say that the US Cold War policies regarding Afghanistan were shortsighted or ill conceived would be overlooking the long history of the US government's support for ultra-right and anti-democracy regimes throughout the MENASA region and Latin America. Herein lie the differences between what I posit as the "imperial gaze" and the "development gaze." As flawed and limiting as the Afghan movements and leaders I have discussed in this chapter may have been, they were concerned with the betterment and development of Afghanistan and its people. On the other hand, the British, Russian/Soviet, and US development and military projects I have discussed, from the Great Game through the Cold War, were launched with an imperial gaze. The goal of the development projects and military campaigns of first British and Russian colonizers and then Soviet and American superpowers was to aggrandize their own geopolitical and economic interests, regardless of the destruction of Afghanistan and its people.

Conclusion

A revisionist retelling of Afghan modern history allows us to see not only the agency of the Afghan people but also the role of foreign powers in the affairs of Afghanistan. Beneath the modern/traditional dichotomy that characterizes much of the historical discourse on Afghanistan lies the complicated geopolitical dynamics of foreign forces at play. The fact that even more progressive accounts only rehash this one-dimensional vector of internal conflict should be cause for suspicion. Foreign interventions and interferences are conveniently not subjected to the same type of rigorous academic or journalistic inquiry, a problem that persists in the present era.

As the failures of the post-9/11 US-Afghan war, the US War on Terror, and US development projects are coming to light, US official accounts and academics are quick to pin the blame on the failures and inadequacies of Afghans and their traditional cultures. For example, Noah Coburn and Anna Larson in *Derailing Democracy in Afghanistan: Elections in an Unstable Political Landscape* (2014) write that local actors hijacked elections by a combination of corruption, fraud, and traditional practices such as voting on the basis of kinship alliances and limiting women's participation. Indeed there is truth in their assertions. The international community invested heavily in creating the infrastructure to hold multiple presidential and parliamentary elections in Afghanistan. According to international election monitoring organizations and public outrage, most of the elections were plagued by fraud and corruption. Local elites, including village elders, warlords, and businessmen, played a big role in sabotaging the elections in their own favor, especially in provincial areas outside of cities. However, Coburn and Larson do not subject the international community and its role in derailing democracy to the same type of academic scrutiny and standards of accountability.

As Rashid Khalidi has written in his book *Brokers of Deceit: How the U.S. Has Undermined Peace in the Middle East* (2013), the US government often directly puts a wrench into the mechanisms of democracy to ensure results that are favorable to maintaining its own geopolitical power and rule in the region. Likewise, Purnima Bose (2020) explains how contrary to its rhetoric, there is a wide and growing gap between the US government's actual foreign policy practices and the pristine image of impartial and well-intentioned bearers of democracy that it projects to the world. She describes how the United States has a long history of covert operations abroad, including influencing the outcome of elections.

As I have written elsewhere (Osman 2014b), Afghans have been outraged by blatant US election engineering, favoring candidates who support its interests in the region. In the wake of 9/11, the US government has engaged in behind-the-scenes election maneuvering in order to protect US assets and interests. Yet in the official narrative, Afghanistan and its people are portrayed as lawless and unruly, incapable of achieving the level of civility to carry out democratic and representative systems of governance—hence the failure of the present era, despite the international development community's admirable efforts.

Nancy Dupree, the American academic and activist who spent many years in Afghanistan, eventually dying and being buried there, said to me in a conversation we had in Kabul, "There is this unbelievable amnesia and arrogance within the American development community, Foreign Service, and academy that we are experimenting with democracy and nation building for the first time in Afghanistan. That's simply a lie. Many generations of Afghans and Americans were doing this type of work and much better I must say since the 1940s. With much less we were able to do so much more. Afghanistan was far ahead then compared to now, when countless billions of dollars have been spent and mysteriously vanished."[9]

As this brief history illustrates, in Afghanistan, a secular modernist reform movement underpinned by human rights and democracy was developing in the twentieth century. Such matters as veiling and purdah were beginning to be accepted as voluntary and not compulsory. Women having a career and working outside of the home was also accepted and becoming the norm, which was partially due to the overall expansion of the educational system. For example, my grandmothers wore the *chadari* (the all-encompassing veil) their entire lives and attended school until only the eighth grade, as was customary at the time. On the other hand, my mother finished the twelfth grade, attended Kabul University, and went to France on a state scholarship for her graduate work. Within a matter of two generations, families that accepted the state's modernist policies were able to increase their agency and therefore acquire the mobility to improve their lives within Afghan society.

Many of the urban television producers I interviewed came of age, like me, during what we call "the good years" and the "golden era." We remember a peaceful, progressive, and modern Afghanistan. As recipients and benefactors of the state's numerous initiatives, including free education and media, we embody that history and those collective memories. For media makers, memories of this era then become a shield in their efforts to launch programming that pushes the culture forward, as well as backward, to a prewar time of governmentally instituted social works and progressive developments and achievements. When inevitably attacked by conservative forces, they can defend their work by arguing that there is a precedent in Afghan culture and history for a multiethnic, multiracial, multireligious, secular, and gender/sexuality-inclusive society with human rights for all. Early Afghan reformers at the turn of the twentieth century needed to ground their ambitious initiatives in the achievements of Turkey and Japan, hoping to appeal to a sense of pan-Asianism and secular pan-Islam. This kind of approach was seen as a challenge to their detractors, who claimed that modernity is a Western invention. Today's reformers point to these early reformers to show that modernity is *mahaly*, of the people and the land, because it was introduced by Afghan leaders, and not Westerners.

These alternative and indigenous modernities of the past are instantiated in the current complex mediascape, where a range of "imagined communities" that address and constitute different notions of what it means to be Afghan in the twenty-first century are at work in the public sphere, speaking to the hearts and minds of contemporary citizens (Anderson 2006; Gaonkar 2001; Larkin 2008). Whereas the Taliban and ISIS (the Islamic State of Iraq and Syria) destroy telecommunication towers that transmit and broadcast signals for wireless telephones, radios, and television, and the International Security Assistance Force, NATO, the Resolute Support Mission, and American armed forces try to protect telecommunication towers either by placing them within the compound walls of their military bases or by having soldiers guard them, the big difference between the "iron horse" of the British Raj and the internationally funded media of today is that the public almost unanimously supports today's media.

CHAPTER 2

Imperialism, Globalization, and Development

Overlaps and Disjunctures

Imperial Ambitions: Foreign Projects, Occupations, and Invasions

In this chapter, I delve deeper into how the dynamics of foreign involvement, past and present, have influenced the contemporary War on Terror moment. In particular I explore whether the current development projects that the international community has implemented, especially in the media sector, are also mired in imperialist agendas or whether they have contributed to rebuilding Afghanistan and improving the lives of people. I conclude the latter.

Known as the "Gateway to Asia," Afghanistan has historically been at the crossroads of imperial ambitions. In what was called the Great Game, the colonial powers of England and Russia would often instigate trouble, pitting the various ethnic groups against one another. Part of their divide-and-conquer strategy involved annexing parts of Afghanistan, thus redrawing the boundaries of the country in their own interests. This strategy was also used in the Cold War and is still frequently deployed by the US government in the War on Terror. Additionally, as I highlighted in the previous chapter, historians have shown how some of the British Empire's and the Soviet Union's modernizing projects were duplicitously designed to serve their larger imperial agendas.

For Afghan rulers and leaders, maintaining the country's sovereignty involved a balancing act of minimizing foreign annexation while also appeasing the interests of a heterogeneous population consisting of semiautonomous ethnic groups such as the Pashtuns, Tajiks, Uzbeks, Hazaras, and Turkmans, among many other smaller groups. Early on, as a result of these border uncertainties (Qassem 2017), the state attempted to implement an isolationist policy. Likewise, as a result of constantly being under the threat of foreign invasions, the people of Afghanistan have always been suspicious of foreign involvement and interference. At the same time, Afghans were and are equally wary of national projects, which they deem as transgressions against their local independence and autonomy.

In actuality, the government's isolationist policy was largely a failure. Afghans themselves have long bypassed scholarly, geographical, and political barriers through their own cultural and economic exchanges with Central Asia, East Asia, India, Iran, and Pakistan, as well as with other countries. While fearful of official state incursions by both Afghan and foreign governments, non-state cross-border connections and flows of people via trade, marriage, arts, culture, and so forth were and are commonplace. Yet in academia and popular culture, the myth of Afghanistan's "isolation" and "irredeemableness" continues to gain currency and has become a formidable paradigm.

In the age of globalization, Afghanistan is even less impervious to cultural influences and changes. As Faye Ginsburg, Lila Abu-Lughod, and Brian Larkin write in the introduction to their 2002 foundational volume, *Media Worlds: Anthropology on New Terrain*, "Our relations with those we study are changing as our cultural worlds grow closer in ways that push anthropology in salutary directions; it is difficult to exoticize others or to maintain fictions of bounded or untouched communities of difference when one includes media in one's purview" (24). Due to Afghanistan's distinctive post-9/11 economy, the vast majority of its media funding and actual media technologies and products come from its regional neighbors as well as from cross-regional interests. As media ethnographers who study transnational media and the effects of globalization have begun to explore, satellite television is rapidly transforming the mediascape in the Gulf countries, from Syria to Iraq (Abu-Lughod 2004; Kraidy 2010; Salamandra 2008).

How are Afghanistan's specific geographic location at the border of Central and South Asia and distinctive sociocultural position, dominated by Indian, Iranian, Turkish, and Western media products and at the margins of Arab and Russian influence, shaping or impeding its development? Is this distinctive geopolitical positioning and cross-cultural engagement laying the foundations of cultural imperialism and "Westoxification"/*gharbzadegi* or fostering freedom of speech, debate, diversity, and democracy for the entire region? Is it sowing the seeds of disunity or regional unity? These are questions that are regularly debated by Afghans in the media, at home, and on the streets; I therefore grapple with them in this study.

The formal Arabic and Persian combined term *bayan almilaly,* or "internationals," is used in institutional settings and on the news. However, the vernacular word *khaareji,* which comes into Persian and Pashto from the Arabic word *khaareji,* meaning "exit" or "outside," is used more widely to designate "foreigners" and "outsiders" in everyday conversations as well as on informal programs such as talk shows and call-in programs. Given the country's long history of fighting colonialism and its current quandary of being a nexus and locus of intense international activity, including the United States' longest war, it was not surprising that the *khaarejis* pervade the Afghan psyche and came up in almost every conversation I had while I was in the country: What are the *khaarejis* planning next? What are their real plans in the region and in Afghanistan? Will they ever leave? What would happen if they left? They have made things worse. They are responsible for the abysmal state of this country in the first place. They think only of their own interests. They have improved things. We need them to stop the rise of the Taliban and other militant extremists.

As a result of the destruction of many of its institutions such as its media, arts, education, and museums, contemporary Afghanistan is, culturally and nationally speaking, particularly vulnerable and unsettled. After over four decades of war and instability, there is serious concern that with the current escalation of NATO and American troops, Afghanistan will remain in a state of perpetual war, breaking into different dimensions and stretching into a fifth decade. Indeed, security is deteriorating considerably. Taliban and Al Qaeda violence is now augmented by the appearance of ISIS in eastern border regions. The international military's support of some ethnic groups and their leaders but not others in the War on Terror is fueling ethnic tensions. Therefore, questions about cultural vulnerability, cultural imperialism, the role of empire, and civil unrest and more wars are legitimate and take on a new urgency in a place and space that continues to be at the crossroads of imperial ambitions, where ethnic violence remains pervasive and the possibilities of redefining national identity and allegiances are wide open. In Afghanistan, national television systems, and politics more generally, are shaped just as much by internal dynamics as they are by relationships with neighboring and more distant countries. While this is true of all nations, it is particularly the case in Afghanistan due to its geopolitical position and significant dependence on foreign aid.

PHOTO 2.1. US private contractors in Asadabad guard an infrastructure development project. The US military in conjunction with the private security forces it contracts engage in military and development projects.

PHOTO 2.2. Children rebuilding a house in Herat.

PHOTO 2.3. **Afghan National Police in Herat.**

Media and Global Flows:
From *Dallas* to Development TV

Since the impact and effects of foreign media projects and international involvement more generally are a central concern of the people of Afghanistan and this book, it is important for me to explicate my position vis-à-vis the heated academic debates on globalization, cultural imperialism, and development communication. Therefore, before analyzing the cultural impact of foreign media and the ensuing cultural wars, I will address what means and methods can best help us understand the effects of globalization and development and the impact of cultural imperialism and why it is imperative to define and distinguish between these grand and loaded terms.

In the field of global media studies, four contested and hotly debated schools of thought can be mapped across its genealogy: *cultural imperialism* and *development communication,* which both are experiencing a resurgence after a period of decline, and the newer *globalization theories* and *hybridity.* Given the state of the world, the ongoing wars in MENASA, the global refugee crisis, and transnational interventions, it is not surprising that both the cultural imperialism thesis and development communication of the 1950s to 1970s have been resurrected and built upon by scholars to make sense of contemporary geopolitics and the role of the media. Oftentimes, however, these schools of thought do not merge and remain oppositional. In my work, I attempt to bridge these schools of thought so that one's claims do not always negate the other's but can exist simultaneously. For example, I demonstrate in this book how the international community's interventions in Afghanistan have resulted in media imperialism and have yielded positive development projects along with problematic ones.

The cultural imperialism school of thought gained impetus internationally from the 1950s through the 1970s as postcolonial social movements sought to redress the asymmetrical power dynamics in the wake of colonialism. In the 1970s and 1980s, cultural imperialism as a concept and social movement was also adopted and promoted by UNESCO. During this time UNESCO commissioned a panel chaired by Nobel Peace Prize laureate Seán MacBride to document the desires of underprivileged countries to enter into global dialogue, have access to information and communication technologies, and be heard. The commission produced MacBride's report, *Many Voices, One World,* which offered a set of recommendations to level the global media playing field by making media representations and information and communications technologies more equitable. Based on MacBride's report, UNESCO passed resolutions such as the New International Economic Order and the New World Information and Communications Order, which sought to "correct inequalities and redress existing injustices (and) make it possible to eliminate the widening gap between developed and developing countries" (MacBride 1980, 16). Ironically, two of the United Nations' wealthiest members, the United States and England, were hostile to the resolutions and left UNESCO, taking their substantial financial contributions with them. Ultimately, the "global conversation" was thwarted by those who had money and therefore power even within the corridors of a global nonprofit organization. This episode highlights the incredible scale of dominance of Western countries over many weaker countries, thus making apparent the limitations of working within "global" institutional bodies that are not equitably global.

In academia, one of the most influential media imperialism theorists was Herbert Schiller. Schiller attributed the overwhelming dominance of Western media to the commercial development of media corporations in the United States. As Schiller notes, "What is emerging on the international scene bears a striking resemblance to the American routine of uncoordinated expansion of production, promotion of the output through the communications media, higher sales, further plant expansion, and then the cycle's repetition" (2004, 482). Many of Schiller's early formulations continue to define the field of global media studies. His concern, and that of many contemporary media activists and cultural critics, is that distinctive heterogeneous cultures are being erased, tainted, or diffused by the homogenizing force of Western capital expansion and media globalization, what is called the homogenization thesis.

If we look at concrete economic factors and worldwide media ownership trends, it is clear that a handful of Western corporations dominate the film, music, and television industries (Bagdikian 2004; Boyd-Barrett 2007; McChesney 2004; H. Schiller 1976, 1989, 2004). These very real structural imbalances enable wealthy Western nations to aggressively produce, distribute, and market media products with alluringly high production quality. Although the consumption of media products might be global, the production and distribution and therefore financial benefits are skewed in the direction of the West. Such capitalistic strategies, techniques, and ventures, coupled with the exploitative history of colonialism and imperialism of the West, have left many former colonies out of the global picture—both literally and metaphorically. The usual suspect and target of the media imperialism argument is American media products, with their Americanizing effects and messages.

One of the first media studies that challenged the cultural imperialism thesis was Tamar Liebes and Elihu Katz's 1993 examination of the American melodramatic series *Dallas*. Liebes and Katz observed the reception of the 1980s American television show by audiences from different national/ethnic backgrounds, including their own native Israel. Although subsequently their study has been critiqued on multiple fronts, including for making culturally essentialist conclusions about Arabs and Moroccan Jews based on their viewing practices, their study was initially praised and is still used as a bulwark of audience agency against the proponents of the media and cultural imperialism thesis.

The *Dallas* study showed how the American dramatic serial coded with apparent American ideologies was decoded very differently by audiences from different cultural backgrounds, thereby refuting the cultural imperialist argument that the meaning of hegemonic cultural exports is foreordained. In their study, Liebes and Katz found that some viewers, after watching the wealthy lifestyle of the show's Ewing family, expressed the desire to be rich, while others felt that their own ascetic life without luxurious material goods was a richer life. This was in sharp contrast to textual analysis of the American television show, which argued that it was a culturally imperialistic text (Croteau and Hoynes 2003). In fact, the link between hegemony and American cultural products was a given. Thus Liebes and Katz were part of the growing media studies discourse of the active audience who is able to negotiate, resist, or reject the dominant message of hegemonic media texts and therefore is not easily duped into acceptance and acquiescence. While I agree with the active audience discourse and situate my own ethnographic work within it, the danger in this formidable framework is that in the process of directing the debate toward audience agency, these studies either entirely negate or leave the big question of culturally imperialistic texts unanswered. As I explain in the next sections, one does not negate the other; they are not mutually exclusive.

Drawing on the *Dallas* study and others, John Tomlinson's book *Cultural Imperialism: A Critical Introduction* (2002) argues against what he calls the cultural imperialism discourse and its proponents; his text further shook the foundations of the school of thought. Tomlinson also raises questions of method. If we assume that one of the dominant ideological messages of *Dallas* is that the accumulation of wealth, social mobility, and the fetishizing of a money-centered life—essentially the US capitalist lifestyle—entails both hazards and pleasures, then both the acceptance and rejection of this message can be interpreted as hegemonic. So how do we determine if a text is culturally imperialistic? Tomlinson suggests, "The theoretical problems of deciding what actually is to count as cultural imperialism—is 'a message to stay down' the same sort of dominance as seduction towards the 'American way'?—are not empirical questions" (56).

Tomlinson is also critical of Ariel Dorfman and Armand Mattelart's classic *How to Read Donald Duck: Imperialist Ideology in the Disney Comic* (1975). The highly celebrated book, which was a best seller in Latin America, is a Marxist indictment of the United States as an imperialist state that exports its imperialist ideologies, including capitalist expansion, individualism, superiority of the American way of life, white saviorism, the incompetence of third world people to govern themselves, and racist and sexist representations. Subsequently, *How to Read Donald Duck* was banned in the United States and also in Chile by the dictator Augusto Pinochet, who was brought to power in a US-backed coup that toppled the popularly elected Salvador Allende.

Based on grounds of method and proof similar to his critique of the *Dallas* study and others, Tomlinson argues that the "Donald Duck study" is not academically, methodically, or empirically grounded but too polemical and politically motivated in its thesis. He asks how we know that Disney comics are imperialistic texts that promote the American ideology of capitalist expansion into "exotic lands." Tomlinson critiques the authors for taking an inductive rather than a deductive reasoning approach, which, according to him, means that their arguments are subject to interpretation and represent "preaching to the choir." However, regardless of how well researched a study is, I would argue that these methodological charges can be brought against any study, including Tomlinson's own polemical study. Indeed, content and textual analysis as a means to determine cultural imperialism is limiting. Likewise, empirical studies like the *Dallas* study and mine where "immediate viewing contexts" are observed are mired in the problem of proof, since their evidence is premised on assumptions and interpretations that are subjective and therefore subject to challenge. While I agree with Tomlinson that, methodologically, media and cultural imperialism is difficult to prove, I do not agree that this is grounds for not studying the issue. There are better methods and ways of examining the complicated subject matter, which I outline in the next section

Tomlinson's final chapter, "From Imperialism to Globalisation," concludes that cultural imperialism is no longer a useful framework. He argues that the language of cultural imperialism makes one think of "the age of high imperialism and colonialism . . . of nineteenth century European missionaries washing out the mouths of children for speaking their tribal language" (2001, 173). Tomlinson prefers "globalization" to "imperialism" because "the effects of globalisation are to weaken the cultural coherence of all individual nation-states, including the economically powerful ones—the 'imperialist powers' of a previous era" (175).

By contending that in the present era the locus of study should not be specific Western nation-states and that globalization, not imperialism, is a more accurate description for global phenomena and dynamics of today, Tomlinson echoes Arjun Appadurai's influential article "Disjuncture and Difference in the Global Cultural Economy" (1990), often called the "scapes" or the "Globalization 101" article. As the first articulation of a definition of globalization, it is arguably the most influential and most cited globalization essay. In it, Appadurai grapples with the questions raised by globalization and aptly describes the dynamic "flows" of people, media, commerce, and technology with the concept of "scapes": ethnoscapes, mediascapes, financescapes, and technoscapes. According to Appadurai, societies today cannot be imagined as isolated in national enclaves, and the reach of mass media can no longer be contained within individual nations. The advancements in mass communication technologies—satellite and internet in particular—coupled with current accelerating transnational movements of people, ideas, and things, result in a far more complex understanding of "imagined communities" than the world Benedict Anderson described in his groundbreaking 1983 book on the role of print media, such as newspapers and novels, in the origins and spread of nationalism (Anderson 2006).

Appadurai similarly argues that America has become an easy target for cultural critics. Distinctions such as East/West and modern/traditional are outdated approaches to the study of the dynamic global phenomena that shape our present-day world. Accordingly, we need to widen our scope to take into account new variables such as transnational flows of people (tourists, refugees, guest workers, and so on), the disorganization of capitalism, and the role of nation-states versus indigenous people: "First, people, machinery, money, images, and ideas now follow increasingly in nonisomorphic paths; of course, at all periods in human history, there have been some disjunctures in the flow of these things, but the sheer speed, scale, and volume of each of these flows are now so great that the disjunctures have become central to the politics of global culture" (1996a, 37).

From Cultural Imperialism to Globalization and Back Again

In this section, predicated on feminist media ethnographies and postcolonial and political economy approaches, I demonstrate why globalization alone cannot adequately describe the structural imbalances, power disparities, or cultural and ideological issues of the media worlds I am studying. From what I have learned in the Afghanistan case, cultural imperialism and imperialism more broadly are still relevant theoretical and empirical frameworks.

These three publications—Appadurai's "Disjuncture and Difference in the Global Cultural Economy" (1990), Liebes and Katz's *Dallas* study (1993), and Tomlinson's *Cultural Imperialism* (2002)—have defined and continue to define the dominant push toward more neutral theories of globalization, which dismiss cultural imperialism as too outdated a framework to understand the dynamics, scope, and unpredictability of current transnational media "flows." Taken together, they argue today's global phenomena lack the logic, order, cohesion, and coherence of the nefarious colonial past. Today's global "flows," which are of an unprecedented "speed, scale, and volume," are marked by their "disjuncture," "nonisomorphism," "diffusion," "decentralization," "disorganization," and "fluidity." They have also criticized Herbert Schiller and others who hold the cultural imperialism position as being too "totalizing" and "monolithic" in their view of capitalism and imperialism's tendency to expand, dominate, and subjugate vulnerable and developing nations.

On the contrary, I believe these scholars who have theorized globalization as a neutral formation have in fact been too totalizing and monolithic in diminishing the hand of empire along with its egregiousness, its formidable power, and global disparities. Based on my ethnographic research in Afghanistan, I find these globalization narratives paint too rosy a picture of today's global and transnational movements and interactions. My intention is not to entirely negate the globalization thesis. In fact I find some of its language and premises useful. Indeed, the United States and West more generally should not be singled out as the only hegemonic global media players. As we will see in the coming chapters, Afghanistan is awash in foreign media from all over the world, and American media products, with the exception of reality TV, are in fact not popular. Rather, my point is to assert the viability and necessity of cultural imperialism as a conceptual framework and school of thought to understand the current state of global dystopia. Nonetheless, in the wake of the collapse of the Soviet Union, the United States, as the last superpower standing with its unmatched military might, having waged wars and military attacks across the world, should be singled out as an imperialist country.

Notable scholars from a variety of disciplines have been writing against the dominant paradigm of globalization and its copious scholarship. Feminist scholars (Ahmed, Castañeda, and Fortie 2004; Scott 2002, 2010; Katz 2001; Friedman 1998; Freeman 2001; Grewal and Kaplan 1994; Mohanty 2003; Shohat 2001; Shohat and Stam 1994) have been at the forefront of calling for new ways of theorizing globalization, including gendering globalization. Critical of Appadurai's "scapes" and "flows" and other formulations that do not account sufficiently for power relations, they have created new terminology to show the "anti-flows," "disparities," and "reverberations" embedded in global phenomena. As Marwan Kraidy writes, "It has become fashionable in some international communication circles to dismiss cultural imperialism as a monolithic theory that is lacking subtlety and increasingly questioned by empirical research. Cultural imperialism does have some weaknesses, but it also continues to be useful. Perhaps the most important contribution of cultural imperialism is the argument that international communication flows, processes, and effects are permeated by power" (2002, 4).

In his book *Humanism and Democratic Criticism* (2004), the late postcolonial scholar Edward Said critiques the "overmastering paradigm of globalization" and calls on humanist scholars to challenge the many ways the United States, as the last standing superpower in the wake of the Cold War, has consolidated its power and launched deadly economic sanctions and military campaigns across the MENASA region, with little journalistic or international oversight. "America's place in the world of nations and cultures . . .—based on the projection and deployment of vast military, political, and economic resources—has amounted to a new variety of mostly unchallenged interventionism" (78–79).

Of equal import are the critical media scholars (Aouragh and Chakravartty 2016; Boyd-Barrett 1998; Chakravartty and Zhao 2008; D. Schiller 2014; H. Schiller 1976, 1991) who argue that imperialism is dead neither in the academy nor in the real world. It was dying only in media studies due to the entrenchment of the globalization paradigm coupled with the rise of "digital utopianism": "In the last 15 years, across disciplines of History to Political Science, Anthropology to Literature, questions about the continuity and transformation of US Empire have been at the centre, as opposed to the margins of scholarly debate. . . . In contrast, the deafening silence [in the field of media and communication] when it comes to the legacy of US Empire in conjunction with a myopic focus on digital media in catalyzing and/or transforming social movements is especially puzzling given the centrality of these same technologies to the ongoing wars in the MENA region, Afghanistan, and Pakistan" (Aouragh and Chakravartty 2016, 560). These scholars have been successfully resuscitating and building upon the earlier discourse of cultural imperialism while taking into account both continuities and transformations in contemporary US empire.

At the same time, these scholars have challenged the prevailing "digital utopianism," interrogating its underlying political project of erasing the hand of empire with its sweeping optimism. In the aftermath of the Arab Spring and Iranian Green Movement, viewing their shortcomings in hindsight, new research has emerged to demonstrate that the revolutionary rhetoric ascribed to digital media was exaggerated and subject to co-optation by larger regimes (Alexander and Aouragh 2014; Osman 2014a; Ramadan 2012). Other scholars have demonstrated that media infrastructures, platforms, and policies, including digital technologies, which have been highly celebrated and touted as the new beacons of media and democracy, are still largely controlled, centralized, and consolidated by Western corporations in private-public partnerships with Western governments (Chakravartty 2019; Chakravartty and Zhao 2008; D. Schiller 2014). Thanks to these scholars, the shadowy coordination and compliance of big information and communications technology corporations—be they in the newer internet and digital communications or older telecommunications—with US imperial interests have come to light.

To say that cultural imperialism is a relic of the past, outmoded, and obsolete is to say that its forebear, imperialism, is dead too. US imperialism is alive and well throughout the MENASA region, including Afghanistan. Today Afghanistan does not have full sovereignty over its airspace, airwaves, or land. The US government has given itself, with its powerful military might behind it, jurisdiction over Afghan airspace above a certain altitude; airwaves, due to its being the largest media donor and builder of media infrastructure, which I describe in the next chapter; and land, via its ever-growing military bases and prisons, including secret black sites. In the two decades of the US war in the Af-Pak region, the US Armed Forces have unleashed a barrage of aerial and ground attacks resulting in the deaths of thousands, subjected people to over 10,000 night raids, and imprisoned and tortured countless others (Osman 2017).

Needless to say, these operations, which have been carried out predominantly in the provincial Pashtun areas of Afghanistan and Pakistan outside the purview of cities and the international press, have been causing uproar and unrest. Pashtuns and their allies have been organizing massive protests, riots, and peace vigils as well as forming social and political movements in order to demand accountability and protection from their respective governments. To distance themselves from charges of collusion with the US government and its violence, in 2011 leaders of the Pakistani army also lashed out against the Obama-era raid that killed Osama bin Laden, claiming that the raid was a gross violation of their sovereignty because it was carried out without the knowledge of the Pakistani government.

Shortly thereafter, in 2012, the Pakistani government entirely cut off diplomatic ties with the Obama administration and closed down its ocean-to-land routes, preventing the US military and NATO from sending their supplies to Afghanistan. Likewise, Pakistan and Iran have shot down multiple US drones allegedly in their airspace. In response, the US government began to decrease its military activities in Pakistan. The Afghan government, being in a weaker, dependent, subject colony position to the United States, did not and does not have the same ability to thwart the rising tide of US military operations and killings. The Afghan National Army relies heavily on the US government for its funding and training and therefore is not in a position to act independently and shoot US drones. This was also the case during the Soviet occupation until the Afghan National Army revolted and joined the mujahideen resistance, called "freedom fighters" by the US government in the Reagan era and now called "insurgents," "terrorists," "Islamists," and "extremists."

Toward the end of his ten-year presidency, Hamid Karzai tried unsuccessfully to stymie the violence of US drone attacks and night raids, which were the

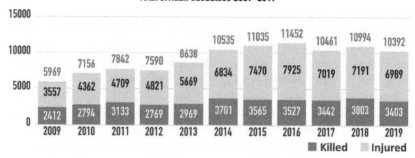

Total Civilian Casualties 2009–2019

FIGURE 2.1. As mandated by the UN Security Council, the United Nations Assistance Mission in Afghanistan (UNAMA) prepares yearly civilian casualties reports "as part of an advocacy-oriented approach to reduce casualties." UNAMA shares its data with the assailant parties "so that they may address the harm they cause and implement measures to better protect civilians." See https://unama.unmissions.org/protection-of-civilians-reports.

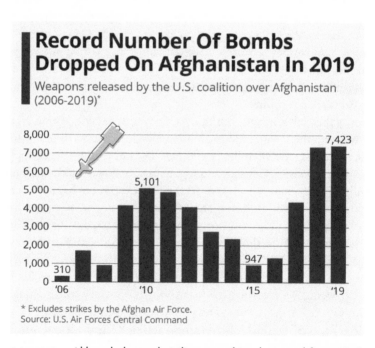

Record Number Of Bombs Dropped On Afghanistan In 2019

Weapons released by the U.S. coalition over Afghanistan (2006-2019)*

* Excludes strikes by the Afghan Air Force.
Source: U.S. Air Forces Central Command

FIGURE 2.2. Although the total civilian casualties decreased from 2018 to 2019, the US coalition forces dropped a record number of bombs on Afghanistan in 2019. Credit: Data journalist Niall McCarthy for Statista.

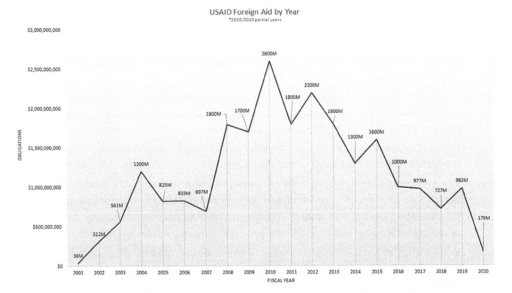

FIGURE 2.3. This graph shows USAID's funding expenditures in Afghanistan from 2001 to 2020. The first major drop in funding began in 2010, then again in 2019. See https://explorer .usaid.gov/cd/AFG for more details.

two biggest public grievances according to both Afghan television programs and my research. In 2013 he refused to sign the Bilateral Security Agreement with the US government, which would grant US officials and soldiers full immunity in Afghan and international courts for war crimes. Thus began Karzai's downfall as the US government turned against him and began to support Ashraf Ghani, who immediately signed the agreement in 2014 upon becoming president. And so the business of war and violence perpetuated against the people of Afghanistan has continued full force through the course of my research and writing. According to UN Assistance Mission in Afghanistan reports, under the Trump administration, civilian casualties are now at an all-time high.

In 2017, the United States dropped the largest non-nuclear bomb on the village of Achin near the Pakistani border. The MOAB—the Massive Ordnance Air Blast, or "Mother of All Bombs"—was the largest scale bomb detonated since World War II. On US network news, President Trump eagerly gloated about the MOAB's power, and a five-second aerial clip of the blast released by the US military also circulated on all the major networks. Aside from these sound bites and clips, in the US mainstream media there was no additional follow-up or further information about this serious matter. Hence it is little known that after declaring there were no civilian casualties, the US government quarantined the entire area. News agencies and television programs in Afghanistan, on the other hand, reported that in the aftermath of the bombing, local and international journalists, as well as many Afghan government officials, were fenced out from the impact zone (Osman 2019c).

As reports of the United States' extensive torture network, rendition programs, and other war crimes, including those that have resulted in a spike in civilian casualties, in MENASA countries continue to leak and surface, the egregiousness and duplicity of the US empire and its embedded corporate media are also becoming apparent. In March 2019, US secretary of state Mike Pompeo announced that the United States would revoke or deny visas to International Criminal Court officials if they continued their investigations into US and allied troops' war crimes in Afghanistan. Pompeo also threatened economic sanctions against the ICC if it proceeded with its investigations. At the same time, the US government is cracking down on whistleblowers and journalists. These facts, along with the corporate media's complicity in uncritically promoting the wars in the MENASA region by touting the US government's fabricated narrative of weapons of mass destruction and its underestimation of the scale and scope of its drone, torture, and killing programs and other war atrocities, have led to the United States falling in international media press freedom rankings (Osman 2019a).

When there are revelations that show the imperialism of the US government abroad and its hegemony at home, which have resulted in the crises in US journalism—namely issues of accountability, representational politics, and accuracy—they are often dismissed as anomalies. As Miriyam Aouragh and Paula Chakravartty have argued, "While there was certainly scholarly interest in the failures of journalistic accountability that led to the marketing of the Iraq invasion and the countervailing influence of Al Jazeera, and subsequent attention to official and leaked information of torture and civilian casualties, most of these works were grounded in liberal normative assumptions that these were but aberrations of US democratic ideals in need of reform" (2016, 561). However, as they explain, this is the status quo of empire. Likewise, Edward Said critiqued the media's ready acceptance of the Bush administration's false narrative of weapons of mass destruction (2004).

Although the rhetoric of present-day US wars and military campaigns across the MENASA region and Latin America suggests otherwise, many of the US government's actions, including the ones I described in this section, are imperialist, not mere "interventions," innocuous cross-cultural engagements, or benevolent involvement in the spirit of humanism, human rights, or humanitarianism. Purnima Bose (2020) explains the covert goals of US foreign policy in Afghanistan: (1) Control over global oil production and distribution, (2) establishing and maintaining military bases to check terrorism and to erode the influence of Russia, and possibly China and India (or any other possible geopolitical competitors), (3) access to Afghanistan's mineral wealth, and (4) profits from infrastructure and rebuilding projects, in which lucrative deals are made with private corporations and corruption overflows.

Post-9/11 studies conducted by the Pentagon and the US Geological Survey have estimated that Afghanistan has an estimated one trillion dollars worth of untapped mineral deposits (Risen 2010). These revelations of mineral wealth spurred the Trump administration to extend the war and use private security firms to secure those areas with violence or by paying off the warlords who controlled them. Likewise, private security and other firms, which the US government routinely contracts to provide all kinds of auxiliary and essential services to its forces abroad, have become a highly profitable war industry. In fact, during Trump's presidency the use of private contracted firms like DynCorp, Blackwater, Halliburton, and many others that were also deployed in Iraq has more than doubled. These private firms with close ties to conservative senior US government officials are even less accountable for their actions and expenditures than government agencies. They often act as the shadow counterpart of the US army.

Thanks largely to the media in Afghanistan, the gap between the rhetoric and the real motives of the US war in Afghanistan is also becoming evident to the Afghan public. In televised proceedings of the Afghan Parliament, the MPs are now describing the US presence in Afghanistan as an occupation, *ishtaghaal* in Persian, whereas earlier in the wake of 9/11, it was called an "intervention" and even "liberation" from the Taliban. Even in the US, with its censored corporate media, the perception of the War in Afghanistan, has shifted from the "good war" to avenge the 9/11 attacks and liberate women to a misdirected and confusing "forever war" stretching on endlessly and ambiguously.

As Achille Mbembe demonstrates in his influential essay "Necropolitics" (2003), imperialism and colonialism are marked first and foremost by violence—the taking of another's sovereignty—be it bodily or territorially, as justified by racism, resource extraction, and market expansion. Mbembe rejects scholarly endeavors that analyze the workings of imperialism and colonialism using the "normative theories of democracy" as inadequate and false. Such accounts demarcate the violence of imperialism as ruptures in an otherwise judicious system of democratic statecraft. On the contrary, Mbembe argues that the violence of imperialism is very much constituted within the social order and institutions of imperialist countries (12–16). Building on Michel Foucault's concept of biopower—"the conditions for the acceptability of putting to death" (Foucault 2007)—he puts forward his concept of "necropower" and "necropolitics," explaining how colonial violence granted itself the right not only to put subject populations to death but also to keep them in an injured state, vacillating between life and death (Mbembe 2003, 17).

In the last part of his genealogical account, Mbembe continues his bleak tour through the necropolitical machinations of late-colonial occupations in apartheid South Africa and Palestine. Here he describes three key tactics of contemporary occupation as enabled by new technologies of war, surveillance, and communication: (1) territorialization, preventing the free movement of occupied communities, (2) infrastructural warfare, destroying all the infrastructural developments of the society, including housing, communications, hospitals, roadways, transportation, and so forth, by new and old technologies of war in order to build new ones, and (3) infrastructural splintering, creating parallel infrastructures for occupied and occupier. As shown above, these same tactics of contemporary occupation are employed in Afghanistan.

Today the United States wields incredible power over all facets of Afghan life, including death, politics, and regional geopolitics more broadly. In other words, aside from the actual technologies of communication, control, and violence, which have changed significantly, in many other ways neoimperialism and the colonialism of the past share the same dynamics, imperatives, and outcomes. Afghanistan today bears a striking similarity to when most of its affairs were under control of the British Empire until the Third Anglo-Afghan War of 1919, known as the War of Independence in Afghanistan. I therefore disagree with the globalizationists' supposition that the dynamics of today's global interventions are vastly different from "the age of high imperialism and colonialism."

However, Afghanistan's asymmetrical positionality is not simply one of unilateral subjugation of a weak state by stronger ones. Furthermore, how the country's positionality has shaped its sense of itself is a complex phenomenon that Afghanistan studies scholars of the region have tried to analyze for a long time. As the revisionist Afghanistan historian Robert Crews has observed in his extensive archival research and interviews, Afghans have "a cosmopolitan sensibility" that "drew strength from an intellectual tradition that has long imagined Afghans as central to global politics. This way of thinking also reflected a sense, built up by the collective memories of millions of Afghan families, of a shared past stamped by various kinds of diaspora experience, of inhabiting all parts of the global far beyond the borders of their country" (2015, 1). Afghans see themselves as neither victims nor free agents but as negotiators, diplomats, and hagglers who have always had to make tough compromises in order to maintain a very shaky sovereignty—this is also true of the media makers I interviewed.

In this section I have outlined the key debates in global media studies and provided my own position within them. I have also shown the problems of method. Critiques of the methodological integrity and soundness of the classic globalization and media imperialism works *How to Read Donald Duck* (Dorfman and Mattelart 1975), the *Dallas* study (Liebes and Katz 1993), "Disjuncture and Difference in the Global Cultural Economy" (Appadurai 1996a), and *Cultural Imperialism* (Tomlinson 2002), which I have distilled here, have raised the issue of how best to study global and transnational media, with the globalization camp arguing that the difficulty of determining cultural imperialism is one more reason why it is not a useful framework. Thus I will conclude this section by providing suggestions for best practices to avoid the methodological pitfalls that global media scholars have taken to task.

PHOTO 2.4. Author and television reporters in a US military Chinook helicopter, invited to join US ambassador Karl Eikenberry's diplomatic mission from Kabul to Kunar in 2009.

PHOTOS 2.5 AND 2.6. A male and a female US Air Force gunners flying over eastern Afghanistan.

PHOTO 2.7. US armed forces in Kabul.

PHOTO 2.8. Ambassador Eikenberry speaking with the Afghan press in Kunar. Eikenberry, who served first as the commanding general and then chief ambassador to Afghanistan, is emblematic of the merging of the military and diplomatic branches.

PHOTO 2.9. During the Obama years, the US military and foreign services were more open and fostered opportunities for the press and researchers.

The impact of transnational global media flows, be it globalization or cultural imperialism, can come into focus only via grounded studies that entail following the money trail, hence a political economy approach, coupled with ethnographic work with producers and audiences, and textual/content analysis, which I have attempted to do in this book. In response to the problems of method in the field, many scholars are advocating for a case-by-case approach that is empirical, localized, and ethnographic (Ginsburg, Abu-Lughod, and Larkin 2002; Kraidy 2005; Skuse, Gillespie, and Power 2011). Ethnographic studies of reception and production offer a nuanced understanding of diverse media practices as they are shaped in everyday life, which grand narratives and macrostructures alone cannot do. Macro-level studies can easily miss the crucial details and differences between places, which are essential to understanding how global forces work in different contexts. Likewise, a zoomed-in localized perspective can miss the structural and infrastructural conditions of the global political economy. Thus a holistic approach that tracks global phenomena on a micro and macro level is the most likely way to unpack and detangle the many layers and tentacles of those phenomena. However, actually tracking how global phenomena take shape in particular cultural locations is logistically challenging and time consuming. It takes a considerable amount of time to build the relationships, language skills, and cultural fluency necessary for this type of research. Thus such ethnographic work is not readily undertaken. Yet this multimodal method is the most effective method to understand the effects and complexity of cross-national media flows.

International Development Projects: The Good, the Bad, and the Imperialist

As scholarly critics of development have rightly demonstrated, development is in many ways a euphemism for keeping structural power arrangements as they are in favor of imperial forces (Barker 2008; Bose 2020; Boyd-Barrett 1977; H. Schiller 1976, 1991; D. Schiller 2000; Shah 2012; Mitchell 2002b; Wilkins 2000, 2010). From this view, imperialism and development are two sides of the same coin, with one usually ushering in the other. A dark joke in Afghanistan is that the Russians brought in development then full-on invasion, war, and occupation, whereas the Americans brought in bombardment and war and then development and now full-on war again. Oftentimes development is only a Band-Aid, a public relations spin campaign designed to cover up and distract from the more nefarious imperialist military, economic, or geopolitical plans and appease the citizenry of the home and subject countries. In fact more than half of US development aid money to Afghanistan was funneled through the Department of Defense.[1]

While I fully agree that the global development infrastructure is deeply entrenched and implicated within the hegemonic infrastructure of imperialism, I also believe it is important to at least partially detangle and distinguish development from imperialism. My fieldwork in Afghanistan has revealed a more complex and contradictory picture. In order to determine their merits and problems, development projects must be evaluated on a case-by-case basis. The main reason some development projects, especially in the media sector, have yielded positive results is because of the political economy that sustains them.

As I describe in the next chapter, Afghanistan has an especially robust media sector, with many competing media outlets, resembling a public service rather than a strictly commercial media model. This is the result of a political economy of media development funding that is international and multilateral in scope, which forces television channels to cater to the public's interests. Countries whose economic, media, and political development is unilaterally funded and dependent on one powerful donor country are susceptible to social influence and geopolitical control by that donor country. As I have written elsewhere, this is the case with Russia and Afghanistan's neighbors to the north, the other post-Soviet Central Asian "stans." These unilateral funding systems replicate colonial structures, wherein the subordinate state's elite class, as chosen vassals of empire, begin to reproduce the authoritarian regime of the donor country (Osman 2019a).

Furthermore, as my project progressed and the United States under the Trump administration shifted its focus to more aggressive, egregious, and destabilizing military approaches, entirely abandoning the development rhetoric and projects that had been launched over the last two decades, I felt it doubly important to extract the generative development projects from the truly problematic ones. Thus while grounding my work in leftist critiques of development communication, I believe it is equally important to defend the entire complicated geopolitical enterprise of development against attacks from the Right. Backed by Orientalist discourses, conservative right-wing US public and private sector officials have long been arguing that development and modernizing projects are futile in "backward," "tribal," and "traditional" countries like Afghanistan. Self-described conservative organizations such as Judicial Watch and conservative media institutions like Fox News are eager to expose the failures, real or imaginary, of USAID (US Agency for International Development) and other development organizations. Yet this powerful and vociferous group of US neoliberals are far from noninterventionists seeking peaceful coexistence. Rather, they are war hawks, who fervently believe in and advocate for war and violence, either by direct attacks or through orchestrated coups. For them, dismantling foreign development is part of a militant xenophobic and racist ideology, embedded in the belief that force is the only way to control unruly MENASA people.

In my fieldwork I witnessed how some of the post-9/11 international development projects have created a semblance of a functioning society in Afghanistan, giving hope to a despondent people who have experienced over four decades of nonstop death, destruction, and loss. In the media sector, many of the proponents of media independence in Afghanistan who train and support journalists' rights as well as monitor and lobby for the media more broadly are NGOs funded by the United States. This is despite continued suppression of media freedoms, journalists, and whistleblowers on the home front in the United States (Curran and Hesmondhalgh 2019; Osman 2019a).

Whereas the campaigns I described in the last section are top-down, shortsighted, and duplicitous and consider only the interests of the imperial country, good development projects are well intentioned, well researched, collaborative, participatory, financially equitable, and ground-up. Recognizing the structural imbalances, some transnational and international organizations are trying to level the cultural playing field by training local Afghans to produce their own media; creating domestic and international venues, festivals, and markets for the media; creating advocacy, monitoring, and watchdog organizations; and promoting human rights.

The Kassel Documentary Film and Video Festival (Dokfest), for example, launched two traveling showcases called Splice In: Film Festival on Gender and Politics in Afghanistan, the Neighbouring Countries, and Europe and Second Take: Gender and Society in Cinema, featuring films by and about Afghan women to travel throughout Europe and the MENASA region. In the fall of 2007, my codirected feature documentary *Postcards from Tora Bora* was selected by Splice In and screened in Europe. The special program then traveled to Kabul in the summer of 2008 under the title of Second Take. The Berlin-based organizers, filmmakers Sandra Schäfer and Elfe Brandenburger, employed a collaborative method by working closely with their paid Afghanistan-based team consisting mostly of Afghans, whom I volunteered with in order to observe their operations. Every logistical phase of the film festival was conducted with the explicit goal of maximizing the participation of Afghan women, especially from low socioeconomic backgrounds.

From the curatorial process, to the design and venue selection, to the corresponding workshops and trainings, their main concern was how to generate a discussion about women's rights from the perspective of those most affected by it. All the screenings, events, and workshops were free to attend for local Afghan women and designed to privilege their voice and give them a platform to speak not only to other Afghans but also to the international development community. The events and screenings were always sold out and filled with Afghan women from many walks of life who felt emboldened by the films, post-screening discussions, and workshops to lead the conversation.

The Splice In and Second Take events were some of the most diverse in terms of women's participation and of centering their problems, hopes, and ideas for moving forward. For example, their corresponding conference, "Strengthening Women's Movements: National and Transnational Experiences," brought together Muslim feminists, women's rights activists, politicians, journalists, lawyers, and film critics from Afghanistan, India, and Iran to build alliances and share ideas for increasing women's participation in civil society. Additionally, they produced multilingual publications to feature interviews and work by leading theorists and practitioners on the topic. Splice In and Second Take fostered a safe space to have difficult conversations about culture, arts, politics, trauma, and healing. Just as importantly, the festivals also enabled many of the local Afghan women, including war widows, to connect directly to the development community, which they are often excluded from, for much-needed jobs and other life-saving resources for themselves and their children, such as food distribution, health care, and the like.[2]

Another amazing NGO I had the privilege to volunteer with and study was the Parisian-based "documentary training and production centre" Ateliers Varan.[3] The participatory anthropologist and filmmaker Jean Rouch and other French filmmakers started Ateliers Varan in 1981 as a collective of French filmmakers with the explicit desire to rectify the imbalances and damages of French colonialism. The 1960s and 1970s self-determination movements of France's former colonies in the MENASA region influenced them. Ateliers Varan's mission is to train filmmakers in postcolonial and developing countries to make their own films and represent themselves. The collective has trained over a thousand filmmakers throughout the world. Having met Jean Rouch

PHOTO 2.10. Martine Malalai Zikria, an Afghan French filmmaker, reporter, and actress, also works for Ateliers Varan, Kabul, 2009.

PHOTO 2.11. Filmmaker and professor Kelly Dolak and TV newscaster and teacher Nadira Jaan cover the Splice In film festival in the Afghan Cinema showcase for *Al Jazeera*, Kabul, 2008.

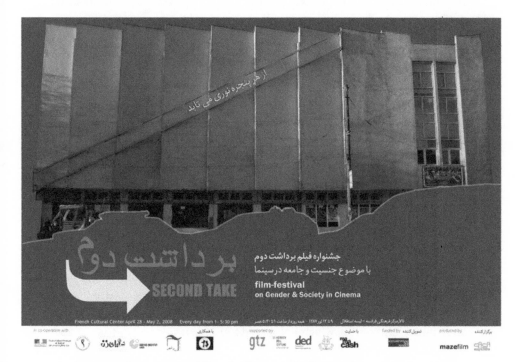

PHOTO 2.12. The promotional flyer for the Second Take: Gender & Society in Cinema Film Festival, Kabul, 2008.

and studied his films under the tutelage of Faye Ginsburg, the participatory anthropologist and collaborator of Rouch, I knew I wanted to be involved with the group even though it was outside of my central focus of fieldwork in Afghanistan.

In Afghanistan its small but lively operations, which began in 2005, were funded by a patchwork of grants from the long-standing French Cultural Centre of Kabul, the German Goethe-Institut, UNESCO, and a few smaller sources. In July 2009 I reached out to Severin Blanchet, the director of the Ateliers Varan Kabul operations and an accomplished filmmaker, who welcomed me to the school. I observed and assisted with the group's filmmaking workshops and attended four of its public showcase screenings during the course of the year. I met the talented filmmakers in training who represented an equal proportion of young men and women, mostly from the minority ethnic Hazara community. The fact that the filmmakers produced incredibly high-quality documentary films on par with top film programs in the United States was a testament to the experience and dedication of Blanchet and his French crew, including Aurélie Ricard and Marie-Claude Treilhou as well as the Afghan French filmmakers Martine Malalai Zikria and Barmak Akram. They taught everything from cinematography and editing to marketing and distribution. In fact, a number of the films went on to win prizes at prestigious international film festivals such as Cannes, and subsequently those filmmakers used their newfound recognition as a way to get out of Afghanistan and make a better life for themselves in Europe. Similar to Splice In and Second Take, the end-of-training screenings were open to the public and well attended and attracted diverse audiences.

On February 26, 2010, Severin Blanchet was killed in a suicide bombing at a new multiuse development called Kabul City Centre. He was one of the brave and dedicated friends I made during my trips to Afghanistan whom I lost to the violence and chaos of war or who were injured. Many development aid workers, who have altruistically taken on the difficult and dangerous task of working in conflict zones, have sadly become casualties to larger forces of violence. The casualties are particularly high among Afghans who are on the front lines, especially those in media and journalism who are frequently targeted by many sides, which I describe in the upcoming chapters. Another dangerous sector is mine clearance, where death rates are high, though of the untargeted variety.

Whereas Splice In, Second Take, and Ateliers Varan were well run and well attended, seeking to reach local audiences as well as the international aid community, the much larger and better funded Kabul International Documentary and Short Film Festival, which I observed from the inside and outside in the summer and fall of 2009, was hierarchal and poorly managed and attended. Despite a larger budget and scale of operations, including the support and involvement of Afghan government officials from multiple ministries, the festival was plagued by power struggles and mismanagement.

Even the beleaguered and maligned USAID, the United States' main development arm, which has been critiqued from inside and outside of academia for fraud, corruption, and its statist enmeshment and propaganda (USGAO 2011; Shah 2012; SIGAR 2018; Wilkins 2010), has been involved in some meritorious development projects too. Nai, an Afghanistan-based journalist training and watchdog organization, receives approximately half of its operating budget from Internews Afghanistan, which is predominantly funded by USAID. According to USAID's website, since its establishment in 2005, Nai, which is also known as Nai-SOMA, Supporting Open Media in Afghanistan, has trained over 11,000 participants. Many journalists I spoke to were alumni of Nai's training workshops and events.[4] During my fieldwork, I interviewed three members of Nai's six-person team, including its executive director, Mir Abdul Wahed Hashimi, and became familiar with the group's important work. Although by comparison with its international counterparts Reporters Without Borders and the Committee to Protect Journalists, Nai is a new and small organization, its on-the-ground work tracking and documenting acts of violence and murders perpetuated against media makers as well as advocating on media makers' behalf far surpasses the scope of the Reporters Without Borders and the Committee to Protect Journalists' research. Nai comprehensively documents statistics on many aspects of incidences of violence and has an online data-mapping project, tracking the last two decades of media freedom and violence in Afghanistan. I rely on its quantitative data in my conclusion chapter, where I analyze the dangerous situation of journalists, and for the media violence charts and graphs shared in that conclusion. Nai's staff, who are trained by Internews' journalist training programs, are all Afghan and paid a living wage, which is often not the case.

Huge disparities exist in pay and labor across international development projects. For example, oftentimes Afghans, despite having the education and skills, are hired in menial labor positions such as *chaiwalas* (tea makers), cooks, cleaners, security, and drivers. Even when Afghans are hired in the same skilled positions as their international counterparts, almost all of the development organizations I encountered had two separate pay scales, which gave Afghans a tiny fraction of the salary of their counterparts.

BBC Media Action, "the BBC's educational and development charity," also has the honorable mission of spreading human rights and equality via international media projects.[5] By all accounts, BBC Media Action's mission is to introduce modernity, democracy, and capitalism to developing, transitional, and post-Communist countries. Afghanistan was a perfect candidate for the mission. Between BBC Media Action and its long-running and trusted World Service, the BBC offers a wide range of services and programming in the local languages of Afghanistan. Its base of operations there is one of the BBC's largest, with a staff of about 200 local project employees. According to its website conflict and chronic instability have characterized Afghanistan's modern history, and therefore the BBC's objectives are to assist the government in creating national unity by bringing an awareness of human rights with special attention to gender rights.[6]

In an effort to meet its mandate, BBC Media Action, which at the time was called BBC World Trust, launched the Afghan Women's Hour in January 2005. The award-winning weekly variety program explored issues concerning women's role in society and broadcast on Radio Television Afghanistan (RTA), Afghanistan's national broadcast station, until 2010. Subsequently in 2011 BBC Media Action launched its popular Azad or Open Jirga, a multilingual live audience political talk show that also broadcasts on RTA. The show is modeled on the *loya jirga* but with the explicit aim of making participation in the discussions more democratic and open to the public. Traditional *loya jirgas*, while representative of different *quowms*, are open only to tribal elders for participation. In 2019, the BBC World Service expanded its collaboration with RTA by rebroadcasting its Dari and Pashto news programs on the RTA network.[7]

Likewise, in 2005 UNESCO helped the nonprofit organization Voice of Afghan Women (VOAW) start Afghanistan's first women's community television channel by paying for broadcasting equipment and governmental registration fees to secure a frequency.[8] In my own research I was surprised to discover that Afghanistan's first television station dedicated to women's rights did not exist. During my multiple fieldwork trips, the VOAW television station was not operational. However, the VOAW organization is quite active in running a successful radio network that broadcasts in the major cities but also targets rural areas. In an interview with Jamila Mujahed, the founder of VOAW and a journalist/presenter for RTA, she explained how significant local radio is to reaching and empowering rural women, who often cannot watch or access television because of repressive community restrictions and also because electricity is even more limited in those areas.[9] Currently there is only one television station in Afghanistan that is owned or run by a woman. Shukria Barakzai, a member of Parliament, is the owner of Aria TV, a children's television channel. In 2017 two television stations, dedicated to women, Zan TV and Banu TV, both meaning women, were launched: However they have been subjected to criticism by Afghan women media makers and activists because they are owned by men and represented in international media by males and most of the senior decision-making roles are held by men (Walsh 2017).

With their socially conscious mandate, most of the transnational organizations I have discussed in this section have a progressive multicultural and plural approach to nation-building. However, the effectiveness or even existence of these media networks and development initiatives and their good intentions cannot be taken for granted.

A bigger problem brought to my attention confidentially was that the development community's interest in "scientific" mechanisms of assessment—be they measuring audiences or accounting expenditures—was often a means of justifying developers' own funding and spending practices and those of their clients or partners. They were not actually accounting and assessing and retrieving real feedback from people. Five of the world's biggest accounting, monitoring, and evaluations firms—Booz Allen Hamilton, Ernst and Young, Deloitte and Touche, KPMG, and Cooper Lybranth—all have large operations in Kabul, enterprises that can easily spend from $25 million to $150 million on contracts in one or two years with no practical results to show for them (SIGAR 2018). A number of projects were recently discovered to exist only on paper. A source I spoke to on the condition of anonymity from one of the accounting firms confirmed that cases of poor performance or obvious embezzlement are sometimes overlooked. Locals will point to many examples of recently "rebuilt" highways, schools, and hospital buildings that are already crumbling due to shoddy construction practices and poor-quality materials.

Development practices of "tied aid" or "conditional aid", whereby donor countries contractually stipulate that about fifty percent of the allocated money be returned to their own domestic revenue, also exacerbate the problems of development in Afghanistan. These cases and practices contribute to making what has been termed "phantom aid" the hallmark of the post 9/11 development era in Afghanistan. Only a small fraction of the large sums of allocated money has actually reached Afghanistan or helped those that need it most. Rather most of it is unlawfully looted or siphoned off via the supposedly lawful but equally egregious modern methods of tied aid and accounting technics. Thus instead of reaching its intended receipts and improving conditions and lives in Afghanistan, international donor aid by prioritizing the economies and national interests of donor countries has lined the pockets of middlemen, high ranking officials, and businessmen.

According to investigative reports released by CorpWatch and Amnesty International, wasteful expenditures, huge overheads, and gross misappropriation of funds plague the system (Nawa 2006). A 2010 study conducted by the U.N. High Commissioner for Human Rights (UNHCR) to assess the first decade of development found that that the despite the enormous expenditures of Western aid money, it had not improved the severe poverty situation in Afghanistan. The UNHCR country representative stated, "Patronage, corruption, impunity and over-emphasis on short-term goals rather than targeted long-term development are exacerbating a situation of dire poverty" (UPI 2010). The UN Office on Drugs and Crime report, which surveyed 7,600 people in twelve provinces, revealed that 54 percent of Afghans think international NGOs "are corrupt and are in the country just to get rich." The report also shows that the number one problem facing Afghans is "corruption," with "insecurity" coming in second and "unemployment" in third place (UNODC 2010, 30).

SIGAR, the Office of the Special Inspector General for Afghanistan Reconstruction, which was mandated in 2008 by the US Congress to provide oversight of US reconstruction expenditures, has exposed numerous cases of fraud and misappropriation of American taxpayer moneys. Some of SIGAR's investigative findings of fraud include the Kabul Bank/International Monetary Fund (IMF) scandal that shut down the bank and USAID's $216 million Promoting Gender Equity in National Priority Programs (SIGAR 2018; Boone 2011). The Afghanistan Papers, a set of 2,000 pages of internal documents from SIGAR obtained by the *Washington Post* through the Freedom of Information Act, further confirms that fraud and corruption was prevalent in US development spending. In a testimony before the House Foreign Affairs Committee, John F. Sopko, the special inspector general, said the more than $132 billion the United States spent on development of Afghanistan was marked and marred by "mendacity and hubris." "As an example, Sopko said U.S. officials have lied in the past about the number of Afghan children enrolled in schools—a key marker of progress touted by the Obama administration—even though they 'knew the data was bad.' He also said U.S. officials falsely claimed major gains in Afghan life expectancy that were statistically impossible to achieve" (Whitlock 2020). When these large-scale cases of fraud and corruption are uncovered and become public, international donors and their Afghan partners are quick to point fingers and lay the culpability on each other.

Many development projects are plagued by problems intrinsic to the international development economy, including national and individual greed, which manifest in a lack of accountability, poor monitoring and evaluation, and corruption/fraud. Sometimes this is because of an imperialist mindset that is not well intentioned and collaborative and dictates that the use of development aid should benefit the sponsoring country. In other instances, the problems are due to poor design and execution. However, while these structural problems persist and exist, overall this period of development has been a turning point for the betterment of Afghanistan. For many young Afghans, this post-9/11 era was their first glimpse of a semi-functional society and peace. The exemplary development projects and organizations I have highlighted in this section are a few of the many artistic, cultural, civic engagement, political, and intellectual initiatives that have flourished. I had not witnessed social and public works projects and activities on this scale since my childhood in Kabul in the prewar era.

Although space constraints do not permit me to elaborate on other meritorious development projects, a few other noteworthy ones deserve at least a mention. The Killid Group and Pajhwok Afghan News are two post-9/11 news organizations that have evolved from small startups into powerful media institutions that employ dozens of Afghans and are known for their hard-hitting investigative reporting for which they have won international journalism awards.[10] I am also grateful for the fastidious media and peacekeeping work of the UN Assistance Mission in Afghanistan (UNAMA).[11] I worked closely with these organizations and rely on their reports and news throughout this book. In terms of music, the Kabul International Music Festival in conjunction with the Afghan National Institute of Music, Sarmast's Music School, and the Music Program of Kabul University have been rehabilitating traditional Afghan music by reconnecting it to its long history of collaboration with Indian, Pakistani, and Iranian musicians. Furthermore, the Turquoise Mountain Foundation and the Aga Khan Development Network both have done incredible work rebuilding Afghanistan's historical sites, such as numerous areas of the Old City of Kabul and the Gardens of Babur, while helping to train a new generation of craftsmen and craftspeople in traditional building practices.

Conclusion

Thus, while all imperial projects are intrinsically egregious, not all development projects are. With a case-by-case approach, it becomes possible to distinguish between beneficial and problematic development projects. Based on the differences I have outlined in this section, I propose two types of gazes, the imperial gaze and the development gaze, as useful categories of analysis to demarcate and identify international interventions, military campaigns, and development projects. Of course development projects can be further classified according to their efficacy. I elaborated on these conceptual frameworks with respect to how Afghan reformers and modernizers have historically put them into practice as compared with imperialists in the previous chapter. I will further elaborate on the development and imperial gazes with respect to how Afghan television producers think in chapter 4.

My conceptual framework of development and imperial gazes are similar to Matt Sienkiewicz's concept of "soft-psy," which he describes as a melding of market-oriented, neoliberal "soft power" entertainment with more militaristic "psyops" approaches to information control and censorship. Psychological operations, coined during World War II by the Psychological War Division and its equally nefarious contemporary counterpart COINTELPRO, deploy covert and overt methods of manipulating content and messages via infiltration, discrediting, and disruption. In his book *The Other Air Force: U.S. Efforts to Reshape Middle Eastern Media since 9/11*, Sienkiewicz takes an impressive comparative systems approach in analyzing how US government funding is influencing the media in Afghanistan, Iraq, and the Palestinian territories. Although our methods are different, Sienkiewicz and I make the same arguments and arrive at the same conclusions, that US development communication efforts post-9/11 do not all fall into another instance of US media imperialism and pure propaganda. As Sienkiewicz explains, "Certainly, America wields a level of military, political, and economic power that constantly inscribes itself on programs produced with US dollars. However, in defiance of orthodox media imperialist understandings, the contemporary American system of media support is one that embraces and depends on important levels of local agency, while nonetheless aiming to assert US hegemony. The opportunities presented by American media-assistance projects in places such as Afghanistan and Palestine result in complex media texts that display surprising levels of personal and communal expressions on the part of Middle Eastern producers" (2016, 2).

Having poured millions of dollars into local television and radio in the Middle East, the US government certainly wants to generate pro-US government content and ideology. However, as Sienkiewicz shows, the results are much more complicated in that local producers in a number of instances are able to assert their own creative and political agendas. As he explains, this is not to say that there are not egregious cases of media censorship and imperialism. There are. Sienkiewicz gives many examples where US government–funded Middle Eastern media organizations are given explicit directives to not cover and report on certain topics, such as the Arabic-language Radio Sawa and Alhurra TV, which are mandated by their US funders to not be critical of Israel.[12]

Likewise, as I explain in chapter 4, US-funded Afghan television stations are incentivized not to cover civilian casualties or other reports that portray the US war in Afghanistan in a negative light. Clearly, these are examples of US propaganda and media imperialism. However, like Sienkiewicz, I believe it is important to distinguish between the malevolent and better media development projects because it is in these spaces, in the gaps and interstices between them, that the agency and freedom to deviate from the prescribed script and message can manifest and thrive. It is this long-leash approach to development communication that can occasionally enable local producers to bite the hand that feeds them, as I describe in the coming chapters.

CHAPTER 3

Afghan Television Production

A Distinctive Political Economy

Introduction

With more suicide bombs, attacks, and killings of civilians by official and un-official Afghan and foreign forces, cases of rampant corruption and blatant disregard of the law by Afghans and foreigners, and a litany of other disasters associated with collapsed, war-torn countries, most everyone agrees that the situation in Afghanistan is becoming more dire. After the initial ouster of the Taliban and renewed promises by the international community to rebuild the country, many Afghans and non-Afghans wishfully imagined that the country was entering a postwar, post-conflict, post–religious extremism era. Yet two decades into international and local efforts to build the nation and bring a semblance of peace to the site of the United States' longest running war, Afghanistan continues to plummet into lawlessness and war. The dream of a functioning democratic nation is moving further from reality. Still, the media is often extolled as the "candle that burns in the darkness."[1]

After over four decades of war, including a six-year blackout by the Taliban of all media except their own Sharia Radio, post-9/11 Afghanistan is experiencing a surge in new media creation with dozens of new free broadcast television and radio stations, mobile telephone providers, and a fledgling but steadily growing internet infrastructure. A new configuration of resources from a combination of foreign, domestic, private, and public sources has enabled this unprecedented proliferation of media. While most television station owners describe their networks as private enterprises that function predominantly on advertising revenue, some investigation made it clear that other sources of support also come from a combination of activities and sponsors, both Afghan and foreign, clandestine and transparent. Iran, India, Turkey, Russia, and the United States, among many other nations, help fund the television stations or programs. It is difficult to ascertain exact figures of funding because donor countries and receiving media outlets intentionally obfuscate them for a variety of reasons, including fear that audiences will charge them with biased reporting and programming and favoring the interests of the donor nation, namely propaganda.

What is abundantly clear, however, is that Afghanistan has an artificially inflated media market with an abundance of media outlets, including a staggering fifty (and growing) private broadcast television stations, which would not be financially feasible without development aid. Where the funding comes from for Afghanistan's burgeoning media outlets, including television stations, is also no secret to the Afghan population. For the most part, they know which television stations are affiliated with which political parties, ethnic groups, underground economies, and foreign powers and watch them accordingly.

Through my research, I discovered that television in Afghanistan is funded in several ways, some that were surely never imagined by media theorists. Overhead and production costs are funded indirectly by arms or opium revenues, directly through investments by foreign governments with particular agendas for winning Afghan hearts and minds, and by commercial ad revenues. Speaking in broad terms, in the West, the political economy of television has been established in two ways: the British public service broadcasting model of citizen "uplift" and the American commercial model in which advertising is crucial for profits. In Afghanistan, a third distinctive economic model is emerging that is rooted in the relationships of patronage that were established during the Cold War, in development aid, and in illicit opium/arms trade.

With over four dozen free new terrestrial television stations and counting, Afghanistan can boast that it offers viewers more choices for programming than many developing or even developed countries. This variety and diversity of content that the television stations provide forms the basis of Jürgen Habermas's theory of the public sphere (1991a, [1962] 1991b): more free channels (in his case study, publications) equals more sources for the dissemination of information, which equals more competition for the creation of a marketplace of debate and ideas. That is, there is a direct correlation between the amount and diversity of international resources that are being funneled into the Afghan media sector and the number and diversity of media outlets and programs that result. The international development community also provides a degree of oversight, protection, and accountability for free speech and local journalists. There are many international media watchdog and media training organizations that genuinely believe in their mission to create an independent media and diverse public sphere in Afghanistan.

Additionally, the UN-mandated post-9/11 constitution has laid many of the foundations of democratic societies. Although the Afghan government is mired knee-deep in corruption, nepotism, factionalism, and partisan politics, the different branches of the government—consisting of the president's office, two parliaments, and the courts—are able to check and curb one another's powers to some degree. The constitution also mandates that at least 25 percent of both parliaments must consist of female MPs. Most importantly, media freedom is legislated in the post-9/11 constitution, although Article 3, which prohibits anything that is deemed "contrary to the sacred religion of Islam," is used by government officials to try to censor, ban, charge, or fine television stations.[2] At the same time, a common joke among Afghan media professionals is that you have freedom to express yourself but no more freedom after the expression. A good example of this is the case of Parwez Kambakhsh, a college student and journalist from Balkh, who was sentenced to death for distributing an article from the internet that was critical of Islam's dictates regarding women. Likewise, Nasir Fayaz, the host of a political discussion program on ATN called *Haqiqat* (The truth) was arrested for criticizing the incompetence of government ministers and ministries. Yet as we shall see in the coming chapters, media owners are able to successfully challenge many of the regressive media dictates brought on by conservative MPs, religious authorities, or other officials. In these particular cases, then president Hamid Karzai, under pressure from Afghan journalist unions and the international community, pardoned Kambakhsh and released Fayaz (Shalizi 2008).

The Ministry of Information and Culture (MIC) and the Ministry of Communications and Information Technology (MCIT) are the two main ministries of the government where decisions pertaining to the media, among other cultural issues, are made. Both ministries, located adjacent to one another, have been attacked numerous times by conservative, liberal, and radical groups. Most recently, in April 2019 the Ministry of Communications and Information Technology was attacked by a suicide bomber. Seven people were killed, many were wounded, and about 3,000 employees of both ministries were evacuated. ISIS took responsibility. In 2006 then president Karzai appointed the conservative minister Karim Khurram, who was backed by the Shura-i Ulama, or Council of Clerics. He began a reign of censorship, banning shows such as popular Indian soap operas and revoking the broadcasting licenses of media outlets that were critical of the government. After much protest and pressure from international

PHOTO 3.1. The heavily reinforced exterior of the Ministry of Information and Culture.

and local media watchdog groups as well as from Afghan private media owners, in 2010 Karzai reappointed Sayed Makhdoom Raheen, whom he had briefly installed during his first term as president. Minister Raheen was responsible for enabling the expansion of free media; however, in his second term he made several rulings in favor of and yielding to conservative forces. Upon being re-elected president in 2019, Ashraf Ghani appointed the moderate Abdul Bari Jahani to succeed Raheen as minister of the MIC and Fahim Hashimy, the owner of 1TV, as minister of MCIT. According to these government ministries, the media and telecommunication industry employs over 200,000 people and generates multi-billion dollars worth of revenues, making it one of the largest and most profitable sectors of the economy.[3]

Moreover, as I have argued elsewhere (Osman 2014a), while globally, governments are cracking down, often violently, on popular uprisings in public spaces, in Afghanistan, public protests are proving to be a powerful social force, mainly because the government is relatively weak and spaces for public gatherings—*maidans*, or town centers—are plentiful. During my field trips, I witnessed a range of uprisings, riots, vigils, and protests over incidents of election fraud,

Quran burning by US soldiers, the Shiite Marriage Law (otherwise known as the Rape Law), civilian casualties, government corruption, deaths of journalists, student tuition hikes at Kabul University, and the banning of popular television programs, among other issues. The outpouring of support and grief for fallen or slain media makers also reverberates throughout the country.

This unique development-saturated media environment has created a robust and vibrant media sector and public sphere in Afghanistan that is unparalleled in the region. Unlike most of its neighbors, Afghanistan has many of the apparent foundations of freedom of expression. In fact, according to Reporters Without Borders' latest World Press Freedom Index, Afghanistan at 121 ranks the highest out of its neighbors in terms of overall press freedom. Applying for a license and registration for a new broadcast television station that is not affiliated with the state is nearly impossible in neighboring China (177), Iran (170), Pakistan (142), Tajikistan (161), Turkmenistan (180), and Uzbekistan (160). Two-thirds of the post-Soviet countries ranked 150 or lower in the index, with scores that keep plummeting. According to an RSF regional report, the "eternal despots" in the region are intensifying their brutal hold on power, identifying Tajikistan, Belarus, Kazakhstan, Azerbaijan, Uzbekistan, and Turkmenistan as the worst countries for media freedom (Reporters Without Borders 2015). In many of those countries the courts are stacked against independent media organizations and producers, and expressing any viewpoint critical of the government is a serious punishable crime. If the public sphere depends on freedom of the press, and that depends on having alternatives to statist media, Afghanistan is certainly far ahead of its neighbors. Since 2006 Afghanistan has been an invited member of the South Asian Free Media Association, a powerful regional media rights organization.[4]

As discussed earlier, Afghanistan's geopolitical history at the crossroads of Asia or as the "Gateway to Asia" has made modern Afghanistan a diverse and multiethnic country. All of Afghanistan's larger ethnic populations—Pashtuns, Tajiks, Uzbeks, and Hazaras—have multiple television stations affiliated with them. Only some of the smaller groups, such as the Turkmen, Baluchis, Aimaks, Pashais, Nooristanis, have affiliated television stations, but Radio Television Afghanistan's local substations compensate for that. The few successful television stations that are owned by smaller ethnic groups and smaller sects of Islam tend to be nationally minded and do not cater to or identify only with their owners' ethnic group.

Furthermore, each of the larger ethnic groups and some of the smaller ones have linguistic/ethnic/cultural ties with neighboring countries that border Afghanistan: Pakistan in the south and east; Iran in the west; Tajikistan, Uzbekistan, and Turkmenistan in the north; and China in the far northeastern corner. These cross-border ethnic relations include the Pashtuns in Pakistan, India, and Iran; Tajiks in Tajikistan; and Uzbeks and Turkmen in Uzbekistan, Turkmenistan, and Turkey. Additionally, many of the people I interviewed believed that Iran supports the Hazara and Shiite television stations. Hazaras do not share an ethnic background with Iranians but have the same religion, Shiism. The majority of the other ethnic groups are part of the Sunni sect of Islam.

Ultimately, though, in this push and pull between national and ethnic, internal and external allegiances, on Afghan television stations the national wins out every time for those established with terrestrial technology that allows them to reach wide audiences across Afghanistan. In the end, most television stations, despite their ethnic affiliations, aspire to be national ones. In order to aggrandize their influence and maximize their profits from donors and advertisers, television stations have to at least feign being oriented toward a national audience. To appear to address only their own ethnic group and their interests is akin to sociopolitical and economic suicide in the eyes of national advertisers and broad-based international donor campaigns that seek to reach such broad audiences. This is especially the case with the most commercially successful private stations such as Tolo TV, 1TV, and Ariana Television Network (ATN), which downplay their ethnic origins entirely.

For analysis purposes I categorize the Afghan television sector into three groups: national, niche, and sectarian. Niche television stations seek to preserve their own ethnic groups' languages, songs, rituals, and other traditions and also to preserve the cultural diversity of Afghanistan and therefore also serve a national purpose. However, some niche television stations veer into the dangerous terrain of sectarianism by catalyzing deep-seated ethnic tensions and violence. The owners of these sectarian stations are usually warlord types. There is some overlap between these categories; however, sectarian television stations lack the open-mindedness to envision an inclusionary multiethnic Afghanistan, where all people live in peaceful coexistence and therefore cannot be categorized as nationally minded.[5]

The Contradictions and Obfuscations of Foreign Aid

In the aftermath of 9/11, the US government identified Afghanistan, Pakistan, and their northern Central Asian neighbors as particularly problematic due to the rise of Islamism in the form of extremist networks such as the Taliban, Al Qaeda, and many lesser-known ones. Thus, Western attention turned to the Central and South Asian republics with promises to bring democratic policies

PHOTO 3.2. Young girls pumping water from a UN-funded well in Bagrami, 2014.

PHOTO 3.3. Young girls at a UNICEF-funded school in Balkh, 2014.

PHOTO 3.4. **A Mine Action SUV in Shar-i Now, Kabul, 2009. Mine Action is a service of the UN Department of Peacekeeping Operations.**

and structures. With this mission, the US government, via the Department of Defense and the State Department, identified the media as a central means of disseminating its messages. According to the Congress-mandated Office of the Special Inspector General for Afghanistan Reconstruction (SIGAR), since 2002 the US government appropriated approximately $140 billion for Afghanistan relief and reconstruction. More than half of the money is allocated to the Department of Defense, while USAID, the Department of State, and other agencies share the rest.[6] This figure does not include the total development aid expenditures because not everything is reported to SIGAR. Nor does this figure account for the total cost of war, which is estimated to be over $1 trillion.

The British government followed suit with its Department for International Development (DFID) and BBC Media Action. Before joining the post-9/11 mission, BBC Media Action, formerly and overtly named the BBC Marshall Plan of the Mind, was first established in 1992 after the fall of the Berlin Wall with the explicit aim of "teach[ing] capitalism to the communists" after the col-

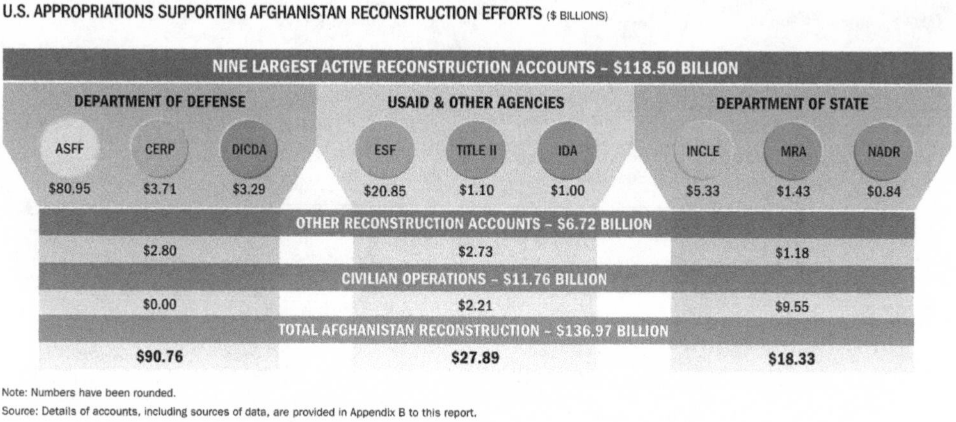

U.S. APPROPRIATIONS SUPPORTING AFGHANISTAN RECONSTRUCTION EFFORTS ($ BILLIONS)

NINE LARGEST ACTIVE RECONSTRUCTION ACCOUNTS - $118.50 BILLION								
DEPARTMENT OF DEFENSE			USAID & OTHER AGENCIES			DEPARTMENT OF STATE		
ASFF	CERP	DICDA	ESF	TITLE II	IDA	INCLE	MRA	NADR
$80.95	$3.71	$3.29	$20.85	$1.10	$1.00	$5.33	$1.43	$0.84

OTHER RECONSTRUCTION ACCOUNTS – $6.72 BILLION		
$2.80	$2.73	$1.18
CIVILIAN OPERATIONS – $11.76 BILLION		
$0.00	$2.21	$9.55
TOTAL AFGHANISTAN RECONSTRUCTION – $136.97 BILLION		
$90.76	$27.89	$18.33

Note: Numbers have been rounded.
Source: Details of accounts, including sources of data, are provided in Appendix B to this report.

FIGURE 3.1. The Office of the Special Inspector General for Afghanistan Reconstruction pulled together information about the largest government funders in the country.

lapse of the USSR (BBC Media Action 2017; UK Parliament 1999). According to the chairman of the Marshall Plan of the Mind, it was formed in order "to transfer skills and knowledge of democratic principles and market economies via national radio and television to assist the transition process [within the former Soviet Union]" (Mandel 2002, 213).

The framework for development aid originated in a series of discussions held in Bonn, Germany, known as the Bonn Conferences. Organized and spearheaded by the United Nations and the United States, Afghan and international civil society organizations and prominent individuals were invited to establish a new transitional government and were tasked with creating a new constitution, which would codify the terms of the new state, from the media to the justice system. In December 2001, over ninety countries promised more than $20 billion at the first Bonn Conference for the reconstruction of Afghanistan, including its media sector. In fact, the information and communication technologies (ICT) sector, which includes everything from telecommunications infrastructure building to media training and literacy, was designated as a key target area for funding. Ten years later, at the second Bonn Conference, held in December 2011, most of the same countries again promised financial aid to Afghanistan. However, as a result of the international economic recession, the promises were much more tempered. Then secretary of state Hillary Clinton said at the conference that the US government could not give exact figures for future aid because, "as everyone is aware, the international community faces fiscal constraints" (2011). Although the numbers and figures are difficult to ascertain because not all of the pledging countries met their projected promises, and because international funding has significantly decreased after the worldwide economic recession of 2008, there is enough information to estimate that 60 to 70 percent of Afghanistan's gross national income consists of international humanitarian aid, with the United States being the largest of the donors.

Even though the US government is legally required to be transparent about how it spends American taxpayer money and to make its expenditures public, following the money trail to find exactly which media projects are funded by which branches of the US government and for how much is nearly impossible, as it provides only certain figures associated with some of its branches. Most funding figures are also difficult to corroborate because they are revealed in a piecemeal manner and tend to be contradictory. Furthermore, there are multiple overlapping branches of the US government that distribute aid money to other governmental and nongovernmental organizations and subcontractors, which make tracking the figures even more difficult.

Likewise, although we know that the media and communication sector is one of the main areas targeted for aid by the United States and therefore heavily funded, the exact figures are equally difficult to determine. According to the Office of the Special Inspector General's audit of US media development expenditures in Afghanistan, the United States spent $2.6 billion on the sector. However as the title of the audit report *Afghanistan's Information and Communications Technology Sector: U.S. Agencies Obligated over $2.6 Billion to the Sector, but the Full Scope of U.S. Efforts Is Unknown* suggests, the information the office was provided was neither comprehensive nor fully reliable (SIGAR 2016a). SIGAR determined that this was due to poor record keeping by the various government agencies allocating the money and a lack of coordination between those agencies. Furthermore, the names of the vast majority of Afghan media organizations, including almost all of the television companies, which are the biggest recipients of the money, are omitted from the SIGAR reports. The only recipients mentioned in the SIGAR reports are small media organizations, media training organizations, and news agencies.

What makes tracking exact figures of funding and its sources and recipients even more challenging in an already opaque system is fear from both funders and recipients that audiences will charge them with biased reporting and programming, favoring the interests of the donor nation—namely, propaganda. Thus, my interviews with senior and midlevel USAID personnel and television station owners and managers were not helpful in this endeavor either. In my multiple interviews and email correspondences with USAID personnel in

Kabul from 2009 and 2010, despite my repeated queries, they did not share any information on which media organizations, television stations, and networks had received funding or how much.[7] The only information that was repeatedly provided to me was an abundance of promotional materials about two new Tolo TV programs that USAID had sponsored and was eager to promote, a travel show called *On the Road* and a police serial called *Eagle Four*.

Likewise, about 50 percent of the television station managers/owners I interviewed admitted to receiving funding from the international donor community, including USAID, UNICEF, UN Women, DFID, the International Security Assistance Force, Resolute Support Mission, UNAMA, the Open Society Institute, BBC Media Action, Internews, Voice of America, and other development arms of national and multinational government organizations. Yet the number of media outlets receiving money from the international donor community as well as from neighboring countries is actually much higher.

Thus, based on my interviews and meetings with USAID and Afghan television personnel along with the information that was reported and not reported to SIGAR by various US government agencies, I believe that there is an agreement between the Department of Defense, the State Department, USAID, and their Afghan media partners not to disclose or release media development funding information. The US government releases only the names of select programs it is promoting and small-scale projects. Yet despite the statistical and quantitative obfuscation, based on the available documentation, I have managed to extrapolate enough information to create a chart that provides an overview of US media funding expenditures (see appendix C). Additionally, my ethnographic research and interviews, which I discuss in the next section, fill in the quantitative information gap about the who's who of media production and funding as well as political affiliations.

Ethnography in the Televisual Village: Television Stations, Owners, Sectarian Politics, and Funding

Within this international donor aid–saturated environment, even though TV owners clamor for donor aid, they simultaneously distance themselves from associations with foreigners. Sekandar Saleh, one of the production assistants whom I was directed to speak to at Tolo TV, one of Afghanistan's most popular and controversial stations (which by many accounts has arguably received the most USAID money), evaded the foreign funding question entirely when I spoke to him; instead he insisted that the station operates commercially and would not admit to or give any figures of international aid received.[8] According

PHOTO 3.5. Afghan media institutions gather at a Government Media and Information Center (GMIC) press conference. The GMIC was established in 2008 by the US government and the UN to help the Afghan government manage and facilitate communication. At the GMIC I interviewed Thomas Niblock and Sardar Wali Seddiqi in November of 2009. I also spoke with two senior American officers from the US embassy and USAID.

to the few audience demographics available, Tolo Television actually has been very successful in gaining a large percentage of the national viewership and capitalizing on that by attracting large national and transnational advertisers (Asia Foundation 2011). However, what it wants to distance itself from is that it is a darling of USAID. Tolo TV received over $3 million from USAID for startup money and continues to receive money for existing and new programs (Altai Consulting 2010, 146; E. Rubin 2010; Auletta 2010).

There clearly is stigma attached to being associated with foreigners. As a way of evading the wrath of government and religious censors, television station owners and executives defend the content of their programming by arguing that they have popular support. In the absence of independent media research companies and technologies that assess viewership, television station owners use their own data and statistics to claim that audiences across different demographics value their television programs because they see a reflection of the issues that are important to their daily lives. Owners also believe that they are in touch with and have their finger on the pulse of what audiences want and therefore represent Afghan voices.

The key to the success or failure of this strategy is to prove they are representing true Afghan culture because they are authentically and unequivocally Afghan. They therefore have to downplay both ethnic and foreign allegiances. Based on my reception interviews that will be discussed in chapter 6, "Reception and Audiences," in many cases television producers and their programs are indeed supported by the demand for and popularity of their work and speak to and for the public by catalyzing debates about topics that are central to the everyday lives of the majority of their viewers. However, in other cases, these claims are a matter of public opinion and public relations management.

By most accounts the Mohseni siblings, Saad, Jahid, Zaid, and Wajma, who grew up in Australia and together created, own, and run the Moby Media Group of which Tolo TV is a subsidiary, are Tajik—or, according to some of their employees, Sayyid.[9] Ownership of Tolo TV is attributed usually to the eldest, Saad Mohseni, an Afghan Australian banker/businessman, because he oversees the production aspects of the station and also represents the company as a spokesperson in media interviews and coverage. For justification, some people pointed to what they deemed as Tolo's partisan positioning in the 2009 and 2014 presidential race and campaigns. They believed Tolo TV favored Dr. Abdullah Abdullah, perceived as an ethnic Tajik, and staunchly criticized Hamid Karzai, an ethnic Pashtun. After making public statements against Tolo's support of Abdullah and his own condemnation, Karzai refused to take part in the widely watched televised presidential debates that Tolo had organized in 2009, for which he was further criticized on Tolo TV for not engaging in the democratic process.

Ariana Television Network, on the other hand, started as an offshoot of its telecommunications sister company, Afghan Wireless Communication Company (AWCC), which is currently the nation's largest cell phone provider. AWCC is a joint venture between the US company Telephone Systems International and the Afghan Ministry of Communications and Information Technology. However, although the Afghan ministry has a small stake in the company, AWCC and ATN are both private enterprises owned and founded by the Afghan American businessman Ehsan Bayat, who is also the head of the Bayat Foundation, a humanitarian and philanthropic organization.[10]

Ehsan Bayat, as his name suggests, is a Bayat, which is a small sub-tribe of the Turkic/Turkman ethnic minority. Most Bayats are also Shiite. As a subgroup of an ethnic minority and religious minority, Bayat is particularly vigilant in displaying his national aspirations and pan-ethnic/pan-religious allegiances. He often televises his charitable work through the Bayat Foundation. Anytime there is a human-made or natural disaster, such as droughts and earthquakes, wherein there is internal displacement and refugees, Ehsan Bayat can be seen flanked by grateful people of all different ethnic groups in different provinces of Afghanistan as he distributes much-needed supplies and rebuilds basic necessities such as wells. Most recently, Bayat has been providing coronavirus pandemic relief by distributing much needed provisions such rice, flour, and oil in hard-hit areas. For his public humanitarian work he is applauded by many people but also ridiculed and caricatured on a few other television programs. While charity is one of the key tenets of Islam, so is humility; thus he has been critiqued for his frequent televisual acts of charity. Critics also point out that he has not made a similar public showing of coming to the site or aid of victims of war, be they civilian casualties from the US war or victims of inter-Afghan violence. His charitable televisual acts are confined to non-war-related disasters, which are deemed apolitical.

AWCC's ubiquitous telecom towers can be found all over Afghanistan, so broadcasting was not a big leap for Bayat, who used the infrastructure of the already established AWCC telecommunications network. When I visited ATN's central production facilities, its ubiquitous telecom tower was prominently featured in the center of the courtyard garden. ATN is located on Darulaman Street, which is a big and active thoroughfare in the heart of Kabul. Often, when there is a protest or riot in Kabul, which happens frequently, the protesters come down Darulaman Street. Even when people are not protesting an issue related to media, such as government policies or civilian casualties, ATN, due to its location and popularity, has been subjected to attacks by rioting crowds on numerous occasions. Of course sometimes the protests are directly related to ATN. In the spring of 2008, ATN abruptly stopped airing the popular Indian soap opera *Kumkum*, due to pressure from the government because of representations of gender. The resulting uproar and clamor by the fan base was brought to ATN's door. The Afghan fans held protests outside of ATN headquarters in Kabul to demand answers. *Kumkum* was reinstated a few months later. As a result, the station has fortified its grounds with high concrete walls surrounding the entire structure. Yet despite its incredibly tight security, the atmosphere inside is surprisingly casual.

In fact, ATN was one of the stations that invited me to interview people and watch its productions on many occasions. The feeling that pervaded its premises was one of excitement. I was able to speak freely with many of the network's personnel during their lunch hour and in between productions. They in turn were not afraid to speak openly with me. The employees I interviewed, from writers to editors and on-screen talent, identified with a range of different ethnic groups and sects of Islam. There was also a high representation of women workers and people of all ages. The diversity of its staff on and off the screen was a testament to the fact that its national and pluralistic aspirations were also put into practice.

During a tea break in the station's garden, I witnessed a heated discussion between a popular video jockey of its most popular music video show, *Seta-rahi-Rangeen* (Colorful stars), and an older producer of ATN's religious call-in shows. The producer was proclaiming why his religious, moral, and educational programming was what audiences craved and needed in these times of disorder, turmoil, and despair. In the process he was also disapproving of the veejay's personal style and his music video program. The producer said, "Just like your show, all your hair gel and fancy Western clothing is a waste of time." To which the veejay replied, "They only have your boring shows on TV to appease a handful of mullahs and housewives. Nobody else watches your shows. Don't you know your ideas are outdated and outmoded? Go to the street and see what people want, how they dress, and what they are talking about. Old man, it's me and shows like mine that they want. We [younger generations] are the future." These types of discussions and debates, representative of larger national debates, were commonplace on the grounds of ATN.

Just like the station's diverse programming, its employees represented a wide range of Afghans from diverse sociopolitical backgrounds. Based on my observations, ATN's inclusive pluralistic approach was not just rhetorical but actually practiced within the walls of its production facilities. The network's gender-inclusive, multiethnic, and multigenerational personnel felt free to express a wide variety of divergent beliefs on and off the air.

The station 1TV, owned by the Hazara businessman and politician Fahim Hashimy, was also open and inviting to me. Hashimy served as the president of the Afghanistan National Olympic Committee before being appointed Minister of Communications and Information Technology (MCIT) by President Ghani in May of 2019. Partially funded by American and European development aid money, 1TV, launched in 2009, was a late entrant into the television scene, compared with the powerhouses ATN and Tolo TV, which launched in 2005 and 2004 respectively. And yet with its high-quality and consistent programming, 1TV quickly rose to position itself in the top tier with ATN and Tolo TV. In 2010, when I first went to observe 1TV's base of operations in the wealthy neighborhood of Wazir Akbar Khan and meet with its personnel, 1TV had just recently launched and was relying on foreign programming and personnel to train their Afghan staff. I spoke with some of the young and inexperienced Afghans who were there with the hopes of building a career and making a living. I also interviewed two of the high-level foreign staff: the station's creative director, Abbas Muzaffar, an experienced Indian television producer, and the station's production director, Siobhan Berry, an experienced British television producer. Berry and Muzaffar among other foreign personnel were in charge of training the 150 new Afghan hires. Inspired by Hashimy's nationally oriented progressive vision, the 1TV staff spoke excitedly of creating a professional media organization that would uplift the country and promote human rights and diversity. Thanks to the dedication of 1TV's foreign and Afghan personnel, in a short time 1TV managed to build a media production facility capable of producing original content creative and high quality enough to compete with the best of ATN and Tolo TV's original programming. Of course foreign programming is still popular and cheaper than original programming and as such makes up a significant percentage of all of the top three Afghan television stations.

All the television stations I went to study were heavily guarded and gated. Many stations also featured a "showcase of media martyrs" located outside their offices, in their courtyards, or in their lobbies. These decorated showcases displayed large portraits or photographs of journalists, telecommunication engineers, producers, or other on- and off-screen media employees who were killed in the line of duty, a symptomatic instance of the larger instability and conflict-ridden state of Afghanistan. Gaining entry into most offices and organizations in Afghanistan entailed being thoroughly searched, submitting to questioning, and waiting for long periods of time to confirm identification, appointments, and purposes of visit. Yet by far, Tolo's security was the most strenuous and time-consuming to navigate, most likely because conservative groups regularly target it and its employees. In January 2016 a Taliban suicide bomber attacked the staff bus of Kaboora Productions, an affiliate of Tolo TV, injuring dozens and killing seven people.

Tolo, like 1TV, is situated in the affluent neighborhood of Wazir Akbar Khan, called WAK by English-speaking foreigners and expatriates who work and live there, since it is part of the Green Zone. The road where Tolo's headquarters of offices and production studios are located is completely blocked off to the public and cars. On the road that leads to the building, one has to pass through multiple checkpoints by foot before being allowed to enter. Once I was inside, an escort directed me to an office. During my visit I was not allowed to see the facilities or interview anyone other than that one designated representative. At least a dozen Tolo employees with whom I had scheduled interviews called to cancel due to pressure from their supervisors. They have to sign contracts of

PHOTO 3.6. This showcase of "media martyrs" outside of Pajhwok Afghan News agency features two journalists and one telecommunication engineer who were killed by the Taliban while working in southern Afghanistan. The writing under all of their pictures says in Dari, "Martyred on the path of serving the people."

confidentiality and were therefore afraid of losing their jobs if they talked to me. Thus the feeling that permeated the Tolo enterprise in many ways was the opposite of the openness of ATN and 1TV. Yet I managed to speak to some Tolo employees off the record and a few others in other contexts such as film festivals.

The national broadcasting station, Radio Television Afghanistan, by virtue of being the governmental station, has to be representative of all Afghan ethnic groups by mandate. Two USAID-sponsored media surveys that were released in 2005 and 2010 indeed show RTA to be building credibility by scoring high ratings among audiences for overall trustworthiness:

> The qualitative research shows that trust in national TV (RTA) tends to be higher than trust in other channels, as RTA is controlled and is the medium for all Afghans. This is a new trend, not observed in 2005 study. At that time,

RTA was liked as "the TV and radio of all Afghans" but with caution, with many thinking that government control was creating a bias. This research shows that, after five years of strong TV development, this control is somewhat appreciated, and is a way for many to avoid un-Islamic programs or profess unity among Afghans. This also explains high audience ratings for the RTA network overall.

"Government TV is better because it belongs to all people across the country and has specific rules and regulations by which it operates. Private TV is free to do as it wishes and works only for the personal benefit of its owners" (Female teacher, Jalalabad). (Altai Consulting 2010, 146)

However, RTA is not always as trustworthy and impartial as this implies. During the presidential elections of 2009, the Independent Elections Commission (IEC), a UN-appointed body that monitored the Afghan elections, stated that RTA favored the incumbent Hamid Karzai, an ethnic Pashtun, by giving his campaign the most coverage.[11] Karzai responded by arguing that as the current president, one would expect more coverage of him and his actions than other candidates.

RTA is located in the Shar-i Now neighborhood of Kabul. Shar-i Now, which means New City, was one of many districts built by the last king, Zahir Shah, in the 1970s as part of the government's modernizing projects in conjunction with American and Russian aid. Now it is colloquially called Shar-i Kona, or Old City, by Kabulis, since many new war- and drug-funded districts have been built post-9/11. RTA also has a vast archive of photographs, radio programs, and television programs from the 1960s and 1970s when RTA, via the government's modernization initiatives, launched many media enterprises.[12] In the lobby of RTA is a gallery of production stills of men and women who worked in radio and television from that era. The women employees, on-screen personalities as well as those who worked behind the scenes, are in sharp contrast to today's women media personalities. The women from the 1960s and 1970s are wearing professional Western clothing or formal traditional Afghan dresses and pants. By contrast, current photographs of female presenters show them donning Islamic attire and conservative clothing.

At RTA I interviewed two general directors, the programming manager, and two of the independent board commissioners, who are elected by the Parliament to make sure RTA is representative of all Afghans.[13] However, my most interesting experience at RTA turned out to be a trip down memory lane with RTA's elderly archivist, Bahudeen. Unlike the other RTA staff, Bahudeen—who was referred to by everyone as Kaka (Uncle) Bahudeen—did not have a business card and resided in the subbasement, which seemed to function as more than his office. As we spent the day walking the corridors of the large RTA building and traversing its galleries, studios, and storage and archival areas, Bahudeen shared stories and described what RTA was like throughout the different eras.

During the facilities tour, Bahudeen, who had worked during the prewar era as well, lamented the changes the country has undergone. In the video archive, as we watched an employee recording a religious television program about Sheikh Asif Mohseni, the owner of Tamadon Television, presented by a religiously attired woman, he said, "It is a shame that we have to document and archive these conservative people and their ideas. Unfortunately they are a part of our culture now."[14] He quickly went and pulled out old Beta tapes of the news from the late 1970s and 1980s and played one side by side with the religious program. He knew all the female newscasters of that era and commented on how much more sophisticated, stylish, and liberated they were.

Across the television landscape there is a direct correlation between commercial success and packaging oneself as a national entity. A number of stations have also been successful by overtly identifying with specific groups, but they still have an overall national message and sentiment that puts Afghan citizenship above ethnicity. Yet subtle and not-so-subtle ethno-religious televisual mudslinging occurs among most of the stations. Within and outside the television screens, such attacks are formulated in accusations of foreign funding, involvement, and allegiance. For example, the battle between the secular Tajik television station Emroz and the religious Tamadon Television is the longest running and most heated. Najibullah Kabuli, the owner of Emroz and a former parliamentarian and businessman, claims that Tamadon TV, owned by the former leader of the Shia Shura-i Ulama, Ayatollah or Sheikh Mohseni, is a "puppet" of the Iranian government (Nazar and Recknagel 2010). Likewise, Mohseni has charged Kabuli for being a spokesperson for Tajik, Israeli, and Pakistani agendas and for using his television as a platform for them. To support their allegations, they both have provided ample unsubstantiated televised evidence, such as secret governmental documents from Iran showing financial backing.[15]

These types of accusations that television stations level against one another of being agents of foreign governments are indirect charges of not being truly Afghan or Afghan enough. Yet some sectarian ethno-nationalist stations go further in inciting hate and violence by not even bothering to veil their speech. They make inflammatory statements that Afghanistan belongs only to their own ethnic group and that other ethnic groups should go back to their respective neighboring countries. They argue that their *quowm* has been in Afghanistan the longest and hence are its rightful inhabitants. This is not unique to any

PHOTO 3.7. The Television Training Studio of Kabul University, funded by the Bayat Foundation. Adam Levin, Center for Global Communication Studies.

one ethnicity. Every group has their racist ethno-nationalists who have made such statements. Pluralism-minded reformers who strive to end *quowm baazi* rightly point out that it does not matter whether an ethnic group settled in Afghanistan recently or ages ago—as long as they espouse unity and diversity, for we are all Afghan.

Such sectarian stations that are polarizing public sphere debates with their ethno-religious messages and televisual attacks on other ethnic groups tend to be marginalized. Even though ethnic affiliations are still a very significant part of Afghan people's identity, years of ethnic violence have made most people highly sensitive to and wary of overtly ethno-nationalist messages by their leaders. People know that at least in public forums they have to be mindful of the hazards of such polemics and to curb public expression of any ethnic/religious bias they might harbor, in large part due to TV's influence.

International support, involvement, or interference is not limited to bordering countries alone. Western countries, such as the United States and many European ones,[16] as well as Russia, India, Turkey, Saudi Arabia, Japan, and

Korea, among others, are interested in Afghanistan and are actively involved in its affairs, including the media sector. Broader transregional affiliations, such as the Saudi government's funding for Sunni hajjis from Afghanistan to Mecca and back, also have a long history.

While the information provided about the breakdown of population demographics as it pertains to affiliations of Afghan television stations is commonly understood and accepted as fact by audiences and the general public, television station owners and operators, with a few exceptions, are not particularly forthright in sharing their financial sources and investors. That said, some television professionals were surprisingly up-front with me in revealing the sources of their funding. One of the production managers of Noor Television replied to my funding question by pointing to a large framed picture of Burhanudin Rabbani above his desk. "Supposedly 40 percent of our funding comes from advertising but you figure it out," he told me.[17] Rabbani, who was assassinated by a suicide bomber in his house in Kabul on September 20, 2011, was a jihad-era commander and religious leader. He also briefly served as president of Afghanistan during the post-Soviet withdrawal of Afghanistan. His political party, Jamiat-i Islami (Society of Islam), known more commonly for being part of the Northern Alliance in the international press, was one of the seven factions that the United States covertly funded via the CIA during the ten-year Soviet occupation and during the rise of the Taliban leading into the post-9/11 era. Jamiat-i Islami adherents are Tajiks, and the Taliban took responsibility for his murder. As with most mujahideen leaders who fought the Soviets, they are revered as heroes by some and considered warlords by others.

Alem Khalili, part owner of Negaah Television and who at the time of our first interview in August 2009 had just begun broadcasting three months prior, when asked how he raised the overhead capital to start Negaah and operate with hardly any advertisers, said, "Look, I am the son of a powerful man within the government."[18] Indeed, he is the son of Karim Khalili, the vice president of Afghanistan at the time and also a prominent mujahideen-era leader. In order to gain the support of ethnic Hazaras, Hamid Karzai appointed Khalili, an important political and religious leader of the Hazaras, as his vice president in 2002, and chose him again as his running mate in the 2004 and 2009 elections. The newly constructed Negaah Television station is situated on top of a hill overlooking the brand-new picturesque neighborhood of Shahrak-i Haji Nabi, or Haji Nabi City. Negaah Television boasts the latest audio/video technology, equipment, editing suites, production studios, conference rooms, office, and landscaped gardens and patios.

Named after Vice President Karim Khalili's brother Haji Nabi Khalili, Haji Nabi City has come under criticism like other newly constructed developments in Kabul, such as Shahrak-i Telayee (Golden City). These opulent new towns with wide boulevards, high-rise glass buildings, marble mansions, fountains, and fine landscaping cater to the nouveau riche of Kabul. Dubbed "poppy palaces" or "narcotecture" by the Western press, these extravagant war- and drug-fueled real estate developments stand in sharp contrast to their war-ravaged surroundings and classic Kabul architecture. Through shady dealings, large areas of public land are essentially bestowed upon or taken by powerful politicians, businessmen, or warlord types with clout and influence within the government. The corruption and illegitimacy of these land grabs are a common complaint of people, especially those displaced by these developments. Sherpur, another new poppy neighborhood that means "the Land of Milk," has been renamed colloquially as Sherchur, a play on words that means "the Land of Theft." With regards to the Sherpur land grab, the Afghan Independent Human Rights Commission publicly condemned the evictions and released a list of twenty-nine senior government officials and powerful people who had received plots (Nathan 2012). However, then president Karzai and the international community turned a blind eye.[19]

Additionally, as mentioned earlier, at least 50 percent of the television station managers/owners I interviewed said they received funding from the international donor community, including USAID, UNICEF, UN Women, DFID, ISAF, UNAMA, and other development arms of national and multinational governments. However, most of the television personnel I interviewed were quick to explain or complain that they receive only a small portion of their funding from that international donor community. Others, like Saba Television and Shamshad Television, readily admitted that a significant portion of their budget comes from international aid.

Fazal Karim Fazal, president of Shamshad Television, established Shamshad TV in February 2006 to reach the Pashto-speaking Pashtun Afghans. While many different languages are spoken in Afghanistan among the many ethnicities and tribes, Dari (a dialect of Persian) and Pashto are the two official languages. Having tapped into a neglected though substantial population, Shamshad subsequently was rewarded by receiving aid from USAID, DFID, and UNAMA, in addition to continued support of about $1 million per year from the Afghan Dutch NGO Organization for Mine Clearance and Afghan Rehabilitation (OMAR), which had provided it with its initial $2 million start-up capital.[20]

Although Shamshad still relies on donor subsidies, Fazal is quick to point out that the station is independent, private, and commercial. By that he means that approximately 50 percent of its income now also comes from ad revenues from various Afghan and international governmental and nongovernmental offices and organizations. Eager to reach Pashto speakers, these organizations pay Shamshad TV for airtime to run official public service announcements and other types of public information campaigns (PICs). Although not commercial in the classic sense, Shamshad has clearly carved out a market. Following its success, Tolo launched its own Pashto-language sister station, Lemar TV.

Shamshad TV is located in the lower-middle-class, 1970s-era Soviet-built neighborhood known as Macroyan. The production facilities are built into the existing structure of their parent organization, the OMAR Mine Museum. When people approach the museum and Shamshad TV from the street, the first thing they notice is their collection of downed Soviet fighter planes displayed prominently on their front lawn. Once inside, more memorabilia from the recent wars as well as from older wars are exhibited for mostly foreign museumgoers. Afghans have little interest in the war museum, since they are surrounded by war and carry personal internal traumas too. Due to its cross-national Pashtun affiliations, Shamshad Television has also opened up a secondary base of operations and production studios in Quetta, Pakistan, on the "Pashtun belt" border of Afghanistan. Shamshad's aspirations to be national and at the same time Pashtun-centric make it a blend of the national and niche types of television stations. In November 2017, ISIS agents posing as police officers attacked Shamshad's Kabul headquarters, killing one person and injuring twenty. Sustaining more deaths and injuries, Shamshad's TV station and adjoining OMAR Mine Museum were attacked again in July 2019, but this time the Taliban took responsibility.

Sanjar Sohail, the director of political affairs and news programming at Saba TV, also readily admitted that a large portion of Saba's budget consists of funding by Western donors such as the Open Society Institute and a few European donors, mostly from the Norwegian and Swedish governments. Saba TV is one of the few nonprofit television stations. It operates its modest facilities, located in the aspiring middle-class Karte 3 neighborhood of Kabul, more like a cooperative by sharing its resources with other media organizations. Its programming consists of mostly educational shows for children and adults as well as a few entertainment programs such as *Ter Yadoona* (Memories of the past), which features classic songs from the "golden eras of Afghanistan, India, and Iran music."[21] I also observed Saba TV to have one of the highest ratios of female employees, represented in all their production departments.

Genres and Their Discontents

What impact is this distinctive political economy, which is partially supported by clandestine war economies, partially by the international donor community, and partially by advertising, having on programming? The answer lies in the opening up of the Afghan economy once the Taliban regime was temporarily pushed out of power by US coalition forces, setting the stage for the entrance of the international donor community, which is embedded in international circuits of capitalism.

All of Afghanistan's television stations function in a very competitive media market due to the high cost of station operations. They need to fill the most air space with the cheapest programs that reach the widest audiences in order to attract advertisers, donor money, or both. So regardless of whether they are mostly subsidized by foreign aid, advertisements, or clandestine war profiteering money, due to the high cost of television production and ownership, their long-term success is ultimately contingent on a commercial model that depends on popularity of programming. Based on my reception studies, which I elaborate on in the coming chapters, the most popular genres of programs within this Afghan television economy are jointly produced public information campaigns, local political talk shows and satire serials, and the news; imported dramatic serials; and foreign reality television formats. Sources of financial support can be mapped across and onto these three popular and controversial genres, each of which engenders its own public debates.

A common complaint I heard frequently from many smaller and less established television stations is the nepotistic and unjust systems of aid distribution that are pervasive in Afghanistan in general and specific to media as well. Lack of transparency and clandestine contracting and subcontracting practices, such as not advertising Calls for Projects proposals, consistently favored certain media outlets and their Western collaborators who both gained by continuing to amass large profits, despite perhaps not adequately demonstrating merit and quality or by barely proving compliance with donor protocols via superficial markers.

Reports have shown that via hiring and contracting practices, the incentive of many foreign nongovernmental organizations and transnational aid organizations is to actually support the growth of their own home countries' economies rather than that of the host country. That is not to say that they do not support local development and growth; however, their priority often clearly points to their own government mandates that dictate the return of a large percentage of the allocated moneys back to the home countries.

Tolo TV, one of the main producers of reality formats and one of the most successful television stations, is often singled out by competing television stations for being favored by American governmental organizations. They claim that Tolo is enabled via American funding practices to exercise monopolistic control or to monopolize the market, thus disabling an even playing field for its competitors. Clearly such conditions provide Tolo with an advantage, but it is arguable whether that advantage is unfair because Tolo in response maintains that its commercial success and popularity with audiences demonstrate the quality of its programming and meet donor protocols, therefore meriting its favored status. Some people also complained that Tolo TV could be more cooperative in sharing their resources and less litigious and proprietary with their content and employee contracts.

However, it is also important to distinguish between different types of capitalism. Whereas the overlapping interests of Western corporations and international donor organizations are responsible for producing Afghan versions of Western reality television programs, locally produced political talk and satire shows are supported by a different type of commercial model. The former requires high costs of production and attracts large international advertisers. For example, large Western corporations such as Simon Cowell's SYCOtv and Sony Picture Television own the rights to 1TV's *Afghanistan's Got Talent* and *Who Wants to Be a Millionaire?* Afghanistan franchises, respectively, while large corporate advertisers such as Roshan, an Aga Khan Fund for Economic Development–owned telecommunication provider, support programs like *Afghan Star*, the Afghan format of *American Idol, Pop Idol*, and the *X-Factor*. On the other hand, Afghan political talk and satire shows are low in cost and enable smaller local businesses to advertise. Despite their modest production values, they are as popular with viewers, a point I will return to later in chapter 6.

It is equally important to note that international donor aid to the media infrastructure is responsible not only for promoting capitalism and the free market but also for creating and fostering a public service model of television. RTA, the national broadcasting station, receives most of its funding from the international community. RTA has thirty-four local affiliate substations, one in every province of Afghanistan, which provide programming in their local languages. Many other stations also rely on international aid to operate; without it they would not be able to provide crucial local and international news and information. These stations tend to produce much-needed educational and informational programs as well as crucial public information campaigns, which are sponsored by international initiatives and aimed at war-zone public safety issues and nation-building more broadly, a point I elaborate on in the coming chapters.

The PSA/PIC, Political Satire and Talk Shows, and News

During the 2009, 2014, and 2019 elections, I witnessed television's new prominent role in boldly staging debates about democracy, capitalism, and nation-building. Via the news and political discussion and satire, Afghan broadcast television very openly critiqued and analyzed all aspects of the candidates' campaign platforms, addressed policy failures, and investigated accusations of corruption and wrongdoing. Numerous television PSAs as part of larger cross-platform public information campaigns teaching democracy were also launched. They ranged from procedural campaigns about voting rights and how to vote to expository ones on what voting and elections are and what they mean. Others explained to people that it is not in their best interest to allow village or tribal elders to "buy" their votes.

The PIC and PSA has become the favorite launching pad for much-needed educational and informational campaigns by the international community. Initially, these PICs were solely sponsored by various Afghan government offices in conjunction with international donor organizations; now, due to their popularity, even the few stations that are outside the purview of international funding are producing PICs and PSAs independently. In addition to the democracy ones, other campaign topics and messages include women's rights, anti-war issues, counter-narcotics, identifying land-mine areas, and national, transnational, racial, and ethnic unity. The women's rights PSAs have addressed everything from street harassment to encouraging women to join the police to more complicated cultural phenomena such as honor killings and *baad* exchanges (offering girls in marriage to resolve blood feuds) (N. Tapper 1991).

The news and PSAs also address the practical challenges of living in a war zone, such as demonstrating how far civilians must stay away from passing US Army convoys and how to identify areas that have been cleared of mines and avoid areas that are still mined. Additionally, the news and special bulletins throughout the day inform people of where there are road closures due to military or insurgent activities. In Afghanistan, television literally helps Afghans navigate daily life and can mean the difference between living and dying.

Programs such as *Zang Khatar* (Danger bell) on Tolo TV and *Talak* (Trap) on Noorin TV are part of this growing genre of political satire that combines investigative journalism and comedy sketches to confront abuses of power stemming from politicians and warlords within and outside of the government.[22] Such programs present the problems that Afghanistan is currently facing and therefore bring up the country's tumultuous recent history for reflection as well. Operating in a fictitious world of humor and parody enables political satire programs to evade the censors to a degree, though their commentary, like the news, can be equally damaging and incisive. In one episode of *Talak*, which aired after the last elections, the hosts went to an animal market to interview sheep and goats about their thoughts on how democracy and nation-building is working out in Afghanistan. Indeed, although political satire in its current televisual form is new, as a genre it has a long history in Afghanistan in print form as well as in oral traditions of short verse poems or jokes (Edwards 1993; M. Mills 1991). It has been a favored venue for critiquing social and political structures and individuals for at least a century. Additionally, while internationally backed reality television programs are enabled by and therefore partially support large-scale capitalism, political satire supports mostly local Afghan actors, producers, writers, advertisers, and audiences as well.

In addition to political satire and political comedy sketch programs, Afghanistan has many political discussion or talk programs. Every channel has at least one. The more successful stations have several. They resemble American talk shows in their form in that there is a host and guests or a panel of guests. However, whereas American talk shows run the gamut from seedy to sublime and include comic late-night variety shows, Afghan talk shows in comparison lack levity and broach serious topics and issues. The guests are prominent politicians and members of civil society including warlords and their representatives. So that the shows can be representative of Afghanistan, people with different viewpoints and from different ethnic groups usually are selected. Some of the political talk shows like RTA's *Open Jirga* and 1TV's *The Mask* or *Naquab* and *Amaj* (Target) have live audience while others like Tolo's *Porso Pal* (Question and search) do not. On the political talk shows with live audiences or call-in components, the question that people ask most frequently in a variety of forms is: Why are warlords given positions of power within the government and allowed to continue to sow violence, lawlessness, and corruption instead of being prosecuted and tried for their numerous war and non-war crimes of the past and present?[23] Sometimes Jerry Springer–esque physical fights breakout among the guests but in ways that seem spontaneous and not premeditated. For example, in one episode of 1TV's *Amaj* where guests from different ethnic groups were invited to discuss the government's controversial 2017 decision to allow Gulbuddin Hekmatyar and his political party to return, a fistfight ensued between Hekmatyar's Pashtun representative and the Hazara representative.

The program's host and third guest Ahmad Saeedi, a well-respected Tajik professor and popular television personality, tried without much success to break up the fighting. One of the most daring and ambitious of the programs in this genre is 1TV's *The Mask*. On the program, which focuses solely on regressive patriarchal practices and violence against women, women guests share their harrowing experiences at the hands of tribal and religious elites while wearing a mask to protect their identity. Legal and human rights experts then provide analysis and offer both psychological consolation and possible solutions.

Reality TV

Reality television formats have also found an avid viewership in Afghanistan. Based on international formats, these serials are locally produced and tailored to Afghan audiences in collaboration with their Western sponsors. A few of the popular ones include *Who Wants to be a Millionaire?* (1TV), *Afghanistan's Got Talent* (1TV), *Afghan Star* (Tolo), and *Dream and Achieve* (Tolo), which is a business entrepreneurship show similar to *The Apprentice*. These competition-based shows, which identify winners by the votes of audiences via mobile phones or a panel of judges or both, are funded by Western media corporations and governments with the explicit goal of promoting both democracy and capitalism. Whether their mission is successful or not is difficult to determine.

For example, the anthropologist Ruth Mandel in her 2002 article "A Marshall Plan of the Mind: The Political Economy of a Kazakh Soap Opera" shows how a mandate by the British Foreign Office to introduce Kazakhs to capitalism via the British-format soap opera *Crossroads* may not have played out as intended. The British writers instructed the Kazakh writers to include in their scripts elements that positively represent free markets and entrepreneurship. However, Mandel explains, it is quite difficult to determine whether the "economic literacy" scenes in which people were writing checks and running shops at a bazaar actually encouraged any of the viewers to open bank accounts or small businesses or even shop, for that matter.

Similarly, it is difficult to ascertain whether *Dream and Achieve*, *Afghan Star*, *Afghanistan's Got Talent*, and *Who Wants to be a Millionaire?* are converting Afghans into rabid consumers and capitalists. All we can say with certainty is that they are providing guidelines for a certain type of success, one that is based on the accumulation of wealth. These Afghan reality TV programs promote not just following one's dreams but how to monetize those dreams, sometimes at any cost. As I show in chapters 5 and 6, some women contestants in *Afghan Star* have subjected themselves to dangerous situations and self-harm in order to realize perhaps unattainable goals. As the television scholar Susan Murray points out in her article "The Politics of Reality Television," reality TV arose from denationalization and the simultaneous neoliberalization of the global economy and therefore replicates the tenets of neoliberal capitalism: "In many ways, reality TV is a perfect fit for the new [neoliberal] economy, which has extolled the virtues of globalization while, at least in the popular imagination, downplayed issues of the unequal distribution of power and wealth between nations" (2019, 273). That is not to say that all reality television formats uniformly follow the genre conventions. Some Afghan reality TV formats tend to be more overt in their neoliberal messages while others are subtler. Also, some tend to be more culturally sensitive and thoughtful regarding their repercussions on and the well-being of participants. The commercials that air during these shows advertise new luxury housing suites, cars, appliances, banking, and telecommunications, promoting a capitalistic model of a materially lavish life, which is far outside the means and reach of the vast majority of viewers.

The ideology that underpins and frames such media campaigns pairs capitalism and democracy as mutually constitutive, one paving the path for the other. In contrast to the undemocratic patronage systems that sometimes sustain the political economy of some of these television productions, the televisual projections of these shows are characterized by celebratory messages of neoliberal capitalist entrepreneurship. According to the award-winning documentary *Afghan Star* (2009), made by the British filmmaker Havana Marking, which is based on the third season of the television show of the same name, apparently a third of the country voted on short message service (SMS) for their favorite singers; for many audience members, this was the first time they had participated in voting. This is cited in the voice-over as demonstrative of the democratizing effects of the program, as if voting for a favorite singer is akin to choosing an elected leader, whose decisions affect every facet of our lives. Lest we forget, the phone company that sponsors the program, Roshan, also makes money from the audience's SMS voting.

It is also important to note that the *Afghan Star* documentary, like the television series, was produced by Tolo TV. Tolo TV is also one of the largest recipients of USAID funding (Auletta 2010; E. Rubin 2010). Specifically, Jahid Mohseni, one of the sibling owners of Tolo's parent company, was an executive producer of the documentary. Their production assistant Sekandar Saleh, who I interviewed, was also part of the production team. Hence, if we follow the funding trail, such assertions in the documentary are not independent observations but can be read as part of the larger US ideological mission. Without a doubt, Western reality television formats have introduced Afghan viewers to a type of cosmopolitanism, expanding their worldview by exposing them to cultures, customs, and trends of the West and other parts of Afghanistan. However, contrary to the assertions of the producers and owners of the television stations who make the reality television programs, I would argue that the cosmopolitanism that has thus far been projected in these Afghan versions of Western reality television formats is a capitalist cosmopolitanism that promotes consumerism rather than its noble counterpart: informed citizenship. As prominent American political economy media scholars have demonstrated unmitigated capitalism in the US has had devastating effects on democracy including freedom of the press (Bagdikian 2004, McChesney 2004, H. Schiller 1991). Conservative forces have also condemned these shows, especially the participation of the female contestants, for their Americanizing or Westernizing effects. This is similar to their argument that Indian, Iranian, and Turkish dramatic serials are turning the public or public opinion in favor of adopting Hindu, Shiite, or secular Sunni codes of being.

Dramatic Serials

Dramatic serials, or soap operas, from many countries, ranging from regional neighbors to Western countries, can also be found on most Afghan television stations. Yet by far the most popular ones are from India and Turkey, with Iran trailing. Islamists and tribal leaders attack them for tainting an imagined pure Afghan Islamic culture and charge them with cultural imperialism, the dark side of globalization theory; they worry about the cultural influences of Hinduism, secular Sunni Islam, or Shiite Islam. The large fan base of these imports, on the other hand, find these dramatic serials valuable and liberating in many ways, particular in generating debates over domestic and gender issues both at home and in the public arena. For Afghan women who face victimization on a daily basis, steeped in a misogynist world of warlordism and Islamism, they also revel in the agency afforded women on these foreign dramatic serials.

Furthermore, there is a long history of cultural and linguistic affinity between Afghans and Indians, Turks, and Iranians. For example, many Afghans can understand the dramatic serials imported from these three countries without the common overdubbing in Dari and Pashto. Dari is a dialect of Persian and mutually intelligible with the Farsi spoken in Iran; Uzbeks and Turkmen share a dialect with Turkish; and many Afghans understand Urdu, which is related to Hindi. However, as the Turkish media scholar Bilge Yesil has demonstrated, beyond the cultural proximity and universal appeal—arguments that are commonly used to explain the transnational popularity of these countries' serials—is a strong economic imperative. Turkish drama exports exceed $300 million annually and reach over 400 million global viewers because they, like Indian serials, are aggressively marketed worldwide due to shifting local and global political economic paradigms (Yesil 2015, 2016).

Dramatic serials are financed or subsidized by the same countries that produce them. Sometimes they are sponsored by the donor country's government and offered for no charge. Other times they are offered for low introductory prices by private foreign production studios. Afghan television managers and owners complained that once they have cultivated a market and a devout following, the private foreign production studios who own the rights of the serials then demand high prices for further episodes and more seasons of their programs, thus disabling the less-affluent television stations from buying them. The foreign serials that make it to Afghan television stations are not always the highest caliber ones from their countries of origin. In fact, they tend to be either B rated serials or older serials that have already had a broadcast run in their countries of origin. And yet the foreign serials' high output and subsidized pricing coupled with their relatively higher production values and overall quality of storytelling make it difficult for Afghan dramatic serials to compete with them in the same capacity, given that the Afghan soap operas have started more recently. The popularity of Indian and Turkish soap operas has to do with these and a variety of other factors, which I will elaborate on in chapter 6.

CHAPTER 4

Producers and Production

The Development Gaze and the Imperial Gaze

Television: The Ideology Machine

Television's unique electro-visual mass appeal—sensory integration, simultaneity of exposure, and broadcasting potential, which imbue it with a false sense of communal live-ness—has always made it a source of social power and cultural imaginings. As television scholars have theorized, the medium has both the eerie ability to conjure a sense of face-to-face community gatherings and the power to reach large-scale audiences (McCarthy 2010; McLuhan 1962; Murray 2018, 2019; Ong 1982; Parks 2005; Williams [1974] 2003).[1]

Every new media technology is celebrated for its utopian promises and liberatory potentials—and also criticized for its dystopian possibilities. Television in the West has been seen through both lenses; in the United States, where commercial models have dominated, it has often been considered "a vast wasteland" (Minow 1961) (with the exception of public and community television), while in the UK, television is imagined as a technology for the uplift and education of the citizenry of a democratic nation.

The legacy of terrestrial television has also been intricately linked with the nation-state and therefore associated with dominant ideologies. Although the modern nation-state was theoretically intended to transcend ethnic, tribal, and other feudal, genealogical, and kinship formations, with the rise of fascism it has been conceptualized as a hegemonic entity that includes elite groups affiliated with the state and excludes or tries to manage minority populations, in extreme

PHOTO 4.1. A Kabuli cab driver plays an Indian music video from the popular program *Hop* on Tolo TV for his riders. Photo credit: Jalal Nazari for the author.

cases even exterminating them (Appadurai 2006). With the rise of Nazism and fascism, prominent scholars from the Frankfurt School (Horkheimer and Adorno [1944] 2002) and their American colleagues (Lippmann 1925; Blumer [1933] 2004; MacDonald 1953; Lasswell 1927; McLuhan 1962) posited that radio and television were degenerative and denigrating forces that either coalesced public opinion around state ideology or created complacency and apathy in society. According to John Corner, "Often, the threat of de-democratization has been perceived: television replacing primary participation with secondary or even tertiary engagement, in which the tele-presence of politicians within a political theatre of tele-events reconfigures and redefines political structure and action" (1999, 25).

Media scholars from a variety of disciplines have been challenging this influential strain of thinking. Sociologists, for example, have demonstrated the integral role of media in enabling critical dialogue and informing citizenry in large-scale societies (Calhoun 1992; Dewey 1927; Habermas 1962; C. Mills 1956; Schudson 1999), the prerequisites for the formation of a democratic public sphere. Anthropologists have likewise explored how people become involved in certain ideological and discursive social movements and how these shape collective action (Burdick 1992; Edelman 2001; Escobar 1992; Nash 2004). More specifically, they have studied the potential of "small media" to mobilize counterpublics and, in some cases, to effect social change (Ginsburg 1998; Michaels, Langton, and Hebdige 1994; Sreberny-Mohammadi and Mohammadi 1994). Such work reveals how diverse groups within a society use the media to negotiate and contest representations of them while also making their own media as a basis for cultural and political claims in the public sphere. These studies have thus been crucial to expanding perceptions about television. However, research that demonstrates the potential of television to mobilize change in large-scale, national, or broadcast settings has been relatively rare and often reveals that indeed television has had dangerous consequences.

Decolonizing Television Studies: Managing Incendiary Relations

Over the latter half of the twentieth century and into the twenty-first, television has spread throughout the world and has been taken up in a variety of cultural settings. It has been shaped by diverse political economic formations at different historical moments and operated in relation to changing technological regimes. Research has similarly expanded beyond the original location of television studies—the United States and to some extent Canada, Australia, the UK, and Western Europe—to include the non-Western world.

The emergence and expansion of research on television in non-Western settings over the last three decades, especially by scholars using qualitative and ethnographic methods, has helped to broaden our understandings of the role that television plays in the contemporary world. This book is indebted to such recent scholarship and builds on the contributions of pioneering scholars responsible for it. Clearly, issues of gender, politics, political economy, and religion are particularly at stake here, in ways that resonate with television's presence in the Middle East (Abu-Lughod 2006; Kraidy 2005; Oren 2004), South Asia (Mankekar 1999; Rajagopal 2001), and Central Asia (Mandel 2002; Skuse, Gillespie, and Power 2011).

In Afghanistan, television is linked to the national contemporary political situation in a number of distinctive ways. First and foremost, it is at the center of violence in Afghanistan: it has generated violence and has also been the target of it. The tele-presence of women (versus their contributions in other media such as radio and print) is stirring emotional and violent responses from Islamists and other conservative groups. Second, sectarian television stations affiliated with specific ethnicities are "retribalizing" Afghanistan, to borrow Marshall McLuhan's term, as ethnic groups deliberately use the medium to catalyze deep-seated ethnic tensions. Third, television stations also accuse one another of being foreign puppets carrying out the interests of other countries, a claim that has veracity. Additionally, television station ownership in Afghanistan—as is the case in most parts of the world—is the province of wealthy elites with ties not only to the domestic and international states and corporate interests but also to warlord networks.

On the surface, then, it appears that the socioeconomic substructure of television once again occludes rational debate, understanding, and social mobilization. Yet, if we look closer at the ground-level specificities of Afghanistan, an entirely different picture emerges. In a country where the vast majority of people are illiterate and where access to computers and the internet is limited, television becomes a sort of equalizer, giving the masses access to information, news, and the means to understand and reflect upon their complex, precarious, and rapidly changing lifeworlds. Television, along with radio, actually reaches the majority of Afghans. The larger question of whether it elevates the terms of debate and creates a public sphere or only refeudalizes the country through sensationalism and public opinion management is thus a second-order question; it will be explored in the coming chapters.

Even though all the owners of Afghanistan's fifty (and growing) television stations are wealthy elites associated with dominant structures, it is important to note that not all of them are conservative. As we shall see in the next section, a number of stations, especially the more commercially successful ones, and even a few of those owned by warlords, are quite progressive and reformist in their programming. Writers, producers, and directors from all the stations frequently complain about the constraints and editorial supervision of their programs from their Afghan owners, government and religious censors, and foreign backers as well. Yet, there remains some agency within these constraints. Anthropologists have complicated simplistic interpretations by examining the potential of cooperation between the state and social activists (Ginsburg 1991; Wortham 2000) and have shown how the cultural production that results from government-funded television in different settings cannot be automatically attributed to the state apparatus because producers struggle to express their own views on their own terms. They have distinguished between state-funded and statist television. Likewise, in Afghanistan, even within some of the television stations owned by Islamists and other extremists, there are progressive programs and therefore individuals who are able to somehow negotiate different perspectives from their supervisors.

As an example of the distinctive role television plays in contemporary Afghanistan, consider its managing of potentially incendiary relations with foreign troops. While some international troops have insinuated themselves into the daily lives of Afghans and built trust by patrolling the streets on foot and mingling with people, the US troops have gained a reputation for being trigger-happy, shooting civilians on the streets or in bazaars on several occasions. In one case—which led to massive riots throughout Kabul—a US armored vehicle in the north of the city fired on and killed a little boy who was giving good fortunes. It is common among street children to give "blessings" by burning *esfand* (wild rue) and other herbs in a canister for passersby. The Americans must have thought this was some kind of homemade bomb. After this incident, the US Army put out a series of public service announcements on RTA, as well as on some private stations, in which they demonstrated how far civilians must stay away from passing US Army envoys.

Although it is hard to determine the exact numbers, Afghanistan is on the UN's list of most land-mined countries in the world (both antipersonnel and anti-tank). Numerous PICs and PSAs show Afghans how to identify and avoid areas that are mined and teach them to identify the signs of the few areas that have been cleared of mines and are safe to walk in. Additionally, news and special bulletins—broadcast throughout the day—inform people where roads have been closed because of military or insurgent activities. In Afghanistan, television literally helps Afghans navigate life; it can mean the difference between living and dying.

Many Afghan television workers, including some owners—victimized by war in some way—are genuinely motivated to lay the foundations for peace, nation-building, and healing through television. As I will demonstrate in the coming chapters, television enables a wide range of new possibilities for Afghan people—from these kinds of practical efforts that help people negotiate the consequences of war, to more ideologically framed programs that counter sectarian and gender violence, to entertainment genres such as melodramas and reality shows that offer alternative modernities.

Before engaging further with my own research, it is important to see how broadcast television has been conceptualized through the work of groundbreaking scholars carrying out qualitative studies of television in non-Western countries. The brief review below makes clear that these studies offer frameworks more applicable to the Afghanistan media world than to Western television studies.

PHOTO 4.2. Syeda Masood, a PhD candidate, watches a classical Afghan music show on Tolo TV at the Colbeh Arman Restaurant, 2019. Photo credit: Jalal Nazari for the author.

Non-Western TV Case Studies:
Managing Minorities and the Disenfranchised

For too long, media studies have focused on Western media. But recently there has been a movement of researchers—anthropologists, sociologists, and media studies scholars—who are widening the discipline by examining the television systems of other countries (Abu-Lughod 2005; Mandel 2002; Mankekar 1999; N. Schiller 2018; Oren 2004; Rajagopal 2001). To name but a few examples, there have been recent studies that analyze critical moments in the development of television and nationhood in Egypt, Israel, India, Venezuela, and post-Soviet Kazakhstan. Such rich television studies have helped expand our knowledge of how media worlds are produced across national boundaries. Moreover, they have furthered our cross-cultural understanding of media practices and also revealed the limits of a Western bias in television studies. My work builds on this growing body of non-Western-centric scholarship. It offers insights that render evident the way that things take shape in the context of Afghanistan.

Contestations over the role of television can be especially revealing during periods of radical change, such as the formative years of a nation, the postwar or postindependence years of a country, or the rise of new political regimes. Focusing research on social dramas around television helps to deconstruct the emerging imaginary of nation-states such as Afghanistan as it is instantiated across the complex range of players who are participating in the construction of a new public sphere. This is truer of terrestrially broadcast television, given the state's ability to control the medium and its accessibility. Thus the nation-state/nationalism serves as a key framework in these studies that took shape in contexts where terrestrial television was the dominant form. In such periods, television can serve as a tool that simultaneously unites the dominant groups of society while dividing, disenfranchising, or at least managing the vulnerable or minorities. Fierce debates thus surround its deployment.

While the specificities of each national context undermine any easily generalizable conclusions about non-Western television, some common threads do unite these cross-cultural studies. They are worth exploring, both for their own sake and as a counterpoint to television's effects in Afghanistan. Therefore, I will briefly discuss some influential media ethnographies in order to better contextualize and highlight the stakes involved in national television discourses, namely how nations are configured and imagined and what are the discourses' effects on different publics.

Tasha Oren, in her book *Demon in the Box* (2004), and Ruth Mandel, in her essay "A Marshall Plan of the Mind" (2002), set out to explore the formative years of television of Israel and Kazakhstan respectively. Oren's is a historical project, which required her to go back to the past, into the archive of documents and people who shaped Israeli state television. Mandel, on the other hand, seized on a serendipitous opportunity to observe how the British Foreign Office's mandate of introducing Kazakhs to capitalism, realized via the production of a Kazakh version of the British soap opera *Crossroads,* played out on Kazakh state television. She observes how the everyday practices of production are filled with contradictions.

Lila Abu-Lughod (*Dramas of Nationhood*, 2004), Arvind Rajagopal (*Politics after Television*, 2001), and Purnima Mankekar (*Screening Culture, Viewing Politics*, 1999) explore the advent of new programs on state-run television channels of Egypt and India, both of which have relatively long histories of broadcasting. The studies were carried out just prior to the paradigm-changing advent of satellite and internet. Oren and Mandel found it relatively easy to determine the ideological mechanisms that motivated their systems of study, whereas for

Abu-Lughod, Rajagopal, and Mankekar, assessing the agenda of the television producers, financiers, and writers was a complex task.

Indeed, Oren explains how her archive was intact and ready to be mined: "As television was implicated in the Israeli state project, primary national concerns were defined in terms of broadcasting, offering a rare and lucid glimpse into the anatomy of such definitions and their significance to the Israeli project. Here I argue that television's ideological utility was never as potent in Israel as in the decade before its actual birth" (2004, 6).

Mandel observed that once British funding ran out and British personnel departed, the majority ethnic Kazakh writers of *Crossroads* fired the minority ethnic Russian writers and quickly killed off the characters of the intermarried Kazakh and Russian couples that the British had wanted to be part of the show. The Kazakhs explained that they were relieved that the "controlling British editorial gaze" had ended; they did not want "the big Russian brother" gaze either. As Mandel explains, succinctly summing up the differences between the Central Asian and British understandings of "developmental" television, "The soap operatic narrative proposed by the British, informed by a pluralist model of national identity and aimed at reinforcing a delicate multiculturalism, proved somewhat at odds with the essentialist model of new nationalist indigenization promoted implicitly by the Kazakhstani government and explicitly by the Kazakh writers" (2002, 223).

Rajagopal contemplates similar themes of ethnic/religious tensions in India, for which he coins the useful heuristic of "the split public." His study is focused on the televised national imagery of the Ramayan (a Hindu epic turned television serial), which accompanied the rise of the Hindu Right and the subsequent violence directed at the Muslim minority. He delineates how the broadcasting of a religious-themed program for the first time on the state-run television station Doordarshan helped to equate "Hindutva" (Hinduness) with Indianness. Expanding on Appadurai, he then explains how the Indian People's Party built on the opportunity presented by Ramayan: "To assert Hindu identity was merely a cultural matter, giving voice to what had been unmarked and taken for granted. Secularism was, in this sense, folded into Hindu culture, and to dispute such an understanding was 'pseudo-secular.' Muslim assertion was therefore disruptive and threatening in this account, implicitly anti-national and requiring to be closely monitored" (2001, 22).

He explores the irony of how a modernist media tool, television, came to incite and embody anti-modernist sentiments in the wide viewership—"If media and markets have typically been conceived as advance guards of modernization and secularism, my analysis here indicates why their political outcomes might lead in unpredictable directions"—and follows by astutely suggesting that "any critical analysis of the work of television therefore entails sifting through historical assumptions that may carry over when transposing a theory from one society to another" (Rajagopal 2001, 6). Here Rajagopal's work resonates with Ong and McLuhan about the retribalizing effects of visual/oral technologies as compared with print media.

Through a feminist lens, Mankekar too examines the implications of the nationwide televising of the Ramayan and another Hindu epic, the Mahabharata. She explains her gendered perspective: "As a woman and a feminist who had returned 'home' to do fieldwork, I was struck by the subject positions assumed by women in this reconfiguration of discourses of social justice, identity, and culture. . . . In fact some of the most visible and vocal spokespersons of Hindu right-wing organizations were women" (1999, 4). Her textual analysis, coupled with interviews with Doordarshan producers as well as with women viewers from different backgrounds, reveal how the program's intention—to construct the proper Indian woman or "the New Indian Woman" and the ideal Indian nuclear family—was interpreted differently by women from a range of backgrounds. This "new woman" was to devotedly serve and unite the family unit, which would in turn serve and unite the Hindutva nation. This construction was also designed to deliver the new family to advertisers. In the televising of the Mahabharata epic, the protagonist Draupadi is cast against the antiheroine, the sexually lascivious woman who threatens the integrity of the family and the nation. Her male counterpart is a lecherous Muslim man who also puts the family and the nation in jeopardy by preying on Hindu women.

In her interviews with middle-class women from diverse New Delhi neighborhoods, Mankekar discovers that though the attempts at "indoctrinating" them were not always as effective as intended, the overall message was successful. For example, she observes that the particularly charged scene in which Draupadi is forcefully disrobed was not read as coded. The dominant discourse surrounding the scene suggests that it is about saving Hindu culture. However, female viewers from across religious and caste lines—single, unmarried, and otherwise—all related to Draupadi's vulnerability and used it as a forum for empowerment. Nevertheless, Mankekar concludes that the ideology embedded in Doordarshan did indeed have consequences: "Viewers' engagement with television narratives was central to their constitution as gendered and national subjects, to their construction of national and communal pasts, and to their understanding of violence committed in the name of the nation—thus revealing

PHOTO 4.3. Masoud Abdulzada, a barber in the Pol-i Sorkh neighborhood of Kabul, has the TV on in the background, 2019. Photo credit: Jalal Nazari for the author.

the political significance of texts dismissed by many social scientists as fictive and therefore inconsequential, as 'mere' entertainment or, less charitably, as kitsch" (1999, 11).

The development of Israeli TV was also implicated in cultural hierarchies, but the underlying motif was one of uniting the Jewish population. The Zionist leaders conceptualized television as a means of containing and managing what they considered to be "problem populations" of "Arab Jews" and Palestinian residents. Oren reveals how these populations were labeled "culturally vulnerable"—meaning that they were susceptible to betraying the precarious nation and therefore had to be vigilantly brought under the radar of the nation-state—because of their contentious geographic positioning and their internal contradictions: racial, ethnic, and religious. Echoing Ella Shohat's assessment of early Israeli cinema (1989), all the "problem populations" were portrayed via racialized stereotypes as "backward" Arabs. Yet for the Jews who emigrated from Arab countries, the state of Israel offered them some "hope" of redemption. Their means of salvation came via intermarriage with the white "civilized" European Jewish immigrants; due to their newfound privilege they could be incorporated into the nation. Since funding did not run out as in the case of the British project in Kazakhstan, the intermarried couples were not killed off on-screen. There was no similar route to salvation for the Palestinians. Palestinians intermarrying Israelis would have challenged the entire structure of the elite ruling class and the state of Israel.

Oren explains that Israeli television faced a critical moment when *Hirbat Hizaa*, a short autobiographical story about an Israeli soldier who doubts the nationalist project, was adapted for television. Though the novel had been controversial in print, it was also celebrated and widely taught at schools for its high literary form and style. Oren thus questions why its television adaptation stirred contentious censorship debates and nearly caused the collapse of the young state-run television channel, even before its production was complete and long before it was to be broadcast. "The debate," she writes, "served as the definitive moment that polarized a newly identified cultural elite in opposition to government ideology, forever fractured a cherished mythology, and exposed a deep rift in the political foundations of the nation" (2004, 156). The program had clearly articulated national anxieties and trauma among warring politicians, journalists, policy makers, and the general public. Some charged that it was anti-Semitic and anti-Israeli, while others welcomed the public airing of their "collective guilt and shame" as a part of a healing process. The skewed controversy of the television adaptation resonates with early sentiments about television's dangerous power compared with print, but note how the story was still from the perspective of an Israeli soldier, a member of the nation-state, and not from a Palestinian perspective, because that would have been too disruptive. As Mandel concludes in the Kazakh case, there are limits to free speech and multiculturalism, plurality, and diversity in controlled national environments.

Abu-Lughod explores the anxieties and desires of the Egyptian state and its diverse inhabitants in her ethnography of popular melodramas aired during the holy month of Ramadan. She explains how a state-run television station's secular producers developed programming to reference an earlier time as a tactic to avoid controversy in the present over the role of Islam and the declining state of the economy. During the 1990s, when Abu-Lughod conducted her fieldwork, the nation was undergoing neoliberal free-market "reforms" heralded by the Sadat administration: "Whereas television was introduced at the same time that Nasser nationalized industry, mandated mass public education and welfare, redistributed land, discouraged imports, and called for Arab socialism, it now operated in an environment much changed by regimes since his death in 1970" (2004, 18).

In the 1990s, forces of transnational capitalism coupled with the policies of the IMF led to the increasing privatization of public services. This privatization also increased already widespread poverty and economic insecurity. As a result, television producers channeled people back to the Nasserist era of the 1960s, which was a triumphant time in Egyptian history and the inauguration of national television. Through her interviews with cosmopolitan producers and writers as well as marginalized viewers from Bedouin and peasant communities, she establishes that the most popular programs were those that referred to this idealized developmental moment with its socialist ideals. The melodramas that Abu-Lughod studied used positively "charged nationalist symbols," such as references to the great female singer Umm Kulthum, the Aswan High Dam, and Nasser's charismatic public addresses to a nation on the verge of war with Israel.

Developmental and educational themes also made up a significant percentage of Egyptian national television. These programs ranged in message: some promoted literacy and education; others extolled the virtues of family planning and buying modern products, of being good public servants, and of respecting tourists and tourism; and some even suggested vacation spots. The intended target audience of these uplift and modernization programs were peasants and women, both of whom had been the object of the colonial gaze and civilizing missions (Abu-Lughod 1998, 2006; Fahmy 2005; T. Mitchell, 1991, 2002b). As in the colonial era, the producers even invoked the language of modernizing "backward" and "traditional" people. Abu-Lughod explains that the producers of these shows were part of the culture industry and therefore shared the "dominant codes" of the nation-state. She goes on to explain that overall they tended to be out of touch with the reality of their intended audiences and actually, contrary to their good intentions, did a disservice to their viewers.

Abu-Lughod is particularly critical of their overemphasis on education as the path of redemption for peasants and women. She explains that this was a possibility in Nasser's time when jobs for new graduates were guaranteed through a state mandate; in Sadat's neoliberal 1990s, it was another example of pulling the wool over the eyes of Egyptians. "Given how understaffed and underfinanced the schools are," she asks, "and how few children can actually succeed there, are all the efforts towards schooling worth it?" (2004, 70). She also cites high unemployment rates among poor college-educated youth who did not have the connections to get the better-paying government jobs. Thus Abu-Lughod rightly expresses concern that rural Egyptian villages and domestic laborers, the subjects of her study, readily accepted the dominant messages of seeking a formal education.

PHOTO 4.4. Fraidoon Azimi, the owner of a real estate business, watching a world news program on Rah-e-Farda TV, 2019. Photo credit: Jalal Nazari for the author.

Abu-Lughod's study offers rare moments of disjuncture and slippage from the didactic authoritative statist agenda, among producers or audiences. Of one television adaptation of a story, she observes that, "though the progressive messages about class exploitation and even gender remained, they were muted and ultimately undermined by the validation of an educated, enlightened middle class" (2004, 89). At the historical moment described in the study, Egyptian television functioned primarily as an ideological and propaganda tool of the state and its elites. Abu-Lughod calls this type of television programming and the structures that support it "development realism." She describes it as a "cultural counterpart of social welfare policies" (81).

The 2011 collection *Drama for Development: Cultural Translation and Social Change,* edited by Andrew Skuse, Marie Gillespie, and Gerry Power, addresses the question of "development realism," "social realism," and "realism" through a number of studies of radio drama serials intended to communicate development goals. The book draws on a three-year collaboration between the Open University, the University of Adelaide, and the BBC World Service Trust (now BBC Media Action) and also on the work of scholars who looked at development media in diverse local cultural contexts, including those of Afghanistan, Burma, Cambodia, Nepal, Pakistan, India, Nigeria, and Rwanda. It brings into dialogue the perspectives of the producers who make "dramas for development," the donors who pay for them, and the audiences who consume them, exploring how the idea of cultural translation means different things for each of these groups as they participate in the project of promoting progressive social change in cross-cultural and postcolonial contexts. They argue that the efficacy of the BBC's "educational entertainment" programs hinges on the "social distance" between donors, producers, and audiences in terms of actual and cultural distance. This is exacerbated by the colonial history of Western development projects, which privilege Western scientific methods and worldview at the expense of "indigenous cosmologies" (Hodgetts et al. 2010). Together these issues pose the biggest challenges to transnational media development (Skuse, Gillespie, and Power 2011). The progressive messages are sometimes lost in the translation or misguided; sometimes they lack cultural understanding or sensitivity. In other instances, the productions succeed in their social justice goals. The redeeming qualities that unite most of these transnational ventures are their collaborative nature and the positive intentions of the cross-cultural producers—which I argue in the coming section is mostly the case in Afghanistan as well.

Motivations of Afghan TV Producers: The Development Gaze and the Imperial Gaze

Are non-Western state-run or national television programs doomed to incite violence in their disparate citizen-viewers or to produce regimes of exclusion or other forms of coercion to bring certain groups into line? The winds of change point back to early Western media studies' fears of television and mass media more generally. Once again, scholars have conceptualized television as a problem because it seems that television has been a problem. These studies show that television, across different national contexts, has had consequences antithetical to the tenets of democracy, diversity, pluralism, and multiculturalism.

Is this also true in the Afghan case? Certainly television is at the center of much violence, real and televisual, directly and indirectly. In post-9/11 Afghanistan, is social engineering via television responsible for creating similar types of management or "duping," regimes of exclusion, or, worse yet, violence toward "vulnerable" or "unstable" segments of the population?

Building on Abu-Lughod's concept of "development realism," I posit the categories of the "development gaze," which is to be differentiated from its more problematic other half, the "imperial gaze." Abu-Lughod builds on Michael Schudson's schema (1999) of major media aesthetics of first and second world nations, wherein socialist realism was "designed to dignify the simplicity of human labor in the service of the state," while capitalist realism glorifies "the pleasures and freedoms of consumer choice in defense of the virtues of private life and material ambitions." She adds the useful category of "development realism" as that which "idealizes education, progress, and modernity within the nation" (2004, 81). Both the development and imperial gazes are premised on the rhetoric of development, modernity, and democracy. The key difference is that there is an inherent duplicity built into the imperial gaze. This is because the agenda of imperial projects, from the outset, is to protect, promote, and expand the economic and political interests of the imperial nation at all costs, even at the expense of the subject population. Equally important is the fact that imperial projects tend to be less collaborative in their approach and implementation. They are characteristically more unilateral with a controlling, editorial Big Brother gaze.

Of course there are varying degrees of overlap between the two types of gazes (depending on the specificities of the projects). After all, they are two sides of the same coin, with one usually ushering in the other. In modern warfare, as with the United States' longest war in Afghanistan, the neoimperial army goes in with a highly mediated public relations campaign based on lofty developmental goals intended to appease both the citizenry at home and in the subject country. Nonetheless, it is crucial to differentiate between the gazes since, as we shall see, their political outcomes and ramifications are worlds apart—as different as actually rebuilding the democratic institutions of destroyed nations versus putting into place a simulacra of democracy that hides beneath its moral veneer a client state with proxy leaders who are beholden to imperial forces.

Fully understanding the imperial gaze, how it functions, and how it's cultivated, requires understanding its Western origins and its genesis in the colonized world. The imperial gaze of today, like that of yesteryear, is directly related to the rise of an elite expert class. Early media studies scholars (Blumer [1933] 2004; Lasswell 1927; Lippmann 1925) defended the need for a rational-minded class of scientific experts to rid democracy of the problem of its demos, or irrational masses. This argument was articulated most notoriously by Walter Lippmann in his classic text *The Phantom Public* (1925), where he laid out his treatise explaining that the solution to the ignorance of the general populace and their inability to run a democracy is to empower technocrats who can use science as a tool for the mastery and control of society. Timothy Mitchell in his influential book, *Rule of Experts: Egypt, Techno-politics, Modernity* (2002b), explains how Western technocrats have transformed their development projects from colonial to neocolonial enterprises, yet continue to wreak havoc on colonized and postcolonial nations like Egypt in the same ways. According to Mitchell, the problems of imperialism and global expansion arise not in spite of but because of the merger between scientific methods, population management, and governance. "Although the offices of the East India Company in London have now given way to the headquarters of the International Monetary Fund in Washington, D.C., or the World Trade Organization in Geneva, and the production and export of technocratic expertise is organized from American university campuses rather than the company's Haileybury College in Hertfordshire . . . the issues raised by postcolonialism are no less relevant today—and perhaps more so" (8).

It is no coincidence that the leading Afghanistan experts and government officials in charge of development in Afghanistan in both the US and Afghanistan hail from the same interconnected halls of the US academia, the World Bank, the IMF, the USAID, and various UN organizations. They form a small, Western male elite network, with overlapping interests interwoven into all of these political, corporate, and military institutions. They are granted enormous resources and bestowed enormous power by the prestigious trifecta of development, higher education, and governance to wield their often top-down and detached expertise on the world's most vulnerable people. With the wave of their development wand, they can and have entirely remade, transformed, and slashed and burned economies, geologies, histories, and infrastructures of ME-NASA countries and the everyday lives of their people. As I show throughout this book, in the case of Afghanistan, this combination of being endowed with godlike power and being allowed virtually no accountability to the tax payers who line their pockets has resulted in a dangerous approach to development that is tainted by hubris and duplicity, which has manifested in an Orientalizing and imperialist gaze.

Today's technocrats build on and borrow from the methods of their predecessors, namely the bureaucracy of British colonizers, which is not far off from the methods of Russian and Soviet imperialists. Their neo-imperial gaze is similar to that of colonial rulers, who viewed other people's lands as open sources for exploitation and canvases for statecraft. Even in the face of mounting evidence of misappropriation and mismanagement, the imperialist technocrats of Afghanistan are quick to use their scientific technic to exaggerate, lie, and absolve themselves. They spin and tout their stockpile of failed human rights and nation-building development projects as accomplishments, while continuing to lambast the failures of indigenous nationalists for their top-down elitist projects. What they do not realize is that they themselves are now the veritable embodiment of C. Wright Mills's dangerous technocratic power elite who use "the increased means of mass persuasion . . . to control, manage, manipulate, and increasingly intimidate" the public (1956, 399).

Markers of development and progress including creating the conditions for fair elections, freedom of speech, human rights, and access to education and healthcare become rhetorical and propagandistic public relations campaigns that require superficial validation and demonstration. The appearance of progress, be it in terms of women's rights or education or elections, takes precedence over actual progress. The lofty goal of democratic nation-building in this respect becomes a technocratic simulacra, an imitation that takes the place of actually building the scaffolding of democracy. European aid workers I spoke to from the Swedish International Development Cooperation Agency (SIDA) and the Danish International Development Agency (DANIDA) critiqued USAID for stamping every development project with their logo with little regard for efficacy or crediting other cooperative international aid organizations.

Yet as flawed and destructive as the interwoven gazes of development and imperialism have been in reaping Afghanistan, I still contend that at least in the media sector, they have yielded some positive results worthy of extraction. My contention is based on the fact that the international development community, for all of their shortcomings, has fostered the creation of prolific media sector and robust public sphere. Therefore, there are many media outlets to challenge the hegemony, propaganda, and manipulation of Mills' power elite and Marx' ruling classes.

Although the efficacy of their programs is not uniform, my fieldwork suggests that—at least in the media sector—the Afghan and transnational productions I studied fall into the category of the development gaze. The vast majority of Afghan producers and foreign collaborative producers I came to know have an inclusive pluralist national mindset. They are well intentioned and genuine in their desire to create a more just future for Afghan people out of the chaos, bloodshed, and ashes of its current dismal state.

My interviews with Afghan television personnel, both low level and high level, suggest that the motivation of most producers (including writers, directors, programmers, and owners) can be categorized by three main agendas: (1) nation-building/unity, (2) education/uplift, and to a lesser extent (3) providing entertainment/distraction. Peace, or *suhl* in Persian and Pashto, seemed to be the underlying objective that framed all their work. Given television's power to broadcast nationally and the presence of the international development community, it is not surprising that Afghan television station owners speak about their motivations, programming, goals, objectives, and visions for the future in developmental terms of raising awareness, education, and the elevation of society. Due to the pervasiveness of the international donor community, high illiteracy rates, and the dystopic state of the country, television is imagined to be a particularly powerful force in the effort to "save" Afghanistan.

In this competitive arena where everyone is vying for international aid, owners frequently compare and contrast their programming with others' and challenge the effectiveness or utility of their competitors' programming while promoting their own. Television station owners, steeped in the rhetoric of development, often seem to be reading from the same script or Call for Projects about nation-building, human rights, and unity that characterize transnational NGO projects in media. The efficacy or lack thereof of these development media projects and the intentions of the producers who design and implement them are central concerns of this study, which I analyze in the rest of this chapter and in the following chapters.

Given the recent history of gender violence, civil war, and ethnic tension, it is also not surprising that two of the main targets of the Afghan and international development gaze are women, particularly the "uplift" and "saving" of them, and vulnerable or "dangerous" ethnic groups that are considered a risk to the nation, namely the Pashtuns. These two groups are also the objects of the imperial gaze, past and present. In fact, many Calls for Projects specifically stipulate reaching and addressing these groups and the problems that face them. Thus I argue that in contrast to the other case studies of non-Western TV that I have discussed in this chapter, in Afghanistan, internationally funded TV production is attempting to be more representative of the whole of the population and offering groups of people who are minorities and vulnerable or deemed as "unruly" and "dangerous" the means to improve their positions in society, although not always to good effect.

Reframing Violence:
The PIC, Political Satire, and News

One genre device that has become the favorite launching pad for such messages and is ubiquitous on Afghan television stations is the public service announcement and the public information campaign. PSAs and PICs were initially sponsored only by various governmental offices in conjunction with donor aid in order to promote blatant nationalistic messages and nation-building projects. Now, due to their popularity, stations that are outside the purview of international funding are also producing PSAs and PICs independently.

Tolo TV's powerful PIC series called "Jung bas Ast!" (Enough war!) comprises short vignettes that feature real newsreel footage of horrific acts from the aftermath of suicide bombings and other types of violence inflicted on Afghans by other Afghans. The culprits remain ambiguous, but the implication is that they are Afghan terrorists or insurgents such as the Taliban or other groups that are motivated by racial/ethnic/religious xenophobia. The PSAs in the series always end with a male announcer stating sternly, "Enough war!" in either Dari or Pashto with accompanying black text in the respective language and an exclamation mark over a white background, which drips red, like blood, from the Perso-Arabic script.

One moving PIC of the "Enough War!" series shows, in slow motion, the aftermath of a suicide bomb in Kabul. The camera pans across images of overturned cars and recently killed or severely injured individuals strewn around the wreckage. Then, the camera abruptly goes into real time, with sounds of screaming and sirens. We see a close-up of an Afghan police officer in uniform crying uncontrollably in the foreground and cars burning in the background. As he cries into the camera, he keeps looking backward and pointing to the apocalyptic scene behind him, stammering in an Uzbek-accented Dari that his friends—fellow police officers—were killed. Though everyone I interviewed identified him as Uzbek, his ethnicity was a nonissue. People first and foremost related to his humanity, loss, and pain. His Afghan National Police uniform probably contributed to his identification as an Afghan who represented the country's shared suffering. While in different contexts people sardonically observe that those on the Afghan National Police force are all Uzbek and will revolt, or that the Afghan National Army is hiring only Tajiks or Pashtuns, this was not the case here. Likewise, even though crying is overall extremely shameful for Afghans of all genders and ages, no one pointed to the fact that a grown man was sobbing uncontrollably.[2] An exception was made. He manages to ask through heartfelt tears, "Why? Why? Why?"

The news, which is a favorite genre of Afghans and can broadcast up to a dozen times a day on any given television station, also does not shy away from showing gory scenes of violence, such as that committed all too often by international troops on Afghan civilians, or Afghan-on-Afghan violence.

For someone who is not used to seeing graphic real violence broadcast regularly and frequently on television, it is simultaneously difficult to watch and captivating. The depictions starkly differ from the overly exaggerated, narrated, stylized, fetishized, or voyeuristic depictions of violence found in American Hollywood films. Rather, they are powerful because of their relatively unedited quality and simple realism, which points to the difference between dramatizing violence and portraying violence for what it is. The creators of these PSAs intend to maximize the full effects and affects produced by such acts of violence without being disrespectful of the victims. By showing violence simply and realistically, without much or any editorial commentary or censorship, they can accomplish this.

In the West, due to the stratified nature of capitalism, news-based televisual violence is censored by both the television stations and the government. For example, the broadcasting of uncensored violence during dinnertime (and many other times), as is commonly done on Afghan televisions, would not happen in the United States because it would not be conducive to putting viewers/consumers into a buying mood or mode. McLuhan's famous metaphor comparing the media in the West to a warm bath or a hot bath on a cold day that comforts and sedates people into complacency is apt here (1969). Former president Obama, who briefly lifted the almost two-decade-long ban on showing the caskets of martyred American soldiers on US television stations, reinstated it, presumably due to Pentagon pressure.

To extend McLuhan's metaphor, then, real graphic and violent imagery is a scalding hot bath or an ice-cold bath that jolts and shocks people into action. Protests and riots usually erupt when the killing of civilians by international troops, usually American, are broadcast in Afghanistan. Angry Afghans take to the streets to demand justice. Sometimes they also destroy shops and businesses in neighborhoods where foreigners live, work, and frequent. As a demonstration of the will of the people, violence can be productive in such protests. Before American television began catering to corporate and government interests, this was also the case with the anti–Vietnam War and the civil rights movements, which television played a critical role in mobilizing.

According to Afghan producers who spoke off the record, American government officials from the Department of Defense and the State Department, which have a large presence in Kabul, have asked them to refrain from broadcasting "civ cas," the shorthand used by the international community for civilian casualties. The logic is that civilian casualties will be used as propaganda by the "insurgents," namely the Taliban and ISIS, to turn public opinion against the international military and even nonmilitary presence.

If, on the other hand, suicide bombings are shown too readily, then they can turn people against the Taliban and toward the US-led international military operations. Several American officials involved in diplomacy and communication in Afghanistan also spoke off the record to express similar sentiments. They also claimed to have intelligence that the Taliban have production facilities where they produce compilation DVDs of civilian casualties for home viewing and then distribute them to generate more followers. Of course the real geopolitics of Afghanistan is more complex than any insurgent/American polarity. Yet this is how those who control media representations imagine televisual violence affects the masses.

Fearful of its undeniably powerful effects and unintended consequences, dominant groups try to curb televised violence instead of their own real violence. The producers' intentions, however, are not to support one group or another or to polarize people in favor of or against one group or another. Based on interviews and programming, it appears that producers—who, by virtue of being Afghan, have also been victimized and have suffered at the hands of war and all its tangles of tragedies—aim to condemn war holistically. They want to remind their compatriots of the horrors of war in a very visceral way and reinforce their collective experiences as first and foremost Afghans. By creating overtly anti-war messages—namely, that any type of violence is unacceptable—they are reclaiming a lost humanity and asserting political authority. When handled with sensitivity, they often accomplish just that.

At the same time, we cannot deny that funding pressures and threats affect what types of violence get more airtime. After all, international funding is contingent to a degree on portraying the international community, including military activity, favorably. Incentives for gaining funding or the pressure of losing funding can make producers occasionally acquiesce to foreign interests. Producers are also vulnerable to the real dangers of being targeted and attacked by the Taliban, ISIS, and other extremists. In fact, almost every television station I visited had been attacked at least once by unknown assailants. Thus as a result of their political economy and in some cases their ethnic makeup, some stations do promote one side or another, at times recklessly. While those opposed to Western values or the US War might try to program material that would turn viewers against the West, others focus on Afghan violence, with a focus on specific ethnic groups. Tolo's evocative and powerful "Jung bas Ast!" (Enough war!) series, which I described above, for example, thus far does not have a single episode that features civilian casualties resulting from US coalition military operations. This is similar to Afghan Television Network owner Ehsan Bayat's televisual displays of charity being limited to non-US-war-related disasters. Clearly decisions were made in these instances to shy away from highlighting civilian casualties caused by US-led international military forces. The obvious reason for such decisions, one can speculate, is that the media producers did not want to provoke US government backers and funders. These cases can therefore be read as instances of media imperialism amid otherwise well-thought-out and well-intentioned media campaigns and projects.

Yet despite the constraints, most Afghan television producers manage to show a variety of violence on most stations—and a lot of it, which is a testament to the still free and competitive nature of the press in Afghanistan. When some stations succumb to internal or external pressure to censor civilian casualties or insurgent violence, other stations will report on it. Subsequently, this creates counterpressure on the censoring stations to uncensor war violence in order to remain relevant in a competitive television market. The overall effect is that of the equalization of all violence; there is no hierarchy between good or bad violence. Via these strategies of televising violence they hope to achieve its opposite: peace and unity. As seasoned anti-war activists know, showing the realities of war and war-related violence is a very effective means of coalescing public opinion against war, if not achieving peace. In the Afghan case, that opposition extends to warlordism as well.

Media organizations also have taken on the very dangerous task of holding warlords accountable for present and past atrocities. For example, the Killid Group, in conjunction with its extensive network of radio stations, the Radio Killid Network, and its two popular nationwide weekly magazines, *Killid Magazine* and *Mursal Women's Magazine*, produced a 125-episode series on war crimes and war criminals. Saba TV, in conjunction with its syndicate newspaper, *Hashte Subh* (Eight in the morning), Afghanistan's largest and longest running daily since the ouster of the Taliban, also regularly produces hard-hitting investigative reports on abuses of power. The Killid Group, Saba TV, *Hashte Subh*, and other independent media organizations also partner with and rely on the research of the Afghan Independent Human Rights Commission (AIHRC), a UN-mandated independent body. The growing genre of political talk shows along with political satire programs that combine investigative journalism and comedy are educating Afghans and elevating the terms and topics up for debate in Afghanistan. They confront abuses of power stemming from the power elite, be they foreign technocrats or domestic politicians and warlords.

As I discuss in the conclusion of this book, these brave media challenges to ruthless warlords and other political elites do not pass without reprisals and punishment. As a show of solidarity, many television stations also readily broadcast incidents of violence perpetuated against Afghan journalists and other media makers. Television producers are taking the bold step of broadcasting the violence to generate debate and to stand up for their fellow media makers. The programs use close-ups and graphic imagery of the injuries sustained, dead bodies, and interviews with victims, their families, and the doctors attending to them in a hospital or in their homes. This strategy has been effective in coalescing public sympathy and opinion in favor of journalists' rights and media rights more broadly.

PHOTO 4.5. The Maarafat family, including in-laws, watch Tolo News together in their home in the Dasht-i Barchi neighborhood of west Kabul, 2019. Photo credit: Jalal Nazari for the author.

For example, after a reporter and a cameraman were physically assaulted and their equipment damaged by the Afghan security forces on December 4, 2009, Sepehr TV featured footage of the event repeatedly on its news. It also proceeded to air a special program on media laws and free speech the following week and for several weeks afterward. The program showed the injuries of the victims who were brutally beaten and the destruction of their equipment along with interviews with media law experts about the illegality of the government's actions. Instead of evading responsibility and danger by brushing the incident under the proverbial Afghan rug, the owner of Sepehr—Dr. Najib Sepehr— and manager Elham Mohammadi made the brave decision to use their station to generate discussion around the violence.[3] In the process, they defended the rights and honor of their own victimized journalists as well as media rights and freedom of expression more broadly. As we shall see in chapter 6, protests are also proving to be a powerful social force. Since the central government of Afghanistan is relatively weak and spaces for public gathering, such as *maidans* or town squares, stadiums, and bazaars, are plentiful, massive protests in urban areas, across the country, happen regularly.

For the media makers and their organizations that continue to produce such damning reports, their desire for justice outweighs their fears. Having been traumatized by decades of war, they, like the rest of the public, are avowedly and explicitly anti-war—a fact they hope to convey through PICs, political satire and talk shows, and the news. Showing the realities of war and war-related violence and producing well-researched reports that document war crimes, as opposed to the edited, sanitized, biased, and sensationalized Hollywood and US news–style violence, represent an important first step for Afghans to reclaim their right to a peaceful life.

Dramatizing Democracy and Diversity

Other public information campaigns and public service announcements address the goals of unity, nation-building, and peace through affirmative messages. For example "We Are All Afghan," another Tolo PIC series, has become a favorite of audiences. In one version of it—directed by Roya Sadat, the acclaimed Afghan independent filmmaker and television writer/director—we see Afghan children from all corners of the country, dressed in their distinctive traditional clothing, emerging from their respective village yurts, tents, caves, and mud houses. They join together in a beautiful valley and walk together to the camera, which pans down as they state in unison in Dari, "We are all Afghan." In another version, also with scenic pastoral and rural landscapes in the background, we see adults, of all ethnic groups and races, engaging in work associated with their provinces, such as carpet weaving, farming, and making clayware. Each person, male or female, stops working to address the camera and say in his or her own language or accented Dari, "I am Afghan." The Afghan Civic Engagement Program, which is funded by USAID, also produced a similar PIC called "We Choose Peace" that ran on RTA along with cross-platform delivery on radio stations, posters, printed flyers, and a Facebook page.

During the summers of the 2009, 2014, and 2019 presidential elections, PSAs explaining or extolling democracy and the election process proliferated on Afghan television. These ranged from expository PSAs about voting and elections to instructional shorts that explained how to vote. Some encouraged women to come out and vote. Others explained to people that it was not in their best interest to allow village elders to "buy" their votes. Though simple and somewhat axiomatic in their content, these PSAs were profound in showing the potential of democracy and the democratic process as an exemplary model for creating the conditions for justice and human rights.

However, in some instances the rosy depictions of human rights and democracy in these well-intentioned public information campaigns juxtaposed with the brutalities of life in Afghanistan elicit complex negative responses from viewers. The animated series *Yassin and Kaka Raouf*, funded by USAID through the Afghan Rule of Law Project, has all the qualities of good Education-Entertainment (E-E) programming. It is entertaining, informative, well-produced, and well-executed. The series, which was produced in 2009 but continues to be broadcast on several Afghan television stations including Tolo TV, has as its protagonists the war orphans Yassin and his sister Amina, who are adopted by the kindhearted and law-abiding Kaka (Uncle) Raouf, who also lost his family in the wars. The series follows the trio, having recently returned from Pakistan, where they were refugees, as they try to make a life for themselves in the new internationally funded, development-rich Afghanistan.

According to the producers, with promises of democracy, security, and the rule of law inscribed in the post-9/11 constitution and formal justice system, the goal of *Yassin and Kaka Raouf* is to turn people away from using violence and informal systems of justice to solve problems by building trust in the law and its fair enforcement (Wild 2018). Each episode explores one article of the constitution, including the rights of returning Afghan refugees, prohibition of child labor, equality between men and women, and freedom of speech, the press, and demonstration. In an episode titled "Getting One's Justice," a corrupt cop who bribes people, including Yassin, is successfully brought to justice, tried, and imprisoned. In another episode, "Good Things Come to People Who Deserve Them," a powerful warlord type and his thugs seize Yassin and Amina's deceased parents' home. When Yassin and Amina want to take the matter into their own hands, they are encouraged by Kaka Raouf to fight the warlord in court, where they succeed in retrieving their home and removing the occupying force.

According to my own family's experiences and everyone I have talked to, the Afghan courts thrive on bribery and the political appointment of judges affiliated with warlords who consistently rule in favor of *zoor awarah* and *zoor mundah*, or strongmen who have money and militias. The only way I know that some people with more means have reclaimed their homes or other property from *zoor awarah* is by hiring other *zoor awarah* to remove them by force, which is a dangerous affair and hardly guarantees their holding on to their homes.

The 2019 case of Mina Mangal further demonstrates the wide gap between the lawlessness of reality and the lawful world projected in these pro-democracy public information campaigns. To support her family, as the eldest of six children, Mina Mangal worked as a freelance journalist and newscaster on Tolo,

Lemar, Shamshad, and ATN. At the same time, Mangal was afraid for her life. Having been engaged as a teenager and subsequently married to an abusive husband, Jawad, with a long history of violence, Mangal had filed numerous domestic violence and abduction charges as well as divorce and protection orders with the attorney general's office and other courts. The police briefly detained a group made up of her husband's family and associates who had kidnapped, beaten, and tortured her. They were released most likely because of bribery, which her family also alleges. Immediately after she was granted a divorce in a lengthy legal battle with the courts and her in-laws, while waiting early in the morning outside of her house for a car to pick her up to go to work, she was shot and killed by two men on a motorbike in broad daylight. On Afghan media outlets her parents are clamoring for her ex-husband and his accomplices to be brought to justice, but so far no one has been charged or arrested.

In the fictitious world of *Yassin and Kaka Raouf,* justice is always served, the innocent prevail, and the malfeasant *zoor awarah* and *zoor mundah* are punished for trampling on people's rights. In the real Afghanistan, as the case of Mangal highlights, justice and the rule of law are a shameless and cruel farce. Thus, while most Afghan audiences appreciate the positive messages of *Yassin and Kaka Raouf,* they also read it as naive and absurd, which elicits responses across a range of emotions from amusement to mockery and contempt.

If the PSAs in the previous section show the dystopic state of Afghanistan and remind the public that this is what happens when we let our differences, hatred, and violence take precedence, then the affirmative PSAs, however naive, still provide a glimpse into a future imaginary, a better Afghanistan where living in a united democratic nation with mutual respect in peaceful coexistence is a possibility. A number of Tolo TV's, 1TV's, and ATN's competitors also pointed out another, perhaps less admirable reason for those stations' staunch dedication to promoting peace and nation-building. "Do you think they will let the country plummet into chaos? No, they are making too much money," said one producer. According to their own assertions and documents, Tolo and 1TV and ATN in particular are experiencing incredible growth, profits, and expansion.

The Moby Media Group, the parent company of Tolo, includes in its holdings Lemar, Tolo TV's Pashto-language sister station; Arman FM Radio; Kaboora, a multimedia production company; *Afghan Scene,* a magazine; Lapis Communications, an advertising and consulting agency; AndeshaGah Internet café chain; several restaurants; and Tolo News, a twenty-four-hour satellite news channel. In 2009 Moby Media Group also partnered with Rupert Murdoch's News Corporation to create a series of Persian-language satellite stations, Farsi 1 and Zemzemeh, which are based in Dubai and target Iran and the Persian-speaking diaspora. It is not surprising that Saad Mohseni, the eldest of the Mohseni siblings who own Moby Media Group, is called the "Murdoch of Afghanistan" and "Afghanistan's first media tycoon" by the international press. Likewise, ATN's sister company AWCC is the nation's largest cell phone provider. Of course they both vertically and horizontally integrate and coordinate media messages through their multiple mediums. It is fair to say that they have built media empires.

This is a larger question not just for Afghan media corporations but also for all the nations who have Afghanistan in their sphere of interest and influence: given that in post-9/11 Afghanistan, large untapped markets for goods and services have opened up and foreign national and transnational corporations, such as food, drink, technology, and mining companies, are cashing in, is it in the best interests of the international community to have a stable Afghanistan? Or conversely, are the illicit markets of opium production and distribution, arms dealing and trafficking, confiscating property and land, and other commodities and industries that wartime environments enable still more profitable? Although some media outlets in Afghanistan benefit from war profiteering, not all do. In addition to expanding and opening markets in Afghanistan and in the region via advertising, media empires like Tolo and 1TV and ATN also wield incredible influence in the region and reshape geopolitics in peaceful conditions.

CHAPTER 5

Reaching Vulnerable and Dangerous Populations

Women and the Pashtuns

The Language of Ethno-national Subjects:
The Taliban, Terrorism, and Pashtuns

Another path to nationalist goals is to reach and educate troublesome, or marginalized populations—what Lila Abu-Lughod and Tasha Oren call vulnerable populations. In Afghanistan, two of the main targets of social uplift and modernization projects of most television stations are women and ethnic Pashtuns—also historically the object of the colonial gaze and civilizing missions. Via Orientalist and colonial mythologies, from Rudyard Kipling to Winston Churchill, Pashtun men and women have been both valorized for their bravery and heroics and also stigmatized as warlike and militant. Thus Pashtuns have gained a reputation as a troublesome and dangerous group capable of threatening the security of Afghanistan and other countries. They are also deemed vulnerable and susceptible to joining insurgent groups like the Taliban, who are almost entirely composed of Pashtuns. Although these are false perceptions, anthropologists have shown that there is truth in the notion that Pashtuns have rigid codes of masculinity and honor (Chiovenda 2019; Tapper 1991). At the same time, due to their homosociability and androcentrism, Pashtuns have also been rendered and gendered as queer and sexually deviant (Manchanda 2015).

The ethnic Hazaras, a historically marginalized and discriminated-against minority, are also the target of many development aid projects. Yet in the popular imagination, for better or worse, the Hazaras are considered to be a model minority who have excelled in the arts, literature, sciences, and many other fields. As such they are not the focus of television uplift programming in the same way as Pashtuns, who are considered unruly and volatile. Rather, in order to compensate for the Hazaras' historical marginalization, a number of development aid organizations either cater solely to them or at least give them precedence for scholarships abroad, media training workshops, and other such opportunities.

It is important to note that historically almost all of Afghanistan's ethnic groups have experienced some form of marginalization or discrimination at the hands of other ethnic groups or various Afghan governments based on their characteristics that make them unique and different. Whether it was the forced conversion of Nooristanis to Islam or hostility toward pastoral nomads like the Kochi, Aimak, and Kyrgyz nomads, there is a history of ethnicity-based biases, which is exacerbated for the substrata who are poor and smallest in numbers. Yet unlike the Pashtuns and Hazaras, who population-wise are larger in numbers, the smaller ethnic groups, with some exceptions, do not have television stations affiliated with them that cater to them.

Fazal Karim Fazal, president of Shamshad Television, established that network in February 2006 to reach the Pashto-speaking Pashtun Afghans. While different languages are spoken in Afghanistan among the many ethnicities and tribes, Dari and Pashto are the two official languages. Yet in practice Dari is by far the more prestigious language in cultural circles and is the dominant language of the state. This has continued to be the case even after Afghanistan's secession from the Persian Empire in the early eighteenth century. Governance, education, literature, and many other spheres of Afghan society are conducted in Dari.

Part of the reason for Dari's dominance is Iran's influence and the fact that Dari is a mutually intelligible dialect of Persian. Iran has a prolific publishing industry that prints everything from popular magazines to highly literary original works to the immediate translation of foreign books, ranging from medicine to novels. Since the country does not abide by international copyright laws, it can print and publish for nominal costs and distribute widely to other Persian-speaking countries. Iranians' experience and expertise in this realm has carried over to the internet and digital technologies. Iranian Persian or Farsi software is readily available and inexpensive, whereas the Dari and Pashto equivalents are nonexistent. Thus, in order to navigate daily life, most ethnic groups, unless they are completely cut off from the nation and live in very remote parts of the country, speak at least minimal Dari or some other variation of Persian in their own dialects.

Fazal, for example, is passionate about the need for Pashto-language television:

> They keep saying media is for the people. What people? Why have broadcasting when no one understands the message? If a viewer does not understand then he will stop trying. Most televisions are in Dari. Even if they understand a little Dari, they won't understand high-level Dari, which is what they use. Only in Kabul they will understand this. And they use many Iranian Farsi words, not Dari. You might understand it but most of us don't. Most people are not educated. We have no imported words in Shamshad. Shamshad gives people ownership in every region in Pashto and in their own accents. We hire presenters from those areas.[1]

Although he is not as passionate about it, Fazal recognizes the importance of teaching the Pashtuns Dari as well. In this respect, his sentiments are more nationalist. In fact, 30 percent of his programming is in Dari, and most of the remaining Pashto-only programs are actually bilingual. For example, if viewers phone in on one of the numerous call-in shows and do not speak Pashto, they can still make their comments or ask their questions, which the hosts will translate and reply to in Pashto.

Shamshad is not the first Pashto-language television station, but its ambitious original programming and rapid expansion to the countryside and remote regions of Afghanistan have made it the most-watched Pashto-language television station, according to the Media Support Partnership Afghanistan British surveys from 2008 to 2014, which were conducted by the British embassy.[2] Having tapped into a substantial neglected population, Shamshad was subsequently rewarded with aid from USAID, the International Security Assistance Force, the Department for International Development, and the UN Assistance Mission in Afghanistan, in addition to continued support of $1 million per year from the Afghan Dutch NGO Organization for Mine Clearance and Afghan Rehabilitation, which had provided it with its initial $2 million start-up capital.

Although the station heavily relies on donor aid, Fazal is quick to point out that it is independent, private, and commercial. By that he means that approximately 50 percent of its income now also comes from ad revenues from various Afghan and international governmental and nongovernmental offices and organizations that pay the network for airtime to run campaigns and other types of PSAs. Although not commercial in the classic sense, Shamshad has clearly carved out a hybrid donor-commercial market. Following its success, Tolo launched its own Pashto-language sister station, Lemar TV, in August 2006.

Fazal explains how other television stations target and prioritize cities because they have better infrastructure and because cities are more likely to generate ad revenues (people there tend to have higher incomes). Likewise, the government and the international donor aid community are based in major cities like Kabul since the security situation is somewhat better there. "Our young government can't reach them," Fazal tells me, "and yes the media has been a success but not for these people, not for the countryside. They are in the dark era. They are disconnected not only from Afghanistan but the rest of the world."

The people he is describing are the Pashtuns, and the area is called the Pashtun belt. It is generally accepted in Afghanistan that the Pashtuns are the largest ethnic group in the country, although it is debatable whether they constitute the majority of the population. A national census was initiated in the 1970s but was never finished due to the Soviet invasion. Therefore, it is difficult to ascertain the precise ethnic composition of the country. Exact numbers are contentious, but estimates range from as low as 30 percent to as high as 55 percent.[3]

The Pashtun belt, or regions where Pashtuns are the majority, encompasses the border areas between Afghanistan and Iran and between Afghanistan and Pakistan, an area that is also called the Northwest Frontier. Seen as a problem population by the British and Persian Empires, due to their numerous rebellions and challenges to British and Persian rule, many Pashtun tribes, clans, and families were literally cut off from one another by the British-imposed Durand Line. At the conclusion of the Third Anglo-Afghan War with the signing of the Treaty of Rawalpindi in 1919, the British—as part of their divide-and-conquer approach—recognized Afghanistan's complete sovereignty and in exchange annexed a part of the Pashtun tribal belt to British India. This border dividing the two regions became known as the Durand Line. After 100 years, the annexed region was supposed to be returned back to Afghanistan, an event that Pashtun nationalists still clamor for in the hope of reconstituting a majority. Fazal, who operates production offices on both sides of the Durand Line, explains, "They are half here and half there [the bordering countries]. Now we can unite them with TV. Television can give them a national feeling because they are neither here or there." The sentiments that Shamshad hopes to inspire are of ethnic unity with a nationalist bent.

The terminology that Fazal uses to describe the Pashtuns might sound eerily similar to that of British civilizing missions. That said, their interests and intentions are worlds apart:

These areas and people are affected by problems, trouble, from fundamentalism, traditional rules and regulations, for a thousand years. But above all that, the problem is they need education. They need guidance. They need instruction. Television can defeat our common enemy, which is lack of education and illiteracy. But television here started with just how to make money. Not what people need. For thirty years we lost our identity, forgot how to love our country, how we can develop this country, how the corruption has affected this generation, how we were cut off from the rest of the world and how we can establish this relation again.

Whereas the imperial British forces saw the Pashtuns purely as a problem and obstacle on the path of their imperial ambitions, Fazal sees the problems that Pashtuns face, which he hopes to alleviate through Shamshad. Fazal genuinely believes that educating and bringing the Pashtuns into the fold of the nation will be beneficial both to this "troublesome" segment of the population and to Afghanistan as a whole. His national sentiments are not opposed to introducing people to foreign influences, but he first wants to strengthen Afghanistan's own national, cultural, and social traditions and institutions. Aside from broadcasting programs such as *National Geographic* and a few other foreign-sponsored imports, the vast majority of Shamshad's programs are original productions. In addition to educational programming, such as game and trivia shows, music video shows, and news programs, Shamshad produces and broadcasts Pashto dramatic serials such as *Da Godar Ghara* (By the side of the spring), *Da Gonde Zoy* (The widow's son), *Swara*, and *Malalai*.

Asked to compare the quality of his programs with those from Iran and India, he responds, "They are advanced and developed and we have lost all that but if we continue to buy their programs, do you think we will ever reach their level again? If anyone [other television stations] cared about representing our society and our needs, we would be self-sufficient. Inshallah, Afghanistan will compete with Iran, India, and Pakistan again."

When Fazal does actually describe the Pashtuns as a problem and a troubled group, he is referring to the Taliban, who are Pashtuns from both sides of the Northwest Frontier and who with their extreme brand of Islam and draconian laws have tormented the population of Afghanistan ever since their rise to power in 1996. However, although the Taliban are almost entirely composed of Pashtuns, not all Pashtuns are Taliban—in fact, most Pashtuns denounce the Taliban's ideological worldview. For people like Fazal and former and current presidents Hamid Karzai and Ashraf Ghani, among other prominent ethnic Pashtuns, it is very important to make this distinction. In conversation with Felix Kuehn, a leading expert on the Taliban who along with his writing partner, Alex Strick van Linschoten, has spent many years conducting ethnography with them in the Pashtun areas of Afghanistan, he explained to me—as he does in his coauthored publications including *An Enemy We Created* (Strick van Linschoten and Kuehn 2012)—the importance of differentiating between the Pashtuns, Taliban, ISIS, and Al Qaeda as well as recognizing their internal variations.[4] In fact, ISIS and the Taliban have separately attacked Shamshad's TV station and the adjoining OMAR Mine Museum.

After the September 11 attacks, with the military success of the American-led campaign against the Taliban, the Pashtuns were marginalized by association with the Taliban. Power was transferred to ethnic Tajiks, who formed the core of the Northern Alliance, known as Jamiat-i Islami (Society of Islam) in Afghanistan. The Northern Alliance and Jamiat-i Islami were enlisted in and fought alongside the American army to oust the Taliban from the capital. As a conciliatory gesture, Hamid Karzai was made the interim president. However, the Pashtuns claim they were left out of most government ministries and arenas of politics. Some argue that this marginalization combined with high civilian casualties in Pashtun areas has led to a regrouping and resurgence of the Taliban in Pashtun areas, similar to that which happened with the disen-franchisement and ouster of Sunnis from the Iraq government and the rise of ISIS. Hence, the Taliban continues to be a problem. If, on the other hand, as people like Fazal argue, the Pashtuns were brought out from the periphery of the nation, literally and metaphorically, and they felt a sense of belonging to the nation-building process, they might be less likely to join the Taliban's violent and fanatical grab for power.

As ethnographies of media and social theory have demonstrated, the media industry plays a significant role in the formation of identity and subjectivity—both in the individual and collective sense. Television studies show us that the medium, when deployed on a national level, can have the adverse effect of polarizing people based on ethnicity, race, religion, and other identity markers. Instead of promoting a democratic model of inclusion and plurality, television stations often align with dominant groups to promote ethnocentrism and other hierarchies of race and religion, which give rise to racism and other forms of bigotry. Ultimately this sets the stage for the exclusion of, marginalization of, or discrimination against minority or less-powerful populations. In the worst cases, as we have examined, television's role in identity politics has fueled dominant groups to enact violence against their weaker counterparts. In the best cases, television, on behalf of the elites, has managed to reign in or control vulnerable or problem groups through education in proper notions of second-class citizenship and marriage, bringing them under their radar or surveillance.

It does not undermine the Foucauldian or Gramscian criticisms of institutionalized educational systems' underlying disciplinary nature to claim that they are not all hegemonic. Some educational projects have a more diverse, multiethnic, and multicultural approach, which is inclusionary of marginalized or disenfranchised groups. By adopting the administered messages of television, we cannot assume that Pashtuns are being duped into states of false consciousness. Here I argue, based on my interviews with Afghan producers, that most of them aspire to establish the mindset for an inclusionary, multiethnic Afghanistan where people peacefully coexist. There certainly are sectarian television stations that stir tribal/ethnic violence, but they tend to be marginalized, as I will discuss in the next chapter. Most niche television stations that are affiliated with specific ethnic groups, such as Shamshad, are trying to simultaneously preserve their cultural diversity—such as ethnic languages, songs, rituals, and other traditions—while providing their viewers with the means to access and navigate the state and government. This is a key difference between the ways that the development and imperial gazes function. Afghan television producers seek to bring Pashtuns into the fold of the nation and preserve cultures, in contrast to the British imperial gaze of the past and the present imperial gaze of the United States, which implements violent divide-and-conquer approaches and the full weight of violence and war in order to protect its geopolitical interests in the region.

In this televisual continuum, educating people in the tenets of multiculturalism and plurality is the only option that considers the best interests of the different ethnic groups and the nation as a whole. For the people of Afghanistan who have been shut out, denied, and deprived of an education due to many years of war, this is a very powerful tool for potential social mobility. It maintains and reinforces the self-sufficiency, creativity, and agency of the various ethnic cultures and teaches them how to access the nation-state in peaceful coexistence with other *quowms*. In the next section, the disparities between the development and imperial gazes will be further illuminated with respect to the way that local and international producers interpellate Afghan women's plight with sometimes dangerous consequences.

The Rhetoric of Saving Afghan Women

In the power vacuum left behind in the wake of the Soviet-Afghan War, which first resulted in the final withdrawal of the Soviets from Afghanistan in 1989 and subsequently triggered the collapse of the Soviet Union, the United States emerged as the Cold War victor. Meanwhile, Afghanistan was thrown into a bloody civil war wherein the seven US-funded mujahideen militias fought for the seat of power. Out of the ashes of the Afghan civil war emerged the now notorious Taliban. At first they were welcomed for bringing a semblance of security to a country racked by chaos and lawlessness with their strict version of Islam. Even some women's rights leaders initially welcomed a brief respite from the rapes, kidnapping, and other acts of war that treated women as collateral. But, as the Taliban consolidated power in the mid-1990s, the draconian nature of their laws, based on extreme interpretations of Islam—for example, literally cutting off the hands of thieves and public executions by stoning and hanging—was becoming apparent.

Afghan women were subjected to domestic confinement by the Taliban's extreme gender codes of marriage and prohibitions on education and work. Almost from the start of the Taliban's rise to power, local Afghan feminist organizations covertly collaborated with international feminist organizations to advocate on behalf of Afghan women. Yet it took the events of 9/11 and the War on Terror for Afghan women to reach the spotlight of Western popular culture. This was evident in the proliferation of media such as fiction films, special television programs, documentaries, books, and news that focused on their plight under repressive Islamic regimes. Tapping into the vast repertoire of imagery from the era of colonialism, claims about saving Afghan women from the misogyny of their culture and brethren were used to justify a military assault on the Taliban and Al Qaeda. In keeping with the rhetoric of masculinist protection (Young 2003), the pretext of saving Afghan women added to the already thundering beat of the war drum calling for the United States to avenge the attacks on the World Trade Center and the Pentagon.

The rhetoric of saving Afghan women, then, was born out of the ashes of the 9/11 attacks on the United States. It is therefore unsurprising that the subject of many international Calls for Projects in the media sector and others is the uplift of Afghan women. These include everything from teaching the society about women's rights in the context of human rights to addressing what are considered dangerous and regressive cultural practices. Seizing this economic opportunity as they did with "the Pashtun problem," Afghan media producers are leading the fight to cheerlead and champion women's issues and rights in disparate ways, with varying degrees of efficacy. I will analyze their attempts in this chapter.

All of a sudden, after a decade of media blackout and virtual invisibility due to their enforced relegation to the domestic sphere, Afghan women and international women are paraded on many of the country's television stations. They are center stage in programs ranging from reality television to news. The post-9/11 UN-supervised constitution also dictated women's active participation in civil society, including a legal stipulation that at least 25 percent of the members of Parliament had to be women, further catapulting them into the public sphere.

"Our Women": Gender and Sexuality

In Afghanistan, Islamists denounce the televisual representations of foreign women on the grounds of immorality; they claim that such representations are gender inappropriate and sexually offensive. Their arguments are ultimately designed to create delineation between "their" culture and "ours" and stir fears of cultural imperialism. This distinction saves foreign female television stars from direct attacks and violence—both physical and emotional—since they are not easily accessible and since they are not within Afghanistan's cultural arena. Foreign and (to a certain extent) expatriate Afghan women, then, have a level of freedom to crisscross Afghan Islamist notions of gender and sexuality. The bodies of local women living in Afghanistan, however, fall directly under the self-appointed jurisdiction of Islamists.

As feminist scholars have shown, it is through cultural contestations at the intersection of gender and sexuality that attempts at setting and defining national/cultural/social identity, often in the singular, occur. And as feminist media scholars have shown, this is especially the case if the women are in the public sphere or in media. This is no different in Afghanistan—except that stakes are much higher there. Cultural clashes over the chador or veiling, purdah or the separation of men and women, dancing, singing, and other expressions of female (and to a lesser extent male) sexuality have become commonplace. Afghan women have become the ultimate markers of the Afghan nation, and in their televisual representation they are burdened with embodying all the cultural codes of the nation. As such, expressions of gender and sexuality have become extremely volatile over the course of the last four decades of warfare. Whether it's on the news, in reality TV shows, or in dramas, every aspect of women who appear on screen is scrutinized for appropriateness and whether it upholds the values of the nation-state. That scrutiny is effected by a patriarchal gaze that categorizes women into the classic sexist and universalist whore/virgin binary. For example, in the third season of *Afghan Star*, the only two women contestants, Lema and Setara, are narratively set up as the archetypical binary of proper and improper Afghan womanhood, with Lema, who hails from conservative Kandahar representing virtuosity and respectability, while Setara, who dares to dance a little during her distraught final performance after finding out

PHOTO 5.1. A young woman, Fatima, looks at the election poster of Bamiyan council member Zainab Noori.

she is eliminated, is labeled a harlot. These dangerous condemnations and categorizations, which resulted in Setara receiving death threats, were expressed by the other contestants and the host of the program who are all male. Of course, on-screen male presenters and personalities have much more creative leeway in their performance and expression of gender/sexuality without fear of being subjected to violence.

Sometimes such national/cultural identity–defining arguments are framed in the affirmative. During his 2009 presidential election campaign, for example, Ha-

PHOTO 5.2. Picture of Vidya, the female lead from the Indian dramatic serial *Banoo Main Teri Dulhann* (I will become your bride), on a storefront in Macroyan, Kabul.

PHOTO 5.3. Picture of Prerna, the female lead from the Indian dramatic serial *Kasautii Zindagii Kay* (The trials of life), silk screen printed on a tambourine drum hangs in a store in the Old City of Kabul.

mid Karzai made girls' education a top priority. He made several public speeches, held press conferences, and offered declarations of this commitment on Afghan television stations. Surprisingly, progressive reformers and activists were not impressed by his campaign promises. Among the people who responded were Fatana Gailani, founder of the Afghanistan Women Council, and her sister-in-law Fatima Gailani, president of the Red Crescent (Red Cross) of Afghanistan. They are from the prominent and well-respected Gailani family. In the early eighteenth century, the Gailanis, leaders of a progressive Sufi order, immigrated to Kabul from their home in Baghdad by the invitation of the Afghan royal family. They continue to have a big following in Afghanistan. For over a century they have used their clout to support democratic platforms in Afghanistan. During the Soviet occupation amongst Afghan refugees, Fatima's father, Pir Sayyid Ahmed Gailani, was the most popular and progressive of the Jihadi leaders. Yet he received the least amount of financing from the US government.

In a television interview, Fatana Gailani said, "The education of girls and women has a long history in Afghanistan. This has been part of our culture for over one hundred years. Karzai acts as if he is radically introducing a new revolutionary phenomenon. If he wants to take a stand for women's rights he needs to stop supporting the Shura-i Ulama's strict family laws."[5] In a follow-up statement, Fatima Gailani argued that Karzai's campaign promises were just another political ploy to appease the international community and to deflect attention from his conservative policies. Both Fatana and Fatima Gailani have their graduate degrees from abroad. In an interview with me, the current Minister of Women's Affairs (MOWA), Husn Banu Ghazanfar, who has a doctorate in philology from St. Petersburg University, Russia, echoed that in the twentieth century, girls' education was indeed beginning to be popularly supported in most provinces of Afghanistan.[6] However, due to today's ongoing lawlessness and warlordism, attacks on girls' schools and the number of school burnings are on the rise.

In a parallel development, Nasrine Abu-Bakre Gross—a writer, activist, and member of another progressive religious Kabuli family—publicly opposed Radio Television Afghanistan's policy that all women on the national broadcasting television station must be veiled. Her stance was effectively a challenge to the Minister of Information and Culture (MIC) Sayed Makhdoom Raheen. The Abu-Bakres also originally hail from Iraq and lead another prominent Sufi order of Islam. Nasrine's famous mother, Roqia Habib, was one of Afghanistan's first elected parliamentarians in the mid-1960s. She, like the Gailanis, does not claim to be left-leaning, since the Left in Afghanistan is inextricably linked with the Soviet invasion and occupation. Instead, the word that is commonly used in Afghanistan today (and historically) is *roshan fikr* or "enlightened thinker," and its opposite, a pejorative, is *tareek been* or "dark seer." This is how the Gailanis and Abu-Bakres refer to themselves and how the public refers to them as well. Their political and religious stature is such that even conservatives and other *tareek beens* opposed to their political ideology cannot directly attack them.

Nasrine Abu-Bakre Gross was on several occasions invited to speak on an RTA television show called *The Other Half* that is sponsored by the Ministry of Women's Affairs.[7] She has publicly stated, on several private television stations, that compulsory veiling is antithetical to Afghan culture. She premises her women's rights activism by referring back to the work that her reformist and intellectual family had done in paving the way for women's rights; this included their opposition to obligatory veiling, as well as the passing of the equal rights amendment to the 1964 Afghan constitution. In early February 2012, Raheen announced that women on all television stations must wear the veil on-screen, which women's groups have contested and many television stations refuse to abide by. This law has been interpreted as the Afghan government's attempt to appease the Taliban, with whom it is trying to negotiate.

A common method of discussing culturally sensitive issues in Afghanistan, as in these cases I have described, then, is for people on different sides of the debate to justify their position by claiming that it represents *true* Afghan culture. Another strategy, and one that is used just as often, is to frame the argument contra-factually: as in, we are not American, Latinx, Indian, Iranian. In this self/other dichotomy projected onto televisual representations of foreign women that some consider culturally inappropriate and unsuitable, on-screen Afghan women must bear the ultimate burden of upholding national and cultural identity by embodying all that is accordingly virtuous, moral, and proper. Of course the question of whether women should be in the public sphere, or on television at all, is a common one among Islamists. Therefore, it is the telepresence of Afghan women that spurs and stirs the greatest controversy. As I show in the next section, visibility itself has proven to be deadly for women, especially women from underprivileged socioeconomic backgrounds who work on-screen.

The Cover Story: The Honor Killings Narrative and the Costs of Going Public

In May 2005, Shaima Rezayee, the twenty-four-year-old host of a popular music video call-in show on Tolo TV, *Hop*, was shot in the head and killed at home. *Hop*, which she cohosted with two male VJs, broadcast requests from callers. It mainly featured Afghan music videos but also those from other parts of the world, including Western, Iranian, Tajik, and Indian videos. Rezayee had been under attack from religious and conservative groups for not adhering to strict conservative dress codes and notions of cultural decorum. Although she wore a chador (headscarf), she mixed in other cultural styles such as jeans and Bollywood-inspired bright accents with traditional Afghan clothes. Fazal Hadi Shinwari, a judge on the Afghan Supreme Court, denounced the show, saying, "It will corrupt our society, culture, and most importantly, it will take our people away from Islam and destroy our country" (Synovitz 2005, 4). In March of that year, Tolo TV had fired her, citing unprofessionalism. But some of her colleagues and fans believe that she was scapegoated to appease the Ulama.

In May 2007, Shakiba Sanga Amaj, a twenty-two-year-old presenter and reporter for the Pashto-language television station Shamshad TV, was shot and killed by a gunman, also in her own home. Amaj's parents had moved to Pakistan as refugees during the Soviet-Afghan War. She was born and educated in the Northwest Frontier Province there and moved to Kabul after the Taliban's post-9/11 retreat. She had been a newscaster and a presenter on several shows, including the popular variety talk show *Da Godar Ghara*. Amaj was not particularly daring in terms of her self-presentation; she adhered to the Islamic dress codes of Shamshad TV.

Less than a week later, Zakia Zaki—the founder and manager of a radio station in the Parwan Province ironically called Sadah-i Sulh, or the Voice of Peace—was shot seven times by gunmen who entered her home while she and her children were asleep. Her husband was apparently not home. Sadah-i Sulh, which Zaki began in 2002 with the technical and financial support of the USAID-funded Internews, was a community radio station that covered local and national affairs and politics. Through her work for the radio station, she had become a community activist and a respected local leader. She and her staff used the radio station as an independent platform to serve the local community. Issues of human rights violations were regularly addressed, along with other concerns of the local community. Zaki, who was an ethnic Tajik living and working in a predominantly Tajik part of Afghanistan, was as critical of Tajik warlords as she was of those of other ethnicities. This put her on the radar of warlords, who threatened her repeatedly.

Rahimullah Samandar, president of the Afghan Independent Journalists Association, said that she and the radio station personnel had contacted the union to report threats from local warlords.[8] However, government officials and police investigators have classified all these cases as honor killings, involving members of the victims' own families. According to the police, Zaki's father believes male relatives are responsible for his daughter's murder. Amaj's father also stated in an interview with Pajhwok Afghan News agency that members of their extended family hired the gunman because they thought she was bringing

PHOTO 5.4. Shamshad TV presenter and reporter Shakiba Sanga Amaj, victim of an alleged honor killing.

shame or dishonor to the family. According to other family members, Amaj was killed over a marriage proposal dispute. In the case of Rezayee, the police said they suspect her two brothers. Baseless rumors also abounded about her having an affair with one of her cohosts or possibly being pregnant.

It is difficult to ascertain whether these cases, despite being classified as honor killings, are actually honor killings, since the label is often an easy way for the authorities to evade responsibility. They can claim that "culturally sensitive" matters fall outside their jurisdiction, since they are private family matters. Thus they attempt to absolve themselves of the dangerous responsibility of finding the real culprits, if the murders were politically motivated. Likewise, it is a convenient way for members of the family, if they actually were involved in the murder of their female relative, to elude the scrutiny of the government, since there is a cultural understanding that the state will not intervene. If the families were not involved (and thus often outraged), they can still be pressured by the murderers into taking responsibility. By claiming that the murder of a female journalist or television personality is an honor killing, the authorities

PHOTO 5.5. Shaima Rezayee, host of Tolo TV's music video program *Hop*, victim of an alleged honor killing.

PHOTO 5.6. Zakia Zaki, founder of Sadah-i Sulh (Voice of Peace) radio station, victim of an alleged honor killing. Photo credit: Christopher Grabowski

can deflect attention from larger political truths, forces, and problems that the victims were perhaps trying to uncover.

Reporters Without Borders has declared on its website that these honor killings should be investigated like any other murder. The Committee to Protect Journalists, on the other hand, surprisingly includes only Zaki on its list of "Journalists Murdered in Afghanistan." It believes that according to its definition, Rezayee was not a journalist and Amaj's murder was personally motivated.[9]

Honor killings are a real cultural phenomenon and have gained currency recently due to the rise of tribal-religious extremism. The actual term in Persian and Pashto is *quatlay namoos,* which literally translates as the murder of a *namoos. Namoos* is an Arabic word that probably entered the Persian/Pashto languages during the Muslim Arab conquest of Persia and its eastern province of Khurasan, which became modern-day Afghanistan in the mid–seventh century. However, the word predates the monotheistic religions; it does not appear in any of their holy books. Likewise, it is erroneous to associate honor killings with any particular region, since they are practiced in many parts of the world and across religions, including Hinduism and Sikhism (in addition to Islam).

Contrary to its popular usage, the word *namoos,* which also appears in Turkish and Greek, does not translate (directly) as "honor." Rather, *namoos* is a noun that describes a person or group of people whose sovereignty falls under another person's jurisdiction based on their respective statuses within a kinship structure. Both parties are required to maintain communal codes of virtue and ethics. Although the word is by definition genderless—which means that men or women can be the defenders of or the objects of *namoos*—in Afghanistan, and in many other countries, *namoos* has evolved into a gendered category that maintains the patriarchal order by regulating female subjects. In Afghanistan specifically, *namoos* connotes possession or ownership of females. For example, daughters, wives, and other female family members including extended family are the *namoos* of the male family members, meaning that the male family members have the power to make females uphold and reflect communal codes of virtue, morality, and honor. Likewise, if the males of a family do not enforce or endorse the communal codes, then other males of that community have the power to pressure and punish them.

Even before the Soviet invasion threw the country into more than four decades of war, honor killings did occur in Afghanistan. But the dynamics of the culture were very different during peacetime. Since statistical data does not exist, it is difficult to ascertain whether cases of honor killings were higher or lower back then. Yet it can be said that honor killings of Afghan female media personalities were, according to my interviewees, nonexistent. This is perhaps because there was only one television station in the 1970s, run by the state broadcasting company RTA. Radio was the prominent medium at the time. There were many independent radio stations in addition to the state-sponsored RTA. With the proliferation and flourishing of the media post-9/11, there are today over four dozen television stations that have women staff members working on set and on camera. As the opportunities to become public figures on television have increased for women, so too have the numbers of television stars and the range of their performativity. That said, women in the prewar decades were also public media figures.

The Right to Dance and Sing:
State Sponsorship of Artists and Culture

Questions of honor, morality, and propriety plagued media personalities, both male and female, of the prewar era as well. As anthropologists of the region have written (Tapper 1991; Tapper and Tapper 1992/1993), the concept of *nang*, which is the Pashto word for "honor," permeates Afghan culture. *Nang* is one of the main codes encapsulated in the Pashtunwali: a pre-Islamic, orally passed-down set of tribal virtues and regulations that together make up the Pashtun way of life. Even though the term originally came from the Pashtuns, who according to most population demographics are the ethnic majority in Afghanistan, other tribes in Afghanistan have adopted the Pashtunwali as well.

In a society where kinship networks and lineage are highly delineated, recorded, and well known, one's reputation and name—as an individual, family member, and member of a tribe or ethnic group—are extremely significant. One's every action and behavior leave an indelible mark on one's kinship networks. The Western notion of being able to act only as an individual is completely foreign here. It is simply not culturally acceptable.

To be called *naik naam* or *paak naam*, variations on the idea of "pure named," is an honorific that Afghans of all genders aspire to. Likewise, the Persian concept of being *sangeen*, which will be described in the next chapter, is another respectful title. This configuration of Islamic and pre-Islamic Persian and tribal practices and codes is at the heart of why Afghans—across tribal, ethnic, and religious lines—are very sensitive to and reverent of the cultural concepts of honor and shame. This also translates to their relationship with the arts of singing, acting, and dancing. While Afghans appreciate the arts, they stigmatize the artists themselves. They hold prejudices against them and prejudge artists as being sexual deviants of various kinds. The neighborhood in Kabul that has been traditionally associated with artists' quarters and the cultural center of the city was and is called Kharabad or the "Place of Sin." Hearsay has made it synonymous with prostitution, sexual excess, and hedonism.

In a famous song, Ahmad Zahir, Afghanistan's most popular singer, who was killed under mysterious circumstances during the rule of the Soviet-backed government in 1979, sings, "I'm a drunk and you're crazy. Who's going to take us home? Let's go to Kharabad." Likewise, Ustad Mahwash, another prewar singer who continues to record songs from France, sings in one of her songs, "I haven't even taken a sip of wine and already my reputation is marred." Fazel Ahmad Zikria, a well-known prewar composer and singer who was killed by the Soviet-backed Afghan government, sang under the pseudonym Nainawaz, "the Flute Player," which is borrowed from a Rumi poem. He sang from behind a curtain during concerts because his father did not approve of his career choice. Having gained recognition and a popular following, he began performing more openly but still preferred to compose for other musicians due to the shame of singing publicly. Mirmon Parween, another singer of that era and the first woman to sing on Radio Kabul, a public radio station, sang wearing a *chadari* (burka) to conceal her face in concerts. Likewise, Jillwa stopped singing on Radio Kabul altogether because her brother apparently did not want her to continue.

Another important woman artist and musician of the era, whom I interviewed, is Samia Mirzad who currently resides in New Jersey.[10] Samia Mirzad participated in the media and creative arts landscape in Kabul since the age of fifteen when she was attending Lycee Malalai in the 1950s. She wrote a play called *Zan-i Malik* (Wife of the king) and acted in it along with four friends in order to raise funds for the lycée. Mirzad actually played the role of the king alongside her friend Latifa Amir Seraj. They raised 300,000 Afghanis for the school. In the 1960s, she sang on Radio Afghanistan with Ustad Khyal, a well-known composer. She also reported the news on Radio Afghanistan. After amassing a fan base through state radio, she began to join the concerts of famous male singers such as Ahmad Zahir and Ustad Shahwali in the 1970s. Mirzad also participated in a number of regional fashion shows including one hosted by Princess Shams of Iran (sister of Mohammad Reza Pahlavi). Despite being chastised by her parents, she was one of the first people in her own social circle to take off her chador (head scarf) in public. With her creative contributions to the Kabul cultural landscape, Samia Mirzad inspired many people but faced disapproval from her family, who in turn also faced abuse and ostracization by the community at large. Yet Mirzad persisted because she felt dedicated to her country and felt that these channels were key to lifting up Afghanistan.[10]

In short, the prejudices against musicians and artists are not new. But the key difference is that no one publicly attacked them, called for their death, or actually killed them over issues of honor back then. If anything, the foundations for support of the arts were being laid. Led by the government's public service broadcasting stations, including Radio Kabul and Radio Television Afghanistan, people were beginning to move toward accepting if not embracing artists as well. Ustad Mahwash, for example, was one of the first female musicians to earn the honorific title "Ustad" in the mid-1970s, which means one has achieved mastery over his or her craft ("Ustad" is also what university professors are called). Countless other female singers and musicians followed suit and began to sing publicly, including on RTA. Once the war broke out, some of them continued to sing in exile, though most stopped. However, their music continued to circulate on audiocassettes and CDs and gain popularity within Afghanistan and in the diaspora. Now most of their music can be found online on YouTube and other platforms.

The differences in the pre- and postwar climate of Afghanistan can also be illustrated by the uproar surrounding the recent rebroadcast of these beloved musicians' concerts and performances from RTA's archive on RTA, Saba TV, and other stations. The Shura-i Ulama, or Council of Clerics, declared that the women musicians' performances were "not according to Islam." This surprised many people because the presentations of these early Afghan celebrities are relatively tame by today's standards. The general public is very familiar with the performing female body due to constant exposure to foreign media. The archival footage, which RTA broadcasts weekly, shows popular Afghan women musicians dressed modestly and barely moving as they perform in front of live audiences. They almost lack performativity in comparison to contemporary and past concert aesthetics of non-Afghan female pop icons.

The irony is that foreign music videos and even pornographic imagery have been available in Afghan society for decades via black market films, home videos, and DVDs. During the post-9/11 media boom, the arrival of internet and cable and satellite television only accelerated the process. Even during the Taliban's strict regime, when ordinances against all visual media and representations of the human body—including on billboards and street signs—were in place, it was not difficult to find all types of bootleg media for the right price on the black market. Today foreign media and pornographic imagery is even more accessible. Financial reasons limit most people's access to the internet and satellite television; yet, they can find such imagery easily on the black market in the form of video compact discs and can download it, including short videos, via their mobile phones.

Under the current political climate, however, Indian, Latin American, and Western music videos of female singers have to be pixelated when broadcast on any Afghan television station; otherwise, outcries of debauchery and impropriety are raised by the religious sector. Some television stations were fined by the government for featuring the pop star Shakira in concert and music videos of Enrique Iglesias. Even though they had pixelated Shakira's entire body, this apparently did not do enough to distract from her gyrating. Enrique's expressive dance moves were not blurred or pixelated.

In another incident, the loy saranwal, or attorney general, of Afghanistan during Karzai's presidency, Abdul Jabar Sabit, was recorded on video dancing jubilantly at a family function. The video was subsequently aired and circulated on the news of several television stations. He was then forced to resign due to the uproar from conservative forces. However, my interviews suggest that most Afghans, from all different backgrounds, did not consider the dancing to be a problem, nor his possible drunkenness (due to this expressive dancing, some people criticized him for being drunk as well, a taboo in Islam). Some believed him to be a *paak* (or clean) man publicly and privately and accused his political rivals of distributing the video to tarnish his reputation. Others were critical of him and his political track record, claiming that he was a corrupt politician and a conservative who publicly shunned and passed strict judgments against such behavior while privately engaging in debauchery. Not everyone condoned his politics. But across the spectrum of people I interviewed, with a few exceptions, most were supportive of his right to dance and drink at a family celebration. They perceived the subsequent political fallout and spectacle as an abuse of *nang* or honor. They also commented that to dance at a family celebration is part of Afghan culture. Many even felt that it would be disrespectful for him *not* to show happiness at such events. Yet these popular sentiments were not heard on television. With the televisual focus only on the outrage of other politicians and the Ulama, an opportunity was missed to express the full range of debate.

Gender Violence: Why Now?

While it is true that Afghans are culturally sensitive to the concepts of shame and honor and have very specific codes and notions of gender and sexuality, why are such expressions so politically charged now? Why does the dancing of a politician at a private function turn into a public spectacle? Why is the recirculation of national concerts stirring a controversy, when in their original context their broadcasting was a relative nonissue?

Gender has always been a contentious issue in Afghanistan. However, due to the country's violent recent history, gender has become a particularly volatile matter. Since the start of the Soviet-Afghan War, when the CIA began to clandestinely fund some of the most conservative elements of the Afghan population, the new gender war began. But it was not until the rise of the Taliban in the mid-1990s, the attacks of 9/11, and the start of the War on Terror that Afghan women reached the mainstream Western spotlight in popular culture, evident in the proliferation of media such as fiction films, television programs, documentaries, books, and news that focus on their plight under repressive Islamic regimes. The powerful visual imagery that is the legacy of this prolific body of work originates from Afghanistan but is produced in Western institutions. Subsequently, it ricochets and reverberates globally between America, Europe, and other nations, circulating widely through genres as diverse as law, popular culture, and high art.

As a result, Afghan institutions are forced to "talk back" to the global circulation of images of Afghan women. Ultra-right tribal or religious Afghan institutions choose to "talk back" with decrees that call for violence—and with actual violence. What more than four decades of warfare has fostered is a heightened culture of violence, impunity, and fanatical tribal religious fascism in Afghanistan. At the core of this ongoing war are Afghan women. For the Taliban and other extremist groups, issues pertaining to Afghan women have become an even more contentious symbol of nationhood and a new marker of the jihad against the infidels, including local Afghan reformers. In other words, the terrain of gender discourse has become extremely politicized and violent. Two decades after 9/11, this gender war is still going strong. Afghan women as a trope continue to reverberate globally at an unprecedented volume and on an unprecedented scale. And the "talking" has taken on more and more frighteningly violent forms of expression.

Women as Projects: The Deadly Intersection of Gender, Race, Ethnicity, and Class

It is within this extremely dangerous arena that brave Afghan reformers, both women and men, challenge oppressive forces to reclaim a more just and equal culture. Their reforms and activism put media makers in the crosshairs of ruthless powerful elites and their militias and thugs who threaten, attack, and kill them for providing people with a platform to raise their voices. Yet high-level media personnel and owners can afford to have protection, while low-level personnel cannot. In most cases, it is they—not the owners of television stations—who bear the burden of developing media independence by exposing abuses of power by warlords, critiquing foreign powers and the national government, and airing diverse lifestyles, cultures, and televisual representations of women. Their secular, nationalist, and reformist agendas are sometimes at odds with both the owners of the television stations they work for and the foreign governments that are the patrons of the stations.

The risks of being a public figure on television are high, both for males and females. Nevertheless, it is particularly daring for Afghan women to work on-screen in television. Often, their decision to work on-screen is determined as much by their courage to stand up for women's rights, artistic freedom, and other issues as it is by their socioeconomic predicaments.

Roya Sadat, a writer for Tolo TV's first post-9/11 dramatic serial, *Raazah En Khana* (The secrets of this house), and a writer and director of Tolo TV's second post-9/11 dramatic serial, *Bahesht-i Khamosh* (Silent heaven), explains how difficult it was to find any actresses for the programs. After holding several auditions where only men showed up, she began to solicit in poor neighborhoods in Kabul.[11] Abada, one of the protagonists of the serial, took the job not because she had a desire to act or a wish to be a star but out of sheer desperation. She was married as a child bride to an abusive, opium-addicted, older husband. Moreover, she had many children, including one who is chronically ill, to support. Since the show's airing, at least two of the actresses on *Raazah En Khana* have been forced to escape to other countries due to threats of violence.

According to Fazal Karim Fazal, the president of Shamshad TV, the station employs a cast of actresses consisting mostly of Pashtun Pashto-speaking women based in Pakistan, because the situation for women is currently not as repressive there by comparison. The opposite was true during the prewar era, when Pakistani media producers would come to Kabul for production because of the freer climate. The actresses are not all born Pakistani. A number of them are Afghan-born refugees who chose to continue living in Pakistan after the Soviet withdrawal. Although the central offices and broadcasting facilities of Shamshad are still located in Kabul, it has opened up a secondary base of operations and production studios in Quetta, Pakistan, for this reason.[12] The opposite was true during the pre-war era, wherein Pakistani media producers would come to Kabul for production.

It is important to note that Shakiba Sanga Amaj, Shaima Rezayee, Zakia Zaki, and Mina Mangal, the young victims of apparent honor killings mentioned earlier, all came from different ethnic groups but were united in their low socioeconomic backgrounds and gender. Amaj and Mangal were from poor Pashtun families and grew up in the refugee camps of the Northwest Frontier in Pakistan. Rezayee was a Hazara and a Shia—an ethnic and religious minority in Afghanistan. Zaki was a poor Tajik woman who with perseverance and hard work had created a powerful local radio station to serve her community and to support a large family.

These and other Afghan women journalists or presenters have also used their fame to improve their sociocultural positions. They hope to achieve more agency and influence in their lives. Yet, at the same time, no arrests are made and no one is prosecuted for media-related crimes—even murders—including the ones mentioned above. Despite their high profile, the low socioeconomic status of media makers leaves them vulnerable to abuse and death. As we have seen in other cases of attacks and violence toward media makers, most media

PHOTO 5.7. Setara Hussainzada, one of the contestants in the third season of reality TV program *Afghan Star*, came under attack by conservative forces for her performance on the program.

PHOTO 5.8. Despite adhering to the traditional mores of her conservative province of Kandahar, Lema Sahar, who was eliminated in the second round of the third season of *Afghan Star*, still faced backlash.

workers advocate for themselves and for their colleagues across media outlets. People also show their support for slain media makers by protesting and holding vigils for weeks. However, this is not always the case with honor killings because people tend to shy away from them. The owners of television stations are also quick to absolve themselves of any responsibility for the murders of their female employees. Fazal Karim Fazal of Shamshad TV and Saad Mohseni, one of the sibling owners of Tolo TV, said almost the same thing about the respective deaths of Shaima Rezayee and Shakiba Sanga Amaj: it was a personal/ family affair.[13] They absolved themselves like the government authorities did. Too often issues such as patriarchy and misogyny are dismissed as personal matters resulting from regressive traditions and cultural practices. However, women's rights, domestic violence, femicide, and lawlessness are also public issues with serious political, economic, and national ramifications.

Havana Marking, the British director of the award-winning documentary *Afghan Star* (2009) and its sequel *Silencing the Song: An Afghan Fallen Star* (2011)— both produced by Tolo TV and aired on HBO—confirmed that Tolo TV is not invested in what happens to the contestants once they leave the shows.[14] The documentaries follow the lives of contestants on the popular Tolo TV reality series *Afghan Star* and extol the supposed democratic tendencies of the show. Yet the documentaries also put a spotlight on the difficulties that female contestants face. Most of the women contestants come under attack from prominent and dangerous warlords, and oftentimes they have had to go into hiding. For example, the then governor of Herat and jihad era leader, Ismail Khan, who is described as a warlord in the films, publicly condemned one of the female contestants, Setara, on television, causing her to go into hiding.[15] Of course, all of the female contestants on *Afghan Star* come from underprivileged backgrounds as well.

Some have critiqued Tolo TV for profiting off of its female television stars while being negligent of their safety. The program director of the semireligious-leaning Hazara private television station Negaah, who is also the author of a series of progressive Islamic books sponsored by USAID, asked me during my interview, "Tell me, what has *Afghan Star* done for Afghan women? Who has really profited from such programs? Has it really elevated the position of women in our society or even elevated the discussion?" He went on to explain how, in this highly politicized gender environment, "women have become a project for many television stations to seek international funding or, worse, raise the stakes and create sensationalism for the sake of advertising money."[16]

Although some of his statements need to be taken in context, since Tolo is a considerably more popular, established, and successful television station than Negaah TV, the program director nonetheless raises important questions. If the goal of a television station really is to improve the position and status of Afghan women, as many television station owners soliciting international aid claim it to be, should not its internal policies reflect a dedication to supporting women's safety and long-term well-being? In other words, what safeguards does the station put in place to ensure women's safety (both in the workplace and outside)? Does its programming include diverse representations of Afghan women, beyond the typical depictions of them singing and dancing? Also, demographically speaking, how many Afghan women, both on- and off-screen, does the station employ? He points out that nearly 50 percent of Negaah's staff are women, one of whom is the host of its most popular current events program, *Challenge*. The station also chauffeurs its female staff members to and from their homes. Whenever possible, it also tries to hire male family members of their female staff, in order to safeguard the latter's security and reputation. Many of their staff members are brother and sister duos. Such safety precautions are also taken by a few other television stations, such as Saba TV.

When hearing of such cases of misogyny and violence against women, it is easy to automatically jump to the conclusion that Afghans are innately conservative or, worse yet, "backward."[17] However, this would be a mistake (one that some journalistic accounts of the media situation have made). Likewise, it is important to distinguish between practices of Islam in everyday contexts and Islamism as a legal and political framework (Asad 1993; Göle and Ammann 2006; Mahmood 2005). After all, we would not judge the entire United States based on the conservative and regressive policies espoused by the Tea Party or by Donald Trump's white supremacist followers.

Anyone who is familiar with Afghan history knows that the long struggle for women's rights (and sexuality) has been an ongoing battle between modernist state policies and the more restrictive and repressive interpretations of Islamic law and tribal laws (Majrooh 1989; Nawid 2000; Osman 2005). Thus, women's lives and bodies have been under the jurisdiction and regulations of tribal/religious elders and historically relegated to the private sphere. Although this is a moot point for the grieving families of these media martyrs, the deaths of female television personalities have not been completely in vain, contrary to what Tolo's critics claim. Ordinarily, such incidents would be considered a private matter and thus brushed under the proverbial Afghan rug in a small village and nobody would have known. Yet, because these women were public figures, their cases received attention and enabled debate.

Arguments about the "un/suitability," "in/appropriateness," "im/properness," and "im/morality" of women's representation and sexuality on Afghan television stations can be understood as arguments about cultural authenticity, grounded in claims about what constitutes "true" Afghan identity. However, national identity cannot ever be reduced to a singular truth. A sense of a nation's sensibilities can come into focus only through the blurry lens of cultural contestations. Culture by its very definition is in flux and discursive. It is never static.

Be it the representation and agency of foreign women or of Afghan women, it is precisely this public engagement with cultural and political issues pertaining to human rights, democracy, and nation-building enabled by the burgeoning televisual media world in Afghanistan that is a source of strife for Islamists and other conservative groups and cause for celebration for the defenders of free media and human rights in Afghanistan including Islamic reformers.

Depending on whom you ask, television is either the best or the worst medium with which to raise issues for national public reflection and discussion in Afghanistan. It provides a counter-hegemonic function in at least two crucial arenas. First, as an institution, it enables local Afghans to "talk back" to the international community that has Afghanistan in its sphere of influence and discourse. Second, it provides a platform for television producers to act as local reformers, presenting indigenous modernities and cultural practices that challenge local conservative groups that have enlarged their power base as a result of more than four decades of war. But clearly, this comes at the high cost of sacrificing women television personalities on the altar of progress.

The Possibilities of a Counter-Hegemonic Public Sphere

I would like to conclude by presenting some alternative models for Afghan TV channels. The utility of television goes beyond just rhetorical gestures of women's rights or visual spectacles of the performing female body that generate debate, rage, and anger, which then manifest in riots and violent cultural clashes, such as the killing or persecution of disadvantaged female TV personalities and journalists. Television also has the ability to lay the foundations of human rights and create the conditions for diverse expressions of gender and sexuality by educating people.

TV, as we have seen, is certainly capable of stirring cultural contestations. But it also has the ability (if not the responsibility) to raise awareness around those same controversies and their ensuing violence instead of shying away from them. When violence toward journalists or women occurs, many stations have taken the bold steps of televising the details of the incidents. In these cases it is disappointing that television stations tend to shy away from "honor killings" of their female journalists. Tolo TV and Shamshad TV did not provide a platform of debate to honor their murdered employees in their death after they had capitalized on their talents in life.

There are many TV programs in Afghanistan that have female hosts, newscasters, and reporters. While most of them are targeted by Islamists and other conservatives, some of them remain outside the scope of attack because of the protections that their stations have put in place and because they tend to be more culturally sensitive. At the same time, they manage to elevate the position of women. A prime example of a television program where the stated mission of the program aligns with its production ethics is 1TV's critically acclaimed *The Mask* or *Naquab*. The political talk show, which focuses solely on empowering women by challenging misogynist patriarchal practices, made the well-being of its female guests its top priority from the outset by having them wear a mask to protect their identity, hence the name. As a program dedicated to providing a national forum for "private" and "domestic" matters, *The Mask* accomplishes that goal in its actual production design, thereby encouraging female participants to speak openly and raise sensitive and dangerous topics for public contemplation, without fear of retribution. Another example of a program that ensures that its end goals are reflected in its production is Negaah TV's popular political talk show *Challenge*, which is hosted by a chador-clad and modestly attired Zara Sepher. Sepher challenges some of the most powerful politicians, religious clerics, and warlords on her weekly show, hence the English title. Her interviewing style is both subtle and incredibly astute and incisive. The discussions that *Challenge* inspires tend to be the topic of watercooler or *chai khana* (tea house) discussions the next day.[18] The journalist and women's rights activist Farahnaz Forotan had also been producing hard-hitting interviews on Tolo TV's *Porso Pal* (Question and search) before joining 1TV's *Goft-i Go-i Wezha* (Special talk). On these political talk shows, she has interviewed people from across the political spectrum, from members of Hekmatyar's Hizb-i Islami party to the brother of the executed Afghan communist leader Dr. Najibullah, to the new director of the Afghan Independent Human Rights Commission, Shaharzad Akbar.[19]

Additionally, numerous PICs aimed at women's rights have found a home on almost every Afghan television station. They are often funded in conjunction with Afghan government offices such as the Ministry of Women's Affairs and international humanitarian and donor organizations such as UN Women. The subject matter ranges from encouraging women to join the women's violence unit of the national and local police forces, to addressing street harassment. Since women were forced to remain at home during the Taliban regime, the latter PSAs attempt to acclimatize people by normalizing women engaging in street culture and in public spaces more generally.

Other PSAs try to tackle more complicated cultural phenomena such as the traditional practice of *baad* exchange. In *baad*, women and girls are used to resolve blood feuds (Tapper 1991). According to a 2016 Asia Foundation survey, even though the practice is illegal in the Afghan constitution and considered un-Islamic, most Afghans still prefer the often-problematic and informal tribal systems of justice over the court system, because the latter has no legitimacy.[20] Like most infrastructure efforts, the corrupt and almost defunct justice system has proven ineffectual in serving justice. Hence, people have more faith in the tribal system's reciprocity of "equal" exchange to remedy crimes, even if that means offering women in marriage to appease the relatives of victims of violent crimes. But this is also the consequence of the sweeping ultraconservative values that characterize Afghanistan's thriving warlordism. In the absence of any viable recourse for justice, the PIC is not able to provide any alternatives for solving blood feuds. However, the PIC shows the damaging effects on women and girls and reminds people that the practice is illegal and that they can be punished for practicing *baad* exchange, although, in reality, just as in the case of honor killings, rarely is anyone prosecuted for it.

Saba TV has a program called *Roshani* (Enlighten) that is entirely focused on the meaning of human rights and human rights violations. Contrary to popular understanding, in a survey conducted by the Afghan Independent Human Rights Commission (AIHRC), Afghans have a strong sense of their rights.[21] The Arabic word *haq*, which means "rights," is part of the vernacular in Dari and Pashto. It is not conceptualized as universal human rights or even individual rights, which *Roshani* addresses, but rights as understood in terms of kinship relationships: such as the rights of a daughter, a son, a spouse, in-laws, specific types of cousins, or other kin.

There are also numerous call-in shows dedicated to the topic of rights and proper conduct. Depending on the television station, they are hosted either by mullahs or by other religious clerics or scholars or by nonreligious experts. The hosts field questions from Afghans on a variety of issues—from "Is it permissible to pluck ones eyebrows?" to "Under what conditions can a woman divorce her husband?" Interestingly, regardless of their religiosity or secularity, the hosts' advice is often not grounded in anything more than their personal preferences; in general, they tend to be progressive and liberatory. However, all the hosts are male, and most of the callers tend to be female. This is not the case with similar call-in shows that are on satellite TV stations, which are mostly produced and aired outside of Afghanistan, among the diaspora.

RTA, the national broadcasting channel, has a program called *Crime Scene Investigation*. It is a real-life investigative program that looks into actual crimes, including domestic violence and abuse. In one episode, it investigated a woman's self-immolation. Self-immolation is one of the top-five biggest problems facing Afghan women.[22] The show examined the details of the incident and also interviewed all the people involved. Based on the evidence, including the interviews, the show accused her husband of domestic violence and claimed that this was the main reason the woman had attempted to kill herself. He was then publicly shamed and dishonored. This is the best example of television serving the public interest. It highlights how cultural codes, like shame and honor, can be used for the benefit of marginalized and vulnerable populations.

In this way, through a focus on production, we can see television's potential and effects in Afghanistan in terms of producers' intentions. However, to determine the real efficacy and effect of television, we need to examine reception as well. Reception studies help us grasp what audiences across different demographics value about television programming. They also determine if people see a reflection of the issues that are important to their daily lives. In the next chapter, I continue to explore the cultural specificities of the Afghan media world, with attention to what Afghan people—whether women, different ethnic groups, or the general population—desire and demand of their media.

CHAPTER 6

Reception and Audiences

The Demands and Desires of Afghan People

How Audiences Are Imagined

It seems that the elite ruling blocs within most nation-states view television as a powerful machine for the dissemination of ideological messages, as well as for the production of a cultural/national imaginary (Anderson 2006). In this respect, their perception of television is in line with the Frankfurt School's fears about broadcast media and with the "magic bullet" theory of communication. In Afghanistan, television producers/owners—as the case studies in this work reveal—do not necessarily have a simplistic view of audiences. Just as media scholars in their theorizations about the relationship of media to society have conceptualized people across a wide spectrum—ranging from masses to publics to audiences to citizens to consumers—media producers too have a range of conceptions.

Yet, because they are in a position to transmit broadcasts automatically across the nation, these media producers are united in their sense of omniscience—one that borders on paternalism—about who their audiences are and what these audiences need. In this conception, audiences are abstracted and their actual desires rendered almost irrelevant. Likewise, Afghan people are framed and grouped into different "types" of audiences by television producers. These include educated and cosmopolitan populations as well as troublesome, vulnerable, and other marginalized populations (as I discuss in the previous chapter).

However, there is some overlap between what television station owners make and what audiences actually want made—as one would hope there would be. Anything that purports to represent people, such as politicians, government institutions, and political parties, requires the approval of the "demos" to establish legitimacy. Broadcast television—being a national medium with a limited frequency that is authorized and sanctioned by the government—is particularly beholden to the interests of the public. This is especially true in Afghanistan, where there is an artificially inflated media environment that forces producers to compete for audience shares. Hence, stations, for their survival, have to be in touch with audience needs and demands. Additionally, in order to attract international donors and private advertisers, television stations must also provide evidence to demonstrate whether they are truly popular.

Thus the desires of television station owners/producers in Afghanistan—whether it is to survive or expand financially or to not get shut down by the government censors—are contingent, at least to some degree, on pleasing people or feigning pleasing people. In other words, their own survival drives them to be aware of audience desires and to at least gesture toward them if not actually meet them. So, although producers often couch their motivations as loftier goals—meeting societal needs, nation-building, creating publics, expanding public spheres, and developing the conditions for democracy— "giving people what they want" is just as much a by-product of capitalism and economic survival.

The key questions then become these: In the absence of technologies of measurement such as Nielsen ratings, how do television station owners/producers prove or establish the popularity of their programming to potential advertisers, international donors, or Afghan government officials? More importantly, what are the channels or mechanisms, if any, in a one-way communication medium, especially one with great hegemonic tendencies, for the self-expression and feedback of audiences? These are questions that preoccupy not only those interested in television but all those involved in mass media.

Audience Feedback, Technologies of Measurements, and the Ratings Industry

In the West, a huge industry that specializes in rating systems/technologies, including PR firms, critics, and statisticians, among others, determines and establishes the hierarchy of popularity that controls the rates for advertisers and thereby feeds and maintains the wider media industry.

Correspondingly, there is also a prominent subfield of media studies with a large body of scholarly literature that analyzes and critiques the structures, efficacy, accuracy, and biases of this subindustry of the media world. Many academics are critical about these technologies that assess viewership. They have been instrumental in questioning the establishment's self-proclaimed and accepted expertise as the barometer of audiences. In *Living Room Wars* (2006), Ien Ang explains this phenomenon: "In short, in its 'tendency to serve either the media industry, its clients, or the official guardians of society and public morality' . . ., mass communication research, by offering so called scientific knowledge about the audience (or more precisely, about what could be done in order to 'administer' the audience), has performed a power/knowledge function, which is particularly characteristic of the modern desire for social order" (28).

In post-9/11 Afghanistan, such an industry has started, but it is still only in its infancy. This is for the better, since audiences are less likely to be abstracted by the technologies of the industry. One company, Altai, named after the eastern Central Asian mountain range, was started by three Frenchmen who met while climbing in the region and who wanted to remain in Afghanistan. Seeing a need for a marketing and consultancy company and coming from those backgrounds, they launched Altai in 2004 with the support of USAID's Office of Transition Initiatives, which contracted them to conduct a comprehensive media evaluation survey. When I contacted Altai in 2009 and then again in 2010, some of its employees were still based in Kabul but the main partners were not. I was told that they had sold off the media consultancy side of the company—and that it was very profitable. However, shortly thereafter, in late 2010, Altai surprisingly released another USAID-sponsored media survey. This means either that they never sold the media side of Altai or that they very quickly bought it back once USAID contracted them again.

Another consultancy and market research group, ACSOR (Afghan Center for Socio-Economic and Opinion Research), launched in 2003. ACSOR is an offshoot of D3 Systems, an American research, design, and data collection company with offices throughout the world. Since 9/11, ACSOR has been contracted annually by the Asia Foundation, also a US-based company, to produce its "Survey of Afghan People." This survey is meant to be a holistic public opinion survey that assesses different sectors of Afghan civil society, including the media sector, and it tends to be comprehensive. Moby Media, Tolo TV's parent company, also has a company called Lapis Communications, which managers run by Lapis, its advertising and media evaluation group. The Lapis market research and surveys are not available publicly, and, as I will discuss shortly, I have been privy only to the parts of the research that Moby Media personnel brought to my attention. Before starting Lapis, Moby Media also briefly had ownership stakes in Altai, which presented a conflict of interest for Altai since it had been paid by the US government to produce independent research, which could then be used to stake claims of high viewership. Viewership data that these companies produced for the international donor community, though not always accurate and sometimes far from accurate, was then used by the international donors and their Afghan partners for many purposes, including justifying further support and donor money and expansion.

In the absence of any nationwide technologies of assessment or any other statistical research, this small pool of surveys is cited by those in the development community in their public relations literature and presentations as evidence of their own successes and as sound on-the-ground analysis, in order to justify their accounting expenditures and future projects/projections. However, the credibility of the data set and research methods of these companies has been questioned by locals and the expatriate community (Smith 2011). Drawing on two decades of media ethnography, the anthropologist Andrew Skuse also cautions against an overreliance on quantitative surveys and number crunching, which can obscure in-depth analysis and understanding of people, nations, and cultures (Skuse, Gillespie, and Power 2011).

Like academic scholars who study the statistical and market research industry, local Afghans are skeptical of such studies. For example, if informed that a survey states that in their region a particular program is the most-watched television genre or television channel, they balk and believe only their own experiences and observations. As individuals with varied insights and wisdom, they do not appreciate being abstracted into statistical figures. In my interviews, people often conveyed to me a concern that their reality is not represented in the surveys. Some Afghanistan experts are also wary of such surveys, especially when they discern discrepancies between what they see and hear from Afghans on the street and what the results of these public opinion polls reveal. In the larger surveys, practices of subcontracting also create issues of transparency and discrepancies as the sources of funding get further distant from actual locations and people.

Yet audiences appreciate opportunities to engage directly with the television stations they watch and to have their viewpoints considered. Producers and owners of television stations also like to provide opportunities for such direct audience engagement. This is true of most Afghan television stations, since most of them fall outside the purview of the international community's surveys and therefore tend to be less represented. Many TV stations believe that these surveys only reproduce the status quo—that is, they prop up only the most powerful stations, which have the most international backing, regardless of whether or not they are popular in some regions of the country. Thus, the majority of Afghanistan's television stations have designated daily and weekly programs specifically for the purpose of giving audiences a chance to publicly voice their opinions. These take the form of call-in shows in the mornings or weekly shows that recap the channels' programming. Presenters and hosts solicit direct feedback from audiences about the effectiveness of their programming via mobile phones and by reading audiences' e-mails and letters to the station.

This democratic approach to gauging audience response enables television to function as a two-way interactive social medium. Unlike the foreign government–sponsored large abstract data sets, which most Afghans have never even heard of, this interactive daily or weekly feedback mechanism that most television channels employ has established credibility among audiences. Audiences tend to trust the direct and observable methods of these shows. This is especially true in the case of those programs that do not screen callers, that actively encourage discussion, and that solicit criticisms and suggestions—not just positive feedback. Television owners and producers who provide audiences with such a platform also establish their own credibility in the process, since most of them are underrepresented or not represented in the large, mostly Western-administered surveys.

Whereas the industry may have silenced complex understandings of audiences, reception studies scholars have taken on the important task of giving them a voice by determining whether media messages actually work on the targeted people and allowing them to actually speak and respond. Building on such work, I engaged with audiences to discuss their own relationships to television programming. Although my work started primarily as a production study, I had to venture into reception studies in order to get some sense of how people understood the work they were watching, since Afghanistan lacks ethnographic studies of their media worlds. In the absence of independent agencies and technologies that gauge audiences, my reception research offers insight into how people respond to television in contemporary Afghanistan.

In regard to methodology, my observation and interviewing took place in viewing contexts and non-viewing contexts, as well as in private and public settings and formal and informal contexts but almost always in group/family settings, since that is how most television is watched. Some of the questions I went in with included these: What distinguishes Afghan audiences from viewers elsewhere? What do they want? What do they respond to strongly? What do they want to see that is not available to them on TV?

As axiomatic as it sounds, one of the main tenets that has emerged from the more nuanced work in reception studies is to rehumanize audiences. Audiences are first and foremost people with very specific needs that are based on their circumstances, cultural backgrounds, and historical experiences. Just as the dystopic state of the country has increased the real or imagined powers of television, and therefore the hopes and fears about the medium, particularly among people on the production side of television, the same conditions have sharpened the interest in particular kinds of programming for people on the reception side of television. My research suggests that after experiencing over four decades of warfare and trauma, Afghan audiences have very high expectations of media and journalism in general and television in particular.

Afghan Audiences Demand Justice

Afghan producers frequently complain that people have unreasonable expectations of them. They are expected to publicly shame every corrupt politician and government official who is still using their power as a stronghold and stranglehold. Forced marriages, forceful land grabbing, murders, kidnappings, poisonings, assaults, torture—people have a litany of grievances against current and former warlord types. Sanjar Sohail, an ethnic Hazara who is the director of political affairs and news programming at Saba TV as well as publisher and executive editor of *Hashte Subh* (Eight in the morning), Afghanistan's largest and longest running independent daily newspaper post-Taliban, explained:

> We get inundated with letters and phone calls regularly from people demanding that we broadcast the abuses of this warlord or that warlord. They want to tell the terrible things that have happened to them or their families at the bloody hands of these *zoor awarah*.[1] They are very angry and adamant. They think that television will finally give them some justice or at least a little peace of mind. I do not blame them. People who have been wronged deserve justice and they deserve to be heard. But it is very complicated and dangerous figuring out how to maneuver the ethnic fault lines as well as substantiate information for when the government or the Shura-i Ulama come after us. Sometimes we investigate and produce a segment. Oftentimes our hands are tied due to larger pressures. We are unarmed media makers. We are not the police or the court of law. We do not have the resources to thoroughly investigate and report every crime, but neither do they.[2]

If the newspaper had more liberty to report abuses of power, he explained, it was partially because *Hashte Subh*'s reach was smaller than Saba TV's. For most of its investigative reports, *Hashte Subh* partnered with the Afghan Independent Human Rights Commission (AIHRC). In the wake of the Taliban regime, the AIHRC was constitutionally mandated by the UN to supervise the transitional government proceedings. Although affiliated with the Afghan government and international governments, the AIHRC was meant to exist as an independent body free of coercion from other institutions. Widely known for its hard-hitting investigative reportage and fastidious research, the AIHRC has earned the respect of Afghans throughout the country.

Ironically, on June 1, 2011, the Shura-i Ulama declared, via Hamid Karzai's office, that *Hashte Subh* would be shut down immediately. *Al Jazeera*'s Afghanistan bureau reported that, under pressure from the Shura-i Ulama, President Karzai sent a message to *Hashte Subh* that "publishing material that is against religion, against national unity, and against the high interest of the nation" would not be tolerated (Mashal 2011). In this particular case, the courts ruled in Sohail's favor; they observed that he was only echoing the findings of a respected human rights organization. However, Sohail worried about the next time, especially since Karzai seemed to be ceding more and more ground to conservative forces with criminal histories. He aptly said, "If we expose and write on sexual assault, war crimes, and other problems, the government's hands should not be on our throats, but rather on the perpetrators'" (Mashal 2011).

In 2012, after a series of battles with the AIHRC, Karzai, who is often extolled for supporting free speech in Afghanistan, fired three of the AIHRC's top commissioners, including the director, Nader Nadery, and appointed new ones.[3] This understandably led to some international dismay and outrage.

People realize that dealing with such powerful and ruthless individuals is beyond the means of tribal justice systems such as *loya jirgas*, or public assemblies of elders. Afghanistan's official justice system, moreover, is corrupt, and international law has failed its people. They thus want television to serve as the judge, jury, and executioner of warlords and war criminals. They know that the American government is complicit in bringing many of these dubious characters, ranging from drug lords to ethnocidal mass murderers, to power in the first place and are appalled that the Afghan government has given many of them official posts since 9/11. Like village *loya jirgas*, where familial or tribal justice is enacted on a small scale, they want a national forum or venue whereby they can publicly bring their grievances against these national criminals and demand retribution.

Retribution for Warlords on TV

Afghan television producers are meeting people's demand to shame warlords by highlighting their injustices and scrutinizing their history via the news, current affairs programs, and special programs on warlords. These programs are revealing the duplicity in the warlords' rhetoric and making broader connections to their nefarious foreign funding sources and treacherous actions against the people. For example, when the Afghan government, led by President Ashraf Ghani, signed a peace deal with the Islamist Gulbuddin Hekmatyar, pardoning him and inviting him to return to Afghanistan in May 2017, massive protests erupted across the country, and many television stations produced special programs detailing the atrocities he and his Hezb-i Islami had inflicted on the population since the 1960s.

The programs recounted how the prime minister of Afghanistan in the 1970s, Daoud Khan, who was later killed in the first Soviet-backed coup, had first exiled and then imprisoned Hekmatyar due to his attempts to overthrow the government and his suspected involvement in a series of acid attacks on Afghan schoolgirls and young women attending Kabul University. Yet, during the Soviet occupation, the US government secretly funded his return and rise to power in order to fight the Cold War. During this time and the subsequent civil war, he not only continued his assault against women but also inflicted ethnic violence. During the civil war, for example, he is estimated to be responsible for the killing of 40,000–60,000 people. The programs also investigated Hekmatyar's suspected involvement in the assassinations of numerous reformers in exile including Dr. Sayyid Bahauddin Majrooh, the founder of the Afghan Information Centre (AIC), Meena Kamal, the founder of the Revolutionary Association of the Women of Afghanistan (RAWA), and Mirwais Jalil, an Afghan journalist who worked for the BBC World Service.

Afghan television stations have also effectively shamed Sibghatullah Mojaddedi, another CIA-backed religious mujahideen leader. Mojaddedi, whom the US government has often referred to as an ally and labeled a "moderate," has taken numerous anti-women positions. In December 2003, for example, as chairman of the upper house of Parliament, he tried to permanently banish Malalai Joya, a democratically elected MP and women's rights and peace activist, for speaking out—in a famous televised speech that went viral internationally on YouTube—against warlords and international militarism.[4] He also called her an "infidel" and "communist." Since the event, she has survived multiple assassination attempts. In May 2006, warlord and warlord-affiliated

MPs physically accosted her after she made a similar speech asking that they be held accountable for their human rights crimes against people.

Mojaddedi has also publicly declared, at every presidential election cycle, that female candidates should withdraw their candidacy since women are not fit for public office. In December 2014, when President Karzai refused to sign the Bilateral Security Agreement—which would grant US officials and soldiers full immunity in Afghan and international courts for acts committed on bases, in prisons, and in other facilities in Afghanistan—Mojaddedi tried to use his religious clout in support of the US government's demand to ratify the agreement. He declared on television that God had come to him in a religious dream or what is known as an *istekhara* and said that Afghans should vote for Ashraf Ghani and sign the Bilateral Security Agreement for the country's well-being. While personal *istekharas* are commonplace in Afghanistan, for a prominent figure to have a public *istekhara* with serious national and international implications is unusual. Media makers on television programs and in other media critiqued his "US financed *istekhara*," raising it in satire and comedy shows as well as on discussion programs. The programs highlighted how contrary to his and the US government's rhetoric that he is a moderate and an advocate for women's rights and other marginalized groups, he has a long history of aligning himself with US interests and conservative positions.

Sheikh Asif Mohseni, another religious leader and owner of the religious Tamadon TV, was televisually shamed as well. Sheikh Mohseni, whom progressives more commonly call Sheikh-i Shaiton or Satan's Sheikh, is responsible for drafting the Shia Family Law and the Shiite Marriage Law—known among activists as the Rape Law—and pressuring Karzai to sign it in March 2009. Outside of Mohseni's main mosque in Kabul, hundreds of women protested against the law, which gives Shiite men the right to force their wives to have sex, among other abusive powers. Diana Saqeb, an award winning filmmaker and women's rights activist, who was one of the protest organizers said that she was disappointed that despite their efforts only a few MPs showed up to support them.[5] The protesters were attacked by young male followers of Mohseni, whom he had incited to violence on his television station. Many other stations supported the protesters by providing airtime on their news and other programs. They featured reformist Islamic experts who denounced the law. Additionally, the program highlighted Mohseni's connections to the CIA (during the Soviet-Afghan War) and his more recent links to Iran's Islamic regime—a major benefactor that has built him grand mosques and seminaries throughout the country. Mohseni was also widely shamed for his nonconsensual marriage to an underage girl in 2010. The girl's father, who had opposed the marriage, spoke publicly.

Likewise, in 2016, the media thoroughly investigated and reported on the latest charges of abduction and rape of a political rival by the vice president of Afghanistan, Abdul Rashid Dostum, who also happens to be a well-known warlord and owner of Ayna TV, which has ties to the Uzbek government.

The fact that Afghan warlords have been sowing the seeds of sectarian and gender violence for several decades and are often funded by the international community is not news to Afghans. Rather, programs that highlight these issues are significant because they publicly counter the *duplicity* of the warlords and the international community. While the US government has effectively funded the rebuilding of the media sector and has launched many human rights campaigns to end ethnic, religious, and gender violence, the media spotlight on warlords reveals how the US government is also ultimately responsible for bringing these dystopic conditions to Afghanistan in the first place and reifying them. In order to achieve its immediate geopolitical goals, the US government has repeatedly funded and supported anti–human rights and antidemocratic warlord types with seedy records ranging from femicide to genocide. With their myopic, immediate result–oriented objectives that perhaps aim to appease the political order back home, some US-led projects and campaigns do not consider the dangerous long-term consequences and effects of their interventions. This is a key difference between the development gaze and the imperial gaze: there is an inherent duplicity built into imperial projects in order to protect, promote, and expand the economic and political interests of the donor states. Thus, the Western imperialist gaze and projects that stem from it directly undermine the efficacy of well-intentioned Western development efforts.

By creating transparency and generating debate, these television programs give people a voice in the political process and larger decisions of the state, including whom they want and do not want as leaders. Public debate is the first step in challenging the status quo that these warlords have been trying to entrench: be they regressive social, cultural, or political norms. These programs make apparent the track record of public officials by sifting through their doublespeak to demonstrate that their own self-interests—and not those of their followers or the country at large—often drive them. In some cases, television programs have literally dug up the skeletons and mass graves in their backyards.

Support for the News and Journalists: The People's Heroes

In this equation, where warlords or *jung salarah* have become the ultimate villains of the Afghan psyche, journalists are the ultimate superheroes of the people. Journalists who have established their credentials through fearless reporting have won large fan followings. People revere them and perceive them as saviors, protectors, and an extension of their own wills. Thus they are highly sensitive to and become incensed when journalists are harmed in any way. The outpouring of support and grief for these heroes reverberates throughout the country. When media makers are targeted, attacked, or killed by *zoor awarah*, or strongmen, media outlets, in solidarity with one another, also advocate for themselves and pay homage to the victims by providing in-depth news coverage of the attacks on media makers and media censorship more broadly, televising the subsequent protests on the news, and producing special programs that investigate the incidents of censorship and violence as well as expository programs that address the role of media freedom in democratic societies. Outside of television, a number of low budget Afghan films have been released that feature journalists as their heroes and even superheroes, while warlord types are usually the villains.

In September 2009, Afghan journalist Sultan Munadi—while on assignment as a fixer for *New York Times* journalist Stephen Farrell—was kidnapped by the Taliban along with Farrell. British special forces safely rescued Farrell in a nighttime raid and in the process shot and killed Munadi as he was attempting to board the rescue helicopter, mistaking him for the enemy. To add insult to injury, his body was left behind with no explanation. Widespread anger ensued as people protested for over a week in Kabul. The news and protests highlighted similar cases of double standards in which Afghan journalists were killed or not negotiated for while their Western counterparts were saved, such as the case of Ajmal Naqshbandi, a fixer and journalist who was killed by the Taliban while the Italian journalist he was working for was negotiated for and released.

In March 2007, Naqshbandi was working with an Italian journalist on a dangerous assignment in Helmand when the Taliban captured them both. Subsequently, the release of the Italian journalist and Naqshbandi was negotiated in exchange for the release of five Taliban prisoners. Yet in the chaos of the actual exchange, while the Italian was recovered, Naqshbandi was accidently left behind and later beheaded by the Taliban. Their driver Sayed Agha was the first to be beheaded. Once the beheadings, captured on video, were released and televised in Afghanistan, the public outcry across the country took the form of riots and protests as well as peaceful vigils and public murals honoring them. Local news, echoing public opinion, expressed a common sentiment that Afghan journalists are considered expendable and disposable in the international news production circuit.

PHOTO 6.1. The poster for Ian Old's 2009 documentary film, *Fixer: The Taking of Ajmal Naqshbandi*, which tells the story of the journalist's capture and killing.

PHOTO 6.2. **Protest in Kabul for Ajmal Naqshbandi.**

PHOTO 6.3. **Protest in Kabul for Sultan Munadi, the Afghan journalist killed by the British military forces.**

The same sense of public outrage was expressed over the January 2011 acid attack on well-known journalist Razaq Mamoon, who was formerly a host of a popular weekly political commentary and interview program on Tolo TV. The gathering and outpouring of support outside of his hospital in Kabul was massive. Contrary to some news reports that he was targeted for personal reasons, most of the news outlets confirmed Mamoon's own account that Iranian agents were responsible, since he had just published a book detailing and condemning the Iranian government's involvement in Afghanistan's affairs. He is a fierce critique of Afghanistan's neighbors interfering in its affairs.

Journalists who have built a reputation for fair, independent, and courageous reporting by virtue of their honorable work move outside the bounds of ethnic, tribal, or religious sectarianism. Afghans applaud and celebrate independent journalists as national heroes. Thus the ethnicities of Munadi (Tajik), Naqshbandi (Pashtun), and Mamoon (Tajik) became irrelevant. People feel strongly and are moved to action when media makers or journalists, regardless of ethnicity, are harmed in any way. It is thus a reciprocal relationship: the media explosion in Afghanistan provides audiences with a platform for issues that are crucial to them; in return, people voice their support for the media. Audiences have coalesced to form a strong public, vociferously rising in opposition to conservative elites and in defense of the media. When respected media makers are harmed, people protest, hold vigils, or riot for weeks.

However, this is not the case for slain women media makers. Due to the security situation and gender segregation, protests for women media makers who have been maimed or killed have not been as prevalent. For example, in the 2009 protests against the Shia Family Law, also known as the Rape Law, women protestors were attacked by mobs of fundamentalized and misogynist young men. This changed with the 2015 public killing of Farkhunda Malikzada, which was also carried out by a lynch mob of fundamentalized mosque-goers who were spurred to violence by one of the mosque's mullahs. Malikzada's killing captured on cell phones and broadcast on Afghan television stations shocked the nation and became a watershed moment for the Afghan women's rights movement. Thousands of women protested for weeks demanding justice for Malikzada and in an unprecedented move that goes against conservative dictates of Islam, publicly carried her casket to its burial site. That event shifted the nature of protests so that women began to participate more. Yet women are still wary because they are disproportionally impacted by the violence of present-day Afghanistan.

Stirring the Ghosts of the Past:
New Afghan Genres

Afghans, by virtue of living in Afghanistan, have all experienced a variety of war-related horrors. While everyone is war-weary, they are not, surprisingly, desensitized to televisual violence. Even the most seasoned foot soldiers find violent imagery very evocative. PSAs, news coverage, and specials remind them of a shared history of violence that they are desperately trying to forget. I had the opportunity to watch episodes of violence with different ethnic groups and sectors of society during my fieldwork; the almost unanimous reaction that I witnessed was that of compassion followed by anger. The coverage always spurred conversations about the local climate of violence in which people condemned *all* warlords—be they prominent Soviet-era commanders or the US-backed jihadis who fought them, including those from their own tribes or ethnic groups—as "bloodsuckers" or people with "blood on their hands." The common sentiment was that all these warlords should be ousted from government positions and punished. Every group, even the smaller ones, has at least one warlord or leader affiliated with it.

That said, television depictions of violence handled without sensitivity could be quite polarizing. Some sectarian stations, for example, produce "historical" or epic-type films that glorify their own ethnic-affiliated warlord. Using newsreel footage as well as interviews with their followers, these pseudo-documentaries portray ruthless individuals in a larger-than-life manner, as if they were gods or prophets ordained by destiny with their incredible skills and talents to lead the masses.

Ayna Television, which is owned by Adbul Rashid Dostum, an Uzbek leader/warlord and Afghanistan's vice president from 2014 to 2020, produced and nationally aired at least three different promotional specials during my fieldwork about the greatness of Dostum. Dostum is someone whose human rights violations, including his ethnically motivated violence during the civil war, have been documented by Human Rights Watch (Sifton 2005, sec. 3A; Human Rights Watch 2006). He also has an infamous record, as general for the Soviet-backed Afghan Communist Party, of torturing Afghan POWs and others who rebelled against the Soviet occupation. Needless to say, the Tajiks, Pashtuns, Hazaras, and many other ethnic groups (including some Uzbeks as well) who have been affected by the atrocities that he and his militias committed do not respond well to these productions. At the same time, Dostum is one of the few secular jihadi leaders who does not believe in turning Afghanistan into a theocracy.

Other ethnic-affiliated television stations have also produced epic narratives about their own warlords. Noor TV and Mitra TV—both partially financed by the Tajik political party Jamiat-i Islami—have been especially prolific, producing docudramas in homage to their late leaders Burhanuddin Rabbani and Ahmad Shah Massoud. As part of the Northern Alliance, Rabbani and Massoud joined and led the US coalition's ouster of the Taliban and Al Qaeda, which resulted in the subsequent assassination of both men by the Taliban and Al Qaeda. Ever since then, they have achieved a venerable martyred status for fighting Islamic extremism and terrorism, which masks their tarnished human rights records and makes mentioning them dangerous (Sifton 2005, sec. 3A and 3C; Human Rights Watch 2006; Nordland 2013).

Indeed, none of the ethnically oriented stations refrain from using their broadcasting powers to aggrandize their political base and influence national politics. During the 2014 elections, many of the ethnic-specific television stations were fined for biased coverage (Khitab 2014). Dawat Radio and Television Group—both owned by Abdul Rasul Sayyaf, an ethnic Pashtun—was charged one of the heftiest fines for exclusively promoting his own campaign (Independent Election Commission 2014). Sayyaf, who is a current MP, also has a notorious record of warlordism (Sifton 2005, sec. 3A and 3C; Human Rights Watch 2006). Against strong public opposition, in 2007 Sayyaf along with other jihadi leaders turned politicians and television station owners managed to pass a sweeping amnesty law that absolves them of war crimes prior to 2002. Needless to say, like most warlords, this group of politicians have been implicated in human rights abuses, extortion, land seizures, voter fraud, and other abuses of power that wreak havoc on ordinary Afghans (Human Rights Watch 2008; Freedom House 2008).

The commercially successful and nationally oriented television stations do not engage in such productions. Indeed, most of the ethnic stations have stopped making or airing this genre of "documentaries." They learned quickly that the broadcasting of these fictionalized films generates debate on other television stations, in other media, and within the general public about the accuracy of the information. As a result, most warlords and their affiliated television stations prefer their seedy track record and history not be subjected to research and scrutiny to such an extent. Overall, stations that blatantly incite ethnic bias tend to be marginalized by viewers and discredited in televised debates by the more reputable stations. My interviews suggest that people are traumatized by years of ethnic, racial, gender, and religious violence. The culture has shifted, in large part due to television's influence, so bias and racism are not tolerated any longer, at least publicly.

Such ahistorical television programs bring to the surface Afghanistan's troubled and bloody recent history. Depending on the context and content, remembering can be healing or can reopen painful wounds. There have not yet been any television documentaries that have followed "truth and reconciliation" models in which both perpetrators and victims are heard in open and honest dialogue. The truth and reconciliation models are premised on enabling victims to share the brutalities they have been subjected to, followed by perpetrators confessing their sins, taking accountability for their actions, and apologizing. Such a television program, perhaps on Radio Television Afghanistan, would require a lot more work to produce with sensitivity than the one-sided, self-aggrandizing docudramas do. But it could be transformative for the healing process of the nation.

Yet there have been numerous television programs that have effectively mined historical material and tapped into the nation's psyche to good effect. This is especially true in the case of music videos. Every television station has at least one program dedicated to them, usually a music video call-in show. A new genre of Afghan music videos, which mash-up the past and present, has been produced for famous songs of beloved singers and musicians from the past. In what seems like a surreal act of modern magic to many viewers, modern media technologies recreate a happier past. The past is a source of pride and hope and is a reminder of a better time in Afghanistan's history. It simultaneously evokes a sense of loss and the tragedy and destruction of the present. By reediting old stock footage in a mash-up of still images, films, and music, the producers of these music videos bring back deceased singers who never had music videos to accompany their popular songs during their lifetimes. Archival concert footage, family pictures, and stock footage of Afghanistan's unique and beautiful landmarks—both manmade and natural—come together and come alive. Whereas the landscape footage of Afghanistan has remained somehow eternally picturesque, with the exception of places that have suffered from war and climate-related drought, we see the monuments, gardens, statues, and other architectural and cultural feats destroyed in "before and after" footage.

Many such mash-up music videos have been made for the iconic Afghan pop star Ahmad Zahir. Known as the "Voice of the Golden Age," Zahir was killed under mysterious circumstances at the start of the Soviet-backed government's taking power in 1979 (Inskeep 2010). Many speculate that his death was due to his protest songs and opposition to the Soviet-backed government. One such mash-up video of the past and present features a slow-motion montage of snow melting off snowcapped mountains, breathtaking waterfalls, colorful deserts, and majestic valleys. The camera zooms into and across Zahir's pho-

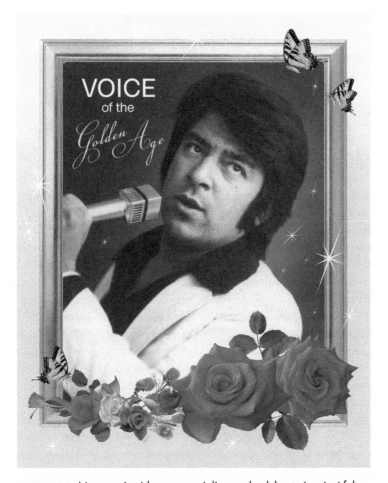

PHOTO 6.4. New music videos memorialize and celebrate iconic Afghan singer, musician, and composer Ahmad Zahir, who was killed at the age of thirty-three in 1979. The deceased pop stars of the prewar "Golden Age" are a source of pride and a wishful invoking of a peaceful past transposed on the dystopic present. Credit: Shabnam Zahir Humphrey (Ahmad Zahir's daughter). Design: Thanh Nguyen.

tographs; this is spliced with slow-motion versions of rare concert footage. In another part of the video, a field of tulips pixelates, and a computer-generated rose multiplies into a screen full of identical roses. To some foreigners and expatriate Afghan observers, the rudimentary effects of cross-fading, pixelating, and multiplying were silly and reminiscent of early video effects. For Afghan audiences, however, these music video mash-ups are a captivating and deeply sentimental experience of modern invention. To see them is to immediately feel nostalgia. These visual montages connect people to the national icons, natural diversity, and wonders of Afghanistan.

Afghan versus Foreign Programming: The Contradictions in Tastes and Identification

For Afghan viewers, the quality of a work is judged less by its production values than by the *Afghaniyat* or "Afghan-ness" of its content. Afghan audiences across different segments of society respond favorably to low-budget local productions, such as music videos, game shows, call-in shows, the news, and public service announcements that speak to their own world of cultural knowledge. As with political satire shows, discussed in chapter 3 and 4, they can share in the Afghan poems, songs, inside jokes, and other national references of these Afghan-led and Afghan-produced shows. The quality of the programs is determined not by glossy, expensive sets or by fancy special effects. Rather, it is the rough, homemade, sketch-like, intimate feel of certain productions, shaped by an Afghan universe of references, that audiences truly appreciate. Unlike Afghan producers, local audiences are not necessarily aware of, nor do they consciously differentiate between, foreign content and productions and Afghan ones. They simply relate to Afghan codes.

Likewise, contrary to how Afghan producers view them, the ethnic Pashtuns, for example, obviously do not perceive themselves as vulnerable, unstable, or dangerous to the nation. Nor do Hazaras or Tajiks or any other ethnic minority. Yet, they all complain about being left out of national processes and therefore appreciate ethnic representation and programming in their ethnic languages and dialects. This appreciation for all things particular to their own subgroups does not negate their broader appreciation for the nationally referenced and coded genres they can share in the lingua franca Dari with all Afghans on more nationally minded television stations.

There are, however, some exceptions. For example, the popularity of Indian and Turkish soap operas far surpasses other dramatic serials, including the fledgling Afghan ones. According to my research, audiences without a doubt value and appreciate the Afghan content of the Afghan dramatic serials. In interviews, they readily noted and expressed enthusiasm for new serials written, directed, and acted in by Afghans. They felt that themes and culturally based story lines—such as ethnic tension, gender violence, generational divides, opium and heroin addiction, lawlessness, and kidnappings, among other war-related, dystopic topics—speak more truthfully to their lives than works imported from elsewhere. Yet their level of enthusiasm and excitement was significantly higher for the more stylized, exotic, and lavish universe of the Indian and Turkish dramatic serials. (Their response to Iranian soap operas was similar to Afghan ones, by comparison not as enthusiastic as for the Indian and Turkish dramas.)

Indian and Turkish productions offer a respite and an escape from Afghans' national burdens. As one Kabuli schoolteacher explained, "I already know what it is like to be a woman here. The hardships of it—I experience it every single day including during the Taliban; I was here. We couldn't get out. But it is nice to see how women are in Indian serials. I especially like the bad ones. They are so wicked," she laughed.[6] We cannot underestimate the value of entertainment in a place like Afghanistan. In a country mired in trauma and violence, including decades of gender violence, television is a more benign drug of distraction than the opiates whose popularity is increasingly growing, fueling a national drug addiction epidemic and crisis.

Of course, the Afghan and non-Afghan producers of these Afghan dramatic serials believe that their serials are at least equally popular with audiences. Fazal Karim Fazal of Shamshad TV insisted that the value of Afghan content and themes on the network's two Afghan-Pakistani dramatic Pashto productions take precedence over other factors for Afghan audiences.[7] Trudi-Ann Tierney, an Australian writer and producer who is senior manager and head of drama at Moby Media, oversees dramatic productions at Tolo TV through Kaboora, Moby's production house. In a series of e-mail exchanges conducted in September 2011 between Wajma Mohseni (one of the sibling owners of Moby), Tierney, and me, Mohseni and Tierney pointed to the 2010 Altai Media Survey and their own 2010 Lapis survey and focus group research that showed *Raazah En Khana*, the Tolo serial, to be the most popular show during the time it was aired, Friday afternoons. The Altai survey also mentioned two other Afghan dramatic serials "with limited audience share" but completely left out the Shamshad dramatic serials such as *Swara* and *Malalai* that were brought to my attention by audiences almost as frequently as the Tolo serials. The fact that the Afghan dramatic serials air only once per week does make comparing their popularity with the Indian serials difficult, since there is a daily dose of attachment to the Indian soaps and their characters. It also makes one wonder why local serials are aired on Friday afternoon, the one day of the week that Afghans have off from work and when most people go shopping in the bazaars, visit family, and go to public parks and other attractions.

It is important to note that Tolo's latest dramatic serial *Khate Sewom* (the third line), launched in March of 2018, is garnering incredible accolades from audiences and critics alike. Directed by the talented award winning Afghan filmmaker Roya Sadat, this is the third Tolo serial that Sadat has worked on but it is the first joint production between Roya Film House and Tolo's Kaboora Productions. Based on my analysis and speaking with viewers, the high caliber story telling and production quality demonstrates a significant improvement in craft and marks a significant moment for Afghan-made dramas. The story revolves around an apartment complex in Kabul where a group of families from diverse socioeconomic backgrounds and ethnic groups live and have to negotiate difficult circumstances and opposing worldviews. What distinguishes this dramatic serial from its predecessors, which dealt with similar war-related issues that plague Afghanistan, is that the characters have agency and are actively striving to challenge the religiosity and prejudices of some of their neighbors. *Khate Sewom* is on par with the best of the foreign dramatic serials I describe in this chapter.

"Trashy Tastes" and Permeable Borders

Dramatic serials created in many countries—from Latin America to the Far East—can be found airing regularly on Afghanistan's television stations. The most ubiquitous ones are American, Indian, Turkish, and Iranian, in that order.[8] Afghan versions of American reality formats tend to be popular, while American television programs such as *24* and *The X-Files*, which also air on Afghan televisions, are not as popular. Turkish serials and some Iranian serials tend to be popular as well. I will discuss a few of them, including the Turkish science fiction–infused, pseudo-religious dramatic serials *Beşinci Boyut* (The fifth dimension) and *Sırlar Dünyası* (The mysterious world) and one Iranian religious epic, based on the life of the prophet Joseph, later in this chapter. Yet Indian dramatic serials are by far the most popular and contentious genre on Afghan television. Thus in the next sections I explore how and why Indian serials have become catalytic in the current Afghan culture wars with their contesting claims on Afghan identity. Conversely, I ask why Afghan and Iranian soap operas have not been either as popular or as contentious.

Although the religious Right has targeted many different genres of television programs—from Afghan versions of Western reality shows such as *Pop Idol* and *Top Model* to music video call-in shows to the news—it is dramatic Indian serials that have consistently borne the brunt of its censorship attacks. A number of private television stations—Tolo, Emroz, ATN, Noor, Rah-e-Farda—are facing government bans, charges, or fines based on Article 3 of the post-9/11 constitution, which prohibits the broadcasting of content that is deemed to be "contrary to the sacred religion of Islam."[9] The Ministry of Information and Culture, among other governmental and nongovernmental bodies, enforces this section of the constitution and ensures that television stations abide by the government's dictates. The Parliament, too, with varying degrees of success, has passed several bills that attempt to ban Indian soap operas.

These popular Indian serials resemble Latin American telenovelas and American soap operas in their melodramatic performances and domestic content and have also over time adopted the lavish sets and costumes stylistically associated with Bollywood films and Egyptian dramatic serials (Abu-Lughod 2004; Das 1995; Ganti 2012). However, unlike Western dramatic serials and similar to Latin American telenovelas, they are not open-ended in form and often last between one and two years.

Love Them or Hate Them:
The Alternative Lives of Soap Operas

As a result of the historical dominance of Bollywood in the region, as well as a new configuration of dynamics, it is no secret that the vast majority of Afghans have loved Indian films and Indian dramatic serials since the explosion of the Afghan television sector. Afghan filmmakers who associate aesthetically with the Iranian avant-garde or Russian socialist realism often complain about the "lowbrow" and "trashy" tastes of their fellow countrypeople who flock to see the latest Bollywood blockbuster but do not possess the "sophistication" and "cultivation" to appreciate high-art films, Iranian cosmopolitan films, global independent films, and documentaries.

People from abroad, both the returning Afghan expatriate community and Westerners working for international organizations, echo a similar distaste. A young Afghan female expatriate from France who works for the United Nations expressed a lack of comprehension of her middle-aged Afghan male driver's love of Indian soap operas. She told me in an interview, "Oh, I know about those Indian programs. All I hear is *Tulsi, Tulsi, Tulsi.*[10] Around a certain time my driver comes into my office to make sure that we're leaving on time. If I have to stay later at work he asks to leave for an hour to go watch *Tulsi*. God forbid, we were running late a few times and he was driving like a maniac and nearly killed us."[11]

The categorization of Indian serials as a lower art form is symptomatic of the development of soap operas and television more generally in the West. As feminist and television scholars have shown, from their onset both the medium of television and the genre of soap operas were gendered as feminine (Corner 1999; McCarthy 2010; Murray 2005; Newcomb 2006; Spigel 1992). In post–World War II United States, television executives and commercial advertisers deployed daytime soap operas as a means of interpellating a new suburban American family by targeting housewives. As the name suggests, soap companies, along with other industries aimed at constructing proper notions of womanhood via the new technology of television, sponsored and created soap operas with the broader goals of selling soap, kitchen appliances, and other modern household products to the nuclear family.

Additionally, during this time, a growing credit industry enabled most Americans to buy television sets they could not otherwise afford. As opposed to theater or concert performances, which were available only to the elites of society, television began to reach the masses and thus became known as "the Poor Man's Theater" (Boddy 1992). The combination of being gendered as feminine along with its low-class status is what led to an overall devaluing of both the genre and the medium in the West. In fact, in her famous study of the popular primetime television soap opera *Dallas*, Ien Ang (1985) discovered that most of the fans she interviewed, recognizing the lowly status of the genre, made excuses about why they enjoyed watching the program. This was also the case with fans of Egyptian and Indian soap operas (Abu-Lughod 2004; Mankekar 1999).

However, this is not the case in Afghanistan. When RTA first started broadcasting a television signal in 1977, most households could not afford television sets. Owning a television set and watching TV was elusive, a sought-after activity that was a sign of high status and wealth. For example, my middle-class Afghan family did not own a set; we would gather with the rest of the extended family at my grandparents' house to watch the nightly programs. Even though the bar for television ownership is not quite as high today, it is still difficult for the average Afghan family not employed by foreign organizations to acquire a television set. Therefore it continues to be a status symbol.

Additionally, the soap operas are aired in the evenings at 7:00 PM and 9:00 PM and target entire households. This is the prime time for broadcasting for somewhat different reasons than in the West. Due to the precarious present-day situation in Afghanistan, in the evenings the majority of people stay indoors and consume media at home. The evenings are also the time when electricity is most consistent.

Since there is no history of stigmatization, the storylines and subject matter of the Indian serials, though still pertaining to domestic issues, are considered worthy entertainment to be enjoyed by both men and women. The fan base of these serials cuts across societal lines. According to one source, a high-ranking judge and a number of prominent warlords and politicians are even known to cut short their evening prayers in order to not miss the start of their favorite Indian soap operas.[12] So while some public figures may publicly dismiss Indian soap operas as a degenerative force, they might privately be fans. Dramatic epic stories of mythic and historic proportions often involving unrequited love between tragic heroes and heroines have a long history in the Afghan literary and poetic spheres, as well in Afghan oral traditions. So, in contrast to their Western counterparts, for the indigenous Afghan population, viewing television soap operas or dramatic serials is a valued and cherished pastime.

Far from Mere Entertainment:
Will Television Save or Destroy Afghanistan?

The popularity of such television programs and television's own intrinsic qualities are recognized by elites interested in Afghanistan. Feminist, cultural studies, and television scholars, particularly from the Birmingham Centre, have also located the medium as a site of cultural contestation (Hall 1997; Morley 1992). In light of television's technological aspects and Afghanistan's current social climate, the heated and volatile nature of debates surrounding television and television programming is not surprising. When a television station abruptly stopped airing another popular Indian soap opera, *Kumkum*, in the spring of 2008—most likely due to pressure from the government—the resulting uproar and clamor could be heard both in online forums and on the streets as fans demanded answers. The show's diasporic fan base (who watch it on satellite television) took to the internet to voice their anger, while the Afghan community held protests outside of the Ariana Television Network headquarters in Kabul.

It is clear, then, that in an increasingly competitive television mediascape, one way to ensure a share of the audience market (and therefore advertising revenue) is through airing Indian dramatic serials. For owners of private television stations, it is a matter of understanding the consumption patterns and tastes of their fellow countrypeople and then delivering programming that appeals to those tastes. For instance, after several years of intense fighting with religious authorities, Tolo TV and ATN, launched in 2004 and 2005 respectively, began self-censoring the content of their Indian soap operas by a combination of blurring, fading, and reediting any "inappropriately" exposed parts of women's bodies and also Hindu religious idols. In order to compete with these popular television stations, Emroz TV, a new entrant on the scene in 2008, took the bold risk of showing Indian serials unedited. The manager of the station, Fahim Kohdamani, was subsequently arrested in March 2009 and imprisoned for two months.[13]

Soon after, in early May 2008, the Afghan government issued a decree completely banning the televising of Indian serials. Many television stations complied, but Tolo TV and ATN refused again, on the grounds that the vague media laws do not give the government the power to ban entire programs but only small portions, which can be altered or removed. Media owners are currently challenging the legality of government censorship. In the process, media laws are being defined in Afghan courts. In the case of broadcast television, the fight is being led by ATN and Tolo TV. Thus, what seems like an act of acquiescing to the religious censors on the part of Tolo and ATN—reediting Indian serials—is in fact an act of defiance.

These kinds of battles over television are not unique to Afghanistan. Media ethnographers have begun to explore how satellite television is rapidly transforming the mediascape in the Gulf countries from Syria to Iraq. They have demonstrated how the continual attempts by religious authorities in Arab countries to block some programming and commission others confirm that television drama is far from mere entertainment (Abu-Lughod 2004; Salamandra 2008; Stanley 2012).

Endogenous Cultural Imperialism

A major grievance that religious groups hold against Indian soap operas is that they are "Hinduizing" Afghan culture and therefore tainting what is imagined as a pure Islamic Afghan culture. Since the Indian dramatic serials address issues such as adultery, divorce, and other domestic matters, the faith-based groups have also charged the programs with "immorality." They have voiced fears that Afghan women and youth are particularly susceptible to emulating the "improper" lifestyles and customs of South Asians.

This type of criticism assumes that certain types of audiences do not possess the media savvy and intelligence to have more complicated readings and therefore are easily duped and swayed. This harkens back to early communication theory, coming from the Frankfurt School and World War I propaganda studies (Horkheimer and Adorno [1944] 2002) and their American colleagues (Lippmann 1925; Lasswell 1927; McLuhan 1962). These studies imagined the media as a weapon in the arsenal of fascism, controlling people's thoughts, behaviors, and actions to be amenable to the suggestions of media producers or societal elites. This simplistic model, which posits an all-powerful media injecting a passive population with messages, has since been complicated by reception and audience research, which has shown that audiences can ward off, appropriate, and reinterpret media messages (Ang 1985; Fiske 1988; Hall 1997; Katz and Lazarsfeld 2005; Morley 1992).

Additionally, by suggesting a pure homogeneous culture, this type of criticism does not take into account Afghanistan's complex media history and shifting consumption and production patterns. From its formative days, Afghanistan's media landscape has been influenced by its powerful neighbors—Iran, India, and, to a lesser extent, the Soviet Union/Russia—and also dominated by their exported cultural products. This was a result of both geographic proximity and cultural affinity. Early Afghan filmmakers, musicians, and other media makers were often trained abroad in one of these neighboring countries for decades. Additionally, Iranians and Afghans share dialects—Farsi and Dari respectively—of the same language, Persian.

During the Soviet occupation, many Afghans sought refuge in Pakistan due to Iran's relatively restrictive immigration policies. According to most statistics, the numbers are two to one, with approximately 3 million Afghans escaping to Pakistan and 1.5 million Afghans taking refuge in Iran. During their decade-long exile, a relatively large part of the Afghan population became fluent in either Urdu or Hindi. In fact, most Afghans can understand the imported Indian dramatic serials without the common overdubbing in Dari. As a result of the immigration patterns, in which more than half of the Afghan population was exiled during the war, the popularity of Indian media is at an all-time high, while the influence of Iranian media is not as substantial.

This brief history illustrates how Indian culture has been a part of Afghan culture for a long time. With the ever-expanding reach of new technologies, globalization theory reminds us that cultures are never insular, impermeable, and static but rather always in flux (Appadurai 1996a; Ginsburg, Abu-Lughod, and Larkin 2002). Media technologies cross borders just like technologies of violence. Despite its reputation—propagated by British and Russian/Soviet colonial mythologies—as a hostile and impenetrable country, and despite its harsh and mountainous geography, Afghanistan is no more impervious to cultural influences than any other country. Yet, this is not to say that the broader charges of cultural imperialism are completely misplaced, as I discuss in the conclusion.

Performances of Non-performativity
and Practices of Unlooking

Despite their cultural exchange, Afghan audiences are quick to draw distinctions between Afghan and Indian forms of cultural expression. Even the most avid fans of Indian serials make very specific delineations between "their culture" and "our culture," thereby Othering their favorite shows as foreign.

They often ground their arguments in the second and third commandments—thou shalt have no other gods and no graven images or likenesses—and Islam's general iconoclastic stance against the representation of the human form (Armbrust 2000; W. Mitchell 2006). In addition, Islamic ways of looking are marked by lowering or averting one's gaze to avoid direct eye contact with another individual or avoid traversing their body with one's own eyes. Such practices, what I have elsewhere called "unlooking" (Osman 2011), are signs of respect and deference because the act of looking directly at the human form or making eye contact, especially if there is the possibility of being excited or pleased, is considered lecherous and dirty. Eyes, as the portals of pleasure, can suggest, project, or solicit pleasure from another human body. As such, eyes and human figures must be controlled and restrained. In traditional Islamic art and architecture, the representation of the human form is strictly prohibited (the third commandment). Similarly, Islamic forms of performance and self-expression can best be described as the performance of non-performativity and unexpression, the exception being the Sufi order (Osman 2005, 2011).

Therefore, in reference to the Indian dramatic serials, "music and dancing," "bright colorful clothes," "ornate accessories," and "lighting of candles," among other expressions of "decadence," are understood as "Hindu forms of worshiping" and signs of "being Hindu not Muslim." Such characterizations of Hindu expressions of devotion and how they permeate Hindu cultural practices actually echo the theological concept of *darshan*, which literally means "seeing" in Hindi but more broadly describes the holistic and embodied experience of engaging with deities. Scholars of Indian culture have illustrated how images and particularly practices of visuality more generally do in fact form an integral part of Hindu modes of being (Eck 1998; Pinney 2004; Rajagopal 2001).

In addition to grounding their difference in Islamic practices, Afghans also readily identify themselves as *sangeen* in contrast to their perceived notions of Hinduness. *Sangeen* is a Persian word that literally means "heavy." It is rooted in the word for rock or stone, *sang*. Connotatively, it is an adjective used to describe qualities of being reserved, rational, unemotional, and stoic. To be described as *sangeen*, and thus be associated with its virtues, is something that Afghans of all genders aspire to. To achieve *sangeen*-ness entails an entire way of being and behaving, complete with its own color schemes and modes of dressing.

Therefore, it is surprising that Afghan audiences reacted relatively unfavorably to the 2008 broadcasting of *Nargess* (Narcissus), an Iranian dramatic serial, which by all standards is imbued with *sangeen*-ness: both aesthetically, in terms of the settings, and in the attributes of the protagonist, Nargess. The common complaint was verbalized as "dill em tang may showed," which literally means, "It suffocates my heart." But it was more broadly interpreted as lackluster, tedious, dull, and dreary. One woman, referring to the *taareek* or dark color schemes of the show, explained, "We have color television but it might as well be a black-and-white set for *Nargess*."[14] Other people made similar comments about the dark chadors and robes of the women and men in the show. In this respect, the concepts of *sangeen* and *darshan* are useful theoretical tools for interpreting the ways in which people perceive their own and other cultures. But they cannot be applied as absolute signifiers of either Muslim or Hindu culture. As my case studies illustrate, in actual practice, no experience can adequately fulfill the hard-to-achieve modes of being completely *sangeen* or in a full state of *darshan*, nor can cultures be reduced to one set of homogenizing conditions.

No wonder, then, that many Afghan television viewers admitted their preference for Indian dramatic serials over the recent Iranian imports, while *simultaneously* proclaiming their Afghan *sangeen*-ness. "What can I say; most people like *cheezahi rangeen* [colorful things] and *rangahiya roshan* [bright colors]," was the comment made to me by one viewer. Many women, especially Kabuli women, associated the aesthetics of "bright and colorful" and unveiled women of Indian soaps with *azadi* or freedom/liberation. When asked why the Iranian soaps felt less liberatory, many could cite only their visual differences. In fact, textual analysis reveals that the heroines in the Iranian dramatic serials tend to have more agency and to be more active in the domestic and public sphere than their Indian counterparts. "Yes, it's true," one woman said to me, "the women drive and work outside of the home in *Nargess*, but I still think *Zora* [an Indian import] is more free."[15] Some Afghan women I spoke to did express a strong preference for the Iranian dramatic serials and could not understand the popularity of the Indian ones. These women had grown up in Iran and felt more versed in Iranian culture, which they genuinely believed was closer to Afghan culture than Indian culture.

Liberatory or Regressive? Weak Heroines
and Strong Villainesses

Albeit for entirely different reasons than the religious critics', some women also expressed—adamantly—that they considered Indian shows to be regressive and as such bad role models for Afghan women. They mentioned popular Indian soap operas, such as *Heena, Banoo Main Teri Dulhann* (I will become your bride), and *Ek Pyara Sa Bandhan* (A lovely bond), known more commonly as *Kumkum*, the name of the female protagonist, represented women in subservient and subordinate positions. They objected to the "weak personalities" and "characters" of the protagonists: Heena, Vidya (from *Banoo Main Teri Dulhann*), Tulsi (from *Kyunki Saas Bhi Kabhi Bahu Thi*, meaning "Because Mother-in-Law was Once a Daughter-in-Law"), Prerna (from *Kasautii Zindagii Kay*, meaning "The Trials of Life"), and Kumkum (from *Ek Pyara Sa Bandhan*). One woman stated, "I cannot believe how much abuse and torture they take from their in-laws," while another commented, "All they do is cry and cry and cry . . . such crybabies."[16] According to these women, most of whom demanded that the shows be canceled, the only "strong" and "intelligent" women in the shows were villainous gun-toting sisters-in-law, mothers-in-law, and aunts-in-law who were perpetually strategizing ways to torment or sometimes kill the new brides in order to gain access to property and wealth bestowed upon their male relatives.

Feminist media scholars have challenged the common perception that women's genres have a "dumbing down" effect on society. Reception studies on romance novels, women's magazines, romantic comedies, and soap operas have revealed that these genres, with their focus on women's issues, can also offer a subversive space where women not only can escape but also can challenge the male gaze and other forms of patriarchal social order and control (Das 1995; Mankekar 1999; Radway 1991). I would argue that this is the case in Afghanistan as well. Despite the critical comments mentioned above, the responses from female viewers were positive overall. Contrary to the women who found the villainesses to be regressive role models, other women viewers found them empowering. Although it is difficult to understand the contradiction in self-(dis)identifications and (dis)tastes among Afghan audiences, with regard to Iranian and Indian soap operas, the liberatory aspects of soap operas for female viewers are strikingly clear.

What Afghan Women Want

For many Afghan women across ethnic lines, they are tired of being not only victimized but also represented as victims, in constant need of saving. In their clamoring for women's rights, producers sometimes unwittingly reproduce the victim narratives that Afghan women are desperately trying to shed. Afghan producers are well intentioned in trying to highlight, via PICs, Afghan soap operas, and other programs that focus on the plight of Afghan women, those regressive cultural practices and other forms of abuse and violence that Afghan women are subjected to. Yet, because these expository and didactic productions sometimes lack creativity in offering alternatives, Afghan women feel boxed in. For Afghan women who face victimization on a daily basis, steeped in a misogynist world of warlordism and Islamism, when afforded the opportunity and privilege of consuming media, they want a media world that is the opposite of their brutal reality. They want a world where they are the heroes and saviors, a world where they have the power to save not only themselves but also the nation.

In this respect, I witnessed that media forms outside of television were more effective in serving the needs of Afghan women audiences. For example, the Afghan women's film industry is producing very popular films that show the full range of women's agency. Whereas the television industry is almost entirely male-run—there is only one female television station owner and few women in positions of power—the film industry is enabling an entirely new generation of female film directors and producers. While some women have made art house films that have gained attention in international venues through nongovernmental organizations such as the French-funded film training program Ateliers Varan, the popular films I am referring to are produced by local DIY production houses with meager resources. Their films are considered too low-budget and poorly conceived to be shown internationally or even on Afghan television stations. Afghan television stations also view them as competition, so they are reluctant to give them any airtime. Yet, they generate high revenues in bazaar media shops and stalls in the form of VCDs, or video compact discs, a cheaper version of DVDs.

Saba Sahar, an actress, director, and police officer, has created her own film franchise, Saba Films.[17] She has a wide-reaching market of female and male fans alike. In her films, she and a cast of female sidekicks are the protagonists and heroes who save Afghanistan from fictional and historic foreign invaders and domestic warlords. She has portrayed a powerful range of characters: a general, a police sergeant, even a traditional horseback-riding woman warrior.

PHOTO 6.5. Still from *Banoo Main Teri Dulhann*, featuring the popular gun-toting antagonist Sindoora, played by Kamya Panjabi, who plots against her sister-in-law and brother, the protagonist couple Vidya and Sagar.

PHOTO 6.6. Tulsi from *Kyunki Saas Bhi Kabhi Bahu Thi* fighting back.

PHOTO 6.7. Sindoora during one of the multiple times she kills her sister-in-law Vidya and her brother, who subsequently are reincarnated and come back to life in new seasons.

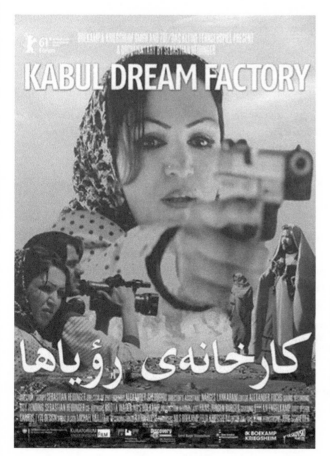

PHOTO 6.8. The poster for the documentary film *Kabul Dream Factory*, which features the trials and tribulations of Afghan filmmaker and police officer Saba Sahar, directed and produced by Sebastian Heidinger.

Additionally, there is a thriving culture of theater in the homosocial worlds of Afghanistan. Having had the opportunity to be invited to the all-women saloons of Kabul and in communal villages, I have learned that there is a long history and thriving culture of women's theater, where the producers, actors, and audiences are all women. They exist outside of the male gaze in upper-, middle-, and low-class urban and provincial settings. The productions, regardless of the resources, ranging from those with the means to have sets, costumes, and props to those in villages that did not even have running water or electricity, were all united in their incredibly well-conceived, well-written, and well-acted productions. Women pass down their craft, stories, and techniques from generation to generation, thereby keeping the culture alive as a way of overcoming oppressive situations. Away from patriarchal control, these theatrical worlds provide women with the freedom to subvert gender roles, experiment with their sexuality, cross-dress, and use satire and comedy to the delight and amusement of audiences.

Although not national in the way that television is, these other media forms provide women on both the production and the reception sides with more agency in expanding their gender roles, representation, and expression.

Turkish and Iranian Secular Muslim Productions: A Realm of Redemption and Peace

Different types of Turkish dramatic serials are also popular in Afghanistan. There are the archetypical varieties of the genre such as Zahra, Paiman, and Quesay Zendagi Maa (the story of our lives), which like their Indian counterparts represent domestic dramas and relationships between people. However another type of drama, which can be best described as secular Muslim science fiction, are also immensely popular. In Turkish serials such as *Beşinci Boyut* and *Sırlar Dünyası*—which air every evening before Indian soap operas on ATN and Tolo TV—we see families and communities torn apart by greed, poverty, drugs, adultery, and other human trials and tribulations. The protagonists are genuinely good, caring, and innocent people who are forced into difficult situations, which the antagonists try to manipulate in order to lead them astray from the righteous path. The serials usually employ the same casts. For example, a particular actress is typecast for the "older woman" role in several serials. However, the stories are not continuous, and each night a different story explores a different issue.

In these stories, mysteriously omniscient hosts watch the dramas unfold from a distance. Supernaturally, they appear and disappear from the scenes. At other times, we see them ruminating in a deck-like structure in the sky. From the trellis and open arches of the structure, beautiful white clouds appear all around. When they interject, be it from their heavenly retreat or in between scenes, they address the camera and the audience directly. Sometimes they provide expository information that drives the narratives, but usually their commentary is more philosophical and spiritual in nature. Although the references are clearly Islamic, in that the older generation of women and men dress traditionally, wear headscarves, and have prayer beads, the hosts' commentary does not have any overtly Islamic overtones. With their calming and peaceful demeanor, they speak about higher powers, being rewarded in the afterlife, and the difference between right and wrong—all the while only occasionally mentioning heaven or hell, punishment for those who are compelled to do terrible things that hurt others, or even God. They have compassion and empathy for all the characters, even the wicked ones. When the stories reach their climax, the hosts materialize and actually engage in the action to save the protagonists.

In one episode of *Beşinci Boyut*, a deadbeat dad with an embezzlement problem returns to his wife and young daughter and promises he has changed. The wife reluctantly takes him back, even though she is falling in love with her boss, a single dad with a young son. Throughout the episode we see how the father is using his family as a ploy to trick people into buying condos in a nonexistent real estate venture. After a while, the wife slowly discovers the truth and prepares to leave her husband. At the end of the episode, the husband is on the run holding a briefcase of money in one hand and the hand of his daughter, whom he has kidnapped, in another. He slips down a mountain and is hanging precariously on a precipice. He must let go of either the briefcase or his daughter. Just as he drops his daughter, the two hosts of the show arrive with the child's mother to catch her. They don't apprehend the father. They let him escape. It is enough that the mother has witnessed the events and the daughter is safe. The last scene is of the wife and her daughter horseback riding into the sunset with her boss and his son, while the hosts look on and smile.

I was curious why these *Twilight Zone* meets *Days of Our Lives*–type serials, with their subtle religious references, are so popular among Afghan audiences. The fact that they were Turkish was not an issue, perhaps because the Turks are Sunnis and there has been a long history of exchange and trust between Turks and Afghans. My interviews suggest that the overwhelming appeal of these shows is that they bring peace of mind, tranquility, and a spiritual order to a traumatized people whose moral universe has been shattered repeatedly and who desperately seek a semblance of a world where justice can supernaturally be enacted without more bloodshed or violence. "I wish they [the hosts] would visit Afghanistan. There's enough here for thousands of exciting episodes. But maybe our problems are beyond them. They would never be able to retire," said a mobile phone vendor.[18]

It is for the same reasons that the epic Iranian religious drama *Hazrat Yousof* (as translated in Dari, or *Yusuf Payambar* in Farsi), which tells the story of the prophet Joseph, has found a home on not one but three different Afghan television stations. One can thus watch the saga unfolding at different stages. This Islamic rendering of the Judeo-Christian religious tale differs a little from the original version from the Holy Book. It incorporates Persian literary accounts, which focus on the love and lust between Yousof and Zulaikha, the Potiphar's wife. Seen as a literary story, it is a well-told drama about the human condition. Love, loss, jealousy, betrayal, power, war, and redemption are its central themes. The morally reprehensible characters, namely Yousof's ten older brothers and Zulaikha—who initially betrays him—are not punished but redeemed through Yousof's generosity, forgiveness, and general compassion.

Afghan audiences find the episode in which Yousof is reunited with his father, who is sick and dying, to be quite moving and stirring. As Yaquob (Jacob), Yousof's father, is traveling in a caravan, they see each other across the desert and their eyes connect. In slow motion, Yaquob stumbles off of his camel and starts running with his arms spread toward his son, who is also running toward him. Yaquob falls, gets up, starts running, and then falls down again repeatedly, until they finally meet and embrace for a long time. Although the production value, sets, directing, and casting of *Hazrat Yousof* are incredibly high by any standard, this epic miniseries, like the religio-sci-fi Turkish dramatic serials, appears kitschy and too overt in its narrative conventions to expatriate and foreign viewers. For local Afghans, however, they are deeply resonant and meaningful, perhaps because the vast majority of Afghans have lost family members to war in a variety of ways, never being able to reunite.

Aside from recounting the emotive power of the reunion scene, male fans had a rather trivial complaint that was clearly disturbing to them, since it was brought to my attention on a few occasions. The issue was that Zulaikha, the Potiphar's wife and Yousof's love interest, was not beautiful enough. According to tradition, the prophet and Zulaikha are supposed to have "divine beauty." All the viewers, men and women, were in agreement that the actor Mustafa Zamani, who plays Yousof, met the mysterious standards of divine beauty; they were thoroughly enamored by his unearthly features and fine assets. Surprisingly, male viewers did not think this was true of the actress Katayoun Riahi, who plays Zulaikha. Contrary to their complaints about her age, historic or textual accuracy was not their main concern, since Zulaikha is supposed to be older than Yousof. I am sure that the producers of *Hazrat Yousof* did not intend for that to be one of the messages or readings. The miniseries also depicts the story from Genesis, in which Zulaikha, who cannot control her sexual desire for Yousof, attacks him and subsequently after her husband catches them, blames Yousof for the impropriety. This famous scene, which has been ubiquitously represented in Western art and literature, perpetuates the sexist trope of the sinful woman. Thus this classic monotheistic tale has all the melodramatic elements of television dramas.

Conclusion

Afghan audiences clearly have a desire for and capacity to contemplate spirituality and justice. At the same time, they need earthly distractions and entertainment. In war-torn conflict zones, the utility of gratification and pleasure that is derived from watching television cannot be underestimated or trivialized. Although producers did not readily admit this, programming and hence the media diet of Afghans consists of plenty of distracting and entertaining programs.

Programs that are deemed too religious are equated with repression; they are not very popular. In fact, if the programs I have mentioned thus far were not couched in some pleasurable narrative conventions, then they would be dismissed. This is not to say that Afghan audiences are not religious. Episodes of Quran burning by American troops set outraged people into riot mode for days. Likewise, most of the people I interviewed preferred the *azan,* or the call to prayers, to be broadcast on television, which the vast majority of television stations, including most of the religious ones, do not do. Yet the religious codes that guide them seem to be gentle and inclusive of other religions. For example, it was reported in newspapers that Afghans across the country were praying for Tulsi, of the Indian dramatic serial, to recover from her coma. To the delight of the public, she does recover. When her husband, Mir, died, people held funerals for him at ziarats, or Islamic holy places of worship, in provinces throughout Afghanistan. I would argue that religion equips Afghans with a semblance of understanding of their chaotic and confusing world. Most cosmopolitan Afghans might laugh off the ignorance of the masses, but many highly educated city dwellers were also rejoicing at Tulsi's recovery.

We cannot underestimate Afghan peoples' need for a higher spiritual order and justice, as well as for entertainment, political satire, and local news. As these popular programs aptly demonstrate, the two categories are not mutually exclusive. Through PICs, the news, and political satire, media makers uncover, investigate, and expose everything from cases of corruption and abuses of power to violence stemming from local and international warlords and government officials. However, the antidote to war and its atrocities is equal parts reflection and distraction and entertainment. With dramatic serials and reality television programs, Afghan media programmers are providing the avid and large viewership of these programs glimpses into the diverse lifestyles, cultures, and televisual representations of gender and sexuality practices of people from around the world. This opens up space crucial for private and public discussion around sensitive cultural issues.

In the conclusion, I synthesize the three types of cultural imperialism I have discussed thus far, with attention to the egregious hand of empire. It could be argued that by aggressively promoting and offering their own media products, programs, and formats at low or no cost, foreign countries are impeding the development of Afghanistan's own media industry, artistry, and media crafts. Additionally, we have seen examples of censorship, both from endogenous and exogenous forces, ranging from pressuring the government to ban programming to directly pressuring producers to do so. Yet the most dangerous form of imperialism, which we have only glimpsed thus far, is more coercive and double-dealing in its political machinations. With a focus through the prism of the media on war profiteering, extraction of wealth, and election engineering, I demonstrate that the imperial project and gaze is alive and well in Afghanistan.

Conclusion

The Future of Afghan Media, the Future of Afghanistan

THUS FAR I HAVE ARGUED televisual media in Afghanistan remains an institution of the public itself, operating to provide and intensify public discussion.[1] As Jürgen Habermas describes it, between the oppression of the state and the tyranny of commercial culture, the public can invoke the public sphere via mass media to express their own opinions in critical dialogue with one another (Calhoun 1992; Habermas [1962] 1991). In this way, the Afghan media is challenging oppressive forces and institutions by making them accountable to the tribunal of the people.

The development of television as a robust feature of the public sphere has been specifically important for contemporary Afghanistan. As a counterbalance to the government, warlords, and foreign interests in Afghanistan, the formation of a vibrant public sphere has the potential to underwrite conversations regarding democracy, national integration, and peace. After experiencing over four decades of war and its brutalities, a traumatized Afghan public has very high expectations of media and journalism in general, and of television in particular. Afghan media producers are delivering on and meeting those high demands. As we have seen thus far, with PICs, the news, and political satire and talk shows, media makers uncover, investigate, and expose everything from the corrupt, fraudulent, and violent activities of warlords and government officials to other cases of direct and indirect abuses of power that ruling elites inflict on innocent individuals and the larger public. With dramatic serials and reality television programs, Afghan media programmers are expanding the worldviews of people by providing them glimpses of diverse global lifestyles and cultures.

Unlike many of its neighbors, Afghanistan has the key factor in the equation for the creation of a public sphere: a free and diverse mass media. The model of development being deployed in Afghanistan is a multilateral development model, whereby resources and funding are dispersed from the international donor community, thereby making it more akin to the public interest model. There is a direct correlation between the amount and diversity of international resources funneled into the Afghan media sector and the diversity and plurality of media. The fact that the various forms of Afghan media are not unilaterally under the influence of one group or country is precisely why Afghanistan has not yet fallen down the slippery slope of commercialization or authoritarianism and its media world remains vibrant and viable, albeit fragile.

Furthermore, being under the gaze of international backers ensures that Afghan media institutions are more accountable to journalistic standards and freedom of speech. There are many international media watchdog and training organizations, including US government–affiliated ones, with genuine commitments to creating an independent and diverse public sphere in Afghanistan. In fact, many of the proponents of media independence in Afghanistan who train and support journalists' rights as well as monitor and lobby for the media more broadly are NGOs funded by the United States, despite continued suppression of media freedoms, journalists, and whistleblowers on the US home front.

In the competitive arena of an artificially inflated media market, for television broadcasters to appear to be beholden only to their own group or worse yet to foreign interests is akin to sociopolitical and economic suicide in the eyes of national advertisers and broad-based international donor campaigns that seek to reach wide audiences. They need to fill the most air space with the cheapest programs that reach the widest audiences in order to attract advertisers, donor money, or both. In the battle for establishing national and cultural legitimacy and authenticity, giving audiences what they want is as much a by-product of capitalism as it is of democracy. And being biased and propagandistic is not good for either. It just so happens that regulated capitalism, where competition is fair and new entrants are able to enter the media market, is mutually constitutive with democracy.

Yet since my initial fieldwork in 2004, three major issues that pose serious threats to the future of a free press and of Afghanistan more generally have become dire and compounded by other factors. In 2012 I identified these issues that could derail the development of the public sphere and media independence as (1) battles over gender and other identity signifiers, (2) the pervasiveness of violence, and (3) US government imperialism (Osman 2012, 2012/2013). In 2020, these issues have indeed become serious problems exacerbated by a number of new underlying factors. The US-led international community has substantially decreased aid to Afghanistan, including the media sector, instead ramping up military campaigns and expenditures via the US Army, NATO, and the Resolute Support Mission. This shift in focus and financial support from development to military approaches has had devastating consequences. With decreased international presence and attention, there are fewer oversight, training, and watchdog groups to protect people and media makers. This state of affairs has emboldened ruling elites, both within and outside of Afghanistan. With the power of militias and armed forces, intra- and extra-governmental forces have become more brazen and ruthless in exercising their power and cultural imperialism with brutality. Regimes of censorship and violence toward the media and media makers have skyrocketed. But before I delve into the details of the sharp increase in violence toward media makers and its enormous threat to the public sphere, it is important to look more carefully at the charges of cultural imperialism within Afghanistan.

Media Diversity versus Media Imperialism

As we have seen, elites in Afghanistan incite fears of cultural imperialism to curtail or ban foreign media imports. Islamists, warlords, and tribal elders pressure the Ministry of Information and Culture to ban foreign programming, particularly Indian, Latin American, and Western media products, without much success. The opponents of foreign media claim that the influx of imports is tainting a (believed to be) pure and monolithic indigenous culture.

The common concern among media activists and cultural critics is that distinctive heterogeneous local cultural ideas and practices are being erased, tainted, or diffused by the homogenizing force of Western capital expansion. Media studies scholars interested in transnational political economy (Bagdikian 2004; McChesney 2004; H. Schiller 1989, 1991) have also demonstrated how structural imbalances enable global media and its profits to flow disproportionately one way, in favor of Western nations. However, new media scholarship is also revealing that the tides of change are dissociating "global media" from the West and that new global players are emerging from non-Western countries. For example, Indian and Turkish media exports are finding avid consumers all over the world (Ganti 2004; Larkin 2008; Osman 2011; Yesil 2015).

Whereas some Central Asian countries like Kazakhstan have placed strict limits on foreign content in order to promote a re-indigenization process, post-independence, Afghanistan's television stations, post-9/11, are awash in foreign media from across the globe. As foreign countries aggressively promote and offer their own media products, programs, and formats at low or no cost, the argument can be made that they are impeding the development of Afghanistan's own media industry, artistry, and media-crafts. As a result of years of war and instability, Afghan television producers cannot compete with the established media industries of India, Iran, Turkey, or the United States. Due to dispossession and displacement as well the destruction of their cultural institutions and the targeted killing of Afghan media stars, personalities, and producers during the different wars, the Afghan media industry has lost tremendous talent and a well-honed tradition of production aesthetics and styles. Therefore, questions about cultural vulnerability, cultural imperialism, the role of empire, and civil unrest and more wars are legitimate and take on a new urgency in a place and space that continues to be at the crossroads of imperial ambitions, where ethnic violence remains pervasive and the possibilities of redefining national identity and allegiances are wide open.

However, opponents of foreign media often use the rhetoric of cultural imperialism to promote, impose, and maintain their own ideologies and autocratic rule. In the case of Islamists in Afghanistan, for example, who are staunchly opposed to the broadcasting of popular dramatic serials from India, Turkey, and Iran, this is a direct attempt at erasing Afghanistan's diverse cultural history and varied experiences with Islam and imposing their own draconian brand. They worry about the cultural influences of Hinduism, secular Sunni Islam, and Shiite Islam. As we have seen, the large fan base of these imports finds these dramatic serials valuable and liberating in many ways, particular in generating debates over domestic and gender issues both at home and publicly.

People I spoke to were appreciative and desiring of diverse media from around the world, both for entertainment and news purposes. Furthermore, while it is true that the postwar fledgling media industry of Afghanistan is no match for the established powerhouse media industries of some of its neighbors or the behemoth global media of the United States, original Afghan programs are not eclipsed and overshadowed. As we have seen, despite the high output and high production value of foreign programming, for Afghan viewers, the quality of local content is judged by its *Afghaniyat* or "Afghan-ness." Afghan audiences across different segments of society respond favorably to low-budget productions such as original news and political satire programs, music videos, game shows, and call-in shows that speak to their own world of cultural knowledge. They can share in the poems, songs, inside jokes, and other national references of these Afghan-made shows. My research shows that people want both foreign and homegrown media.

Furthermore cross-cultural media ethnographies and textual analysis reveal there is not a simple causal relationship between the presence of foreign media and ideological belief systems (Ginsburg, Abu-Lughod, and Larkin 2002; Skuse, Gillespie, and Power 2011; Tomlinson 1995). In other words, there is not a direct correlation between consuming foreign programming and indoctrination in its dominant messages (Hall 1997, 2006). Depending on their ideological perspective and other predispositions, viewers engage with a program differently. Most people have the ability to find various aspects of foreign media useful and enjoyable and still think critically about the impact of foreign involvement and policies. Of course, foreign media has some influence as people become more familiar with the language and culture of the sponsoring countries, but that does not affect most people's ability to be discerning. It is safe to say that foreign programming is not turning Afghans into rabid and mindless followers of foreign countries.

This does not mean that unrestricted foreign media is benign. Rather, the real dangers lie in political machinations and manipulation. For the imperial powers of the United States and Russia, their aid and patronage are contingent on promoting and protecting their vested geopolitical interests in the region, including their military dominance and the growth of their own economies. While the US government uses the benevolent rhetoric of supporting democratic sensibilities and "winning hearts and minds," the reality is far more complicated. Indeed, as I have described, some of its development projects have yielded positive results, supporting the media, human rights, and other rebuilding projects. However, often foreign governments mandate the return of a large percentage of the allocated moneys back to the home countries, as well as extraction of wealth through mining natural resources from oil to metals and gems. As anthropologists have demonstrated, "gifts" never come without debts (Mauss 1954). Applying this to the Eurasian context, Bruce Grant has shown how the power dynamics between Russia and its satellite Caucasus countries reflect imperialism and social control but are couched under the banner of giving and altruism (2009). The US and Russian governments wield their political control over the media in order to manage public opinion and lay the groundwork for maintaining and expanding their economic and political dominance. The egregiousness of the hand of empire comes into sharp focus in election engineering and war profiteering.

The post-9/11 presidential elections in Afghanistan present an illuminating comparative case study with which to understand how local elites and the US government exert their economic, political, and cultural dominance and to what extent local media producers are able or unable to negotiate, resist, or contest their hegemony. Without a doubt, as confirmed by numerous international bodies, the post-9/11 elections in Afghanistan have been marked by fraud. For the former rival Cold War superpowers, the United States and Russia, managing and controlling elections in order to guarantee compliant proxy presidents is central to maintaining and aggrandizing their power in the region. While Russia lost most of its influence in Afghanistan because of its invasion and ten-year occupation of Afghanistan, until recently the US government enjoyed a level of goodwill from Afghan people. US support for Afghan presidential candidates has been contingent on their support for the US-led war, the longest in US history, and continued maintenance and expansion of American military bases and prisons. Likewise, during Tajikistan's last elections, despite Emomali Rahmon's stronghold on power, he was able to secure Russia's backing only after his appointed Parliament approved the Russian bases remaining operational till 2030 (Adinabay 2013).

However, during the 2009, 2014, and 2019 Afghan presidential elections, as I have discussed, the Afghan broadcast media very openly critiqued foreign interference as well as the top presidential candidates. For example, many people in the media alleged that Hamid Karzai stopped being the US favorite in the 2009 elections over his refusal to sign the Bilateral Security Agreement that would grant US officials and soldiers full immunity in Afghan and international courts for crimes committed on bases, in prisons, and in other facilities in Afghanistan. It is no secret that the United States has its favorites and uses various mechanisms to influence the results (Rohde and Gall 2004). Likewise, there was widespread uproar on the streets and in the media when a series of pre-election surveys sponsored by the US embassy in Kabul were deemed as having manipulated the results of the first round of voting in the 2014 election (Osman 2014b).

Afghan television stations that are predominantly funded by the US government are also pressured not to air footage of violence perpetuated by the US military on their news programs, namely civilian casualties. In the United States, due to the stratified nature of capitalism, news-based televisual violence is censored by the overlapping interests of the advertising industry, television executives, and the government. However, despite the restraints, Afghan television producers manage to show a variety of newsreel violence, and a lot of it. As media scholars have shown, seasoned anti-war activists know, and government

PHOTO C.1. On April 30, 2018, an ISIS suicide bomber, disguised as a journalist, detonated himself in Kabul, killing nine media makers: two people from 1TV, two from Mashal TV, one from Tolo TV, three from Radio Free Europe/Radio Liberty, known as Radio Azadi in Afghanistan, and one from Agence France-Presse. Among the dead and wounded, in the foreground an Al Jazeera cameraman calls for help, while in the background a passerby helps a journalist from Radio Azadi up. Photo credit: Omar Sobhani for Reuters.

PHOTO C.2. These are the nine Afghan media makers killed in the April 30, 2018, suicide attack plus BBC reporter Ahmad Shah, who was killed in a separate attack in Khost on that day.

officials have learned, showing the realities of war and war-related violence is a very effective means of coalescing public opinion against war and, in the Afghan case, warlordism, even if such images do not achieve peace.

The Future of Afghan Media, the Future of Afghanistan

Thus far we have seen examples of censorship and political machinations and manipulation, both from external and internal forces, ranging from pressuring the government to ban certain programming and content to directly pressuring producers to do so. Yet with the recent acceleration of war, warlordism, and imperialism, which has given national and foreign ruling power elites more impunity than ever, the regimes of censorship have taken more violent forms. The extent and extremity of violence against media makers—some of whom I came to know during my research in Afghanistan—was one of the surprising findings of my fieldwork. The Ministry of Information and Culture, which oversees television broadcasting, has been repeatedly targeted by different groups. Almost every media institution I visited has a showcase of "media martyrs" displayed prominently in either its lobby or outside area. For women working on-screen, visibility itself can be deadly. The semiotics of televisual representation have become highly volatile. As we have seen, a number of Afghan women, ranging from news broadcasters to presenters, have been victims of alleged "honor killings." Afghan media producers, writers, editors, reporters, engineers, and fixers have been kidnapped, attacked, wounded, and killed by forces ranging from the Taliban and other extremists to agents of surrounding countries and international military units.

High-level media personnel and wealthy media owners who are often prominent public figures, such as politicians, warlord or drug lords, religious leaders, or businessmen, hire bodyguards and live in gated mansions. They also have the resources to leave the country and often have a secondary foreign residence as well. Low-level television personalities and reporters, on the other hand, cannot afford the same privileges or protections. Thus they are subjected to threats, physical attacks, and death for providing people with programming they want to watch and that gives them a platform to raise their voices. Hence it is the mid- and low-level media professionals who bear the ultimate burden and sacrifice for the emergence and quick expansion of a public sphere in Afghanistan—and not the owners of the television stations they work for nor the foreign governments that are the patrons of the stations. Caught between warring ideologies, ranging from Islamist to commercial to "developmentalist," the low socioeconomic status of Afghan media personalities and journalists leaves them vulnerable to abuse and death, despite their high media profiles.

Just like most Afghans, media makers are not strangers to threats and violence; yet by virtue of their profession Afghan media makers—the good ones at least—fall directly in the crosshairs of dangerous foreign and domestic forces on a regular basis. In the examples previously mentioned, Najiba Ayubi, the managing director of the Killid Group, who produced the 125-episode series on war crimes and war criminals, was repeatedly visited and threatened by a group of *zoor awarah*. Sanjar Sohail, the director of political affairs and news programming at Saba TV and its corresponding newspaper *Hashte Subh*, came under attack by the Shura-i Ulama in June 2011 with threats of heavy fines and closure for reporting on the findings of the Afghan Independent Human Rights Commission (AIHRC). Subsequently in 2012, after a series of battles with the commission, Hamid Karzai, often extolled for enabling free speech in Afghanistan, fired three of its top commissioners, including Nader Nadery, the chief investigator on the human rights abuses report, and appointed new ones, to international dismay and outrage.

Not surprisingly, across Afghanistan AIHRC's offices and vehicles have also been the target of attacks by unknown groups who have not taken responsibility. Thus far they have lost nine of their human rights workers including a commissioner, donor coordinator, receptionist, and driver. Cases of *zoor awarah* thugs and their militias, inside and outside the government, who threaten or beat up media makers or destroy equipment, are all too common. Others in the media industry, as we have seen in the cases of alleged honor killings, journalists, and fixers, have paid with their lives.

These are some of the high-profile cases of attacks and murders of media makers, but there are many others that go virtually unnoticed. Reporters Without Borders, the Committee to Protect Journalists, and Nai, an Afghan-based journalist watchdog group supported by Internews/USAID, have been documenting rising statistics in acts of violence and murders perpetuated against media makers, including news anchors, journalists, singers, and actors. In the Reporters Without Borders' 2016 list of deadliest countries, Afghanistan ranks number two, with war-torn Syria leading in first place and cartel-ridden Mexico trailing in the number three spot. In the Reporters Without Borders' 2018 roundup of deadliest countries for journalists, Afghanistan ranked number one. Afghanistan has also consistently made it on the Committee to Protect Journalists' Global Impunity Index of countries with the most unresolved cases of journalists murdered, including the 2020 index. Since 2001, Nai's extensive online data mapping project has collected evidence of 742 incidents of violence

Number of Incidents of Violence Against Journalists

Afghanistan, 2001-2019

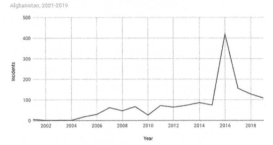

Violence Against Journalists by Incident Type

Afghanistan, 2001-2019

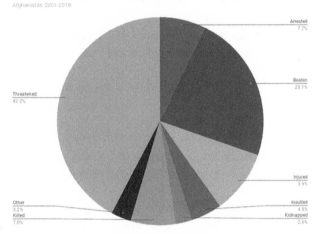

Incidents of Violence Against Journalists by Suspected Assailant

Afghanistan, 2001-2019

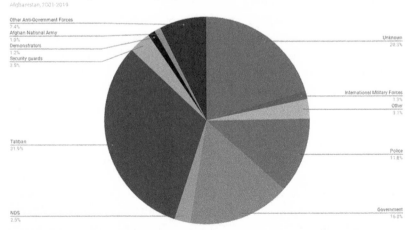

FIGURES C.1, C.2, C.3. These graph and pie charts that illustrate the statistics on violence against media makers were created for the author by Alexandra Budz, based on Nai's research, data, and reports. Nai is an Internews-supported, Afghan-based media watchdog organization; see http://nai.org.af/data/. Nai has recorded a total of 1,477 incidents of violence against journalists up until December 2019.

against journalists. Its "Top Five Organizations Experiencing Violence" are Tolo TV, Ariana TV, 1TV, Pajhwok Afghan News agency, and civic activists.[2]

As I have demonstrated throughout this study, without a doubt the combined power of public space, protest, and broadcast media is a very effective social tool for collective action in Afghanistan. Yet there are serious limits to both the media's self-advocacy and the public's strong and unwavering support. The media-related crimes and murders mentioned in this book are just a few of many. Yet in most such cases, no arrests are made and no one is prosecuted. *Zoor awarah* can continue to censor media makers with impunity and without fear of retribution. Broadcasting the incidents of violence and censorship against media personnel and the media writ large as well as the subsequent protests and producing investigative and expository programs are indeed generative in creating dialogue and raising awareness about media rights and the important role of a free media in a society, but they are clearly not enough. The *zoor awarah* of ruling elites and extremists like the Taliban and ISIS also destroy telecommunication satellite towers that transmit and broadcast signals for wireless telephones, radios, and televisions. The International Security Assistance Force, NATO, and American forces try to protect telecommunication towers from the Taliban by either placing them within the compound walls of their military bases or having soldiers guard them.

The big difference between the "iron horse" of the British Raj and the internationally funded media of today is that the public almost unanimously supports it. It is time to also protect the flesh and blood of the people who run the one institution with the most democratic potential to protect people and restore peace and justice in this dystopian country. Television channel owners, the Afghan government, and the international community must be held accountable for the safety of Afghan journalists, presenters, singers, and actors. This is not just a problem of personal safety; the future of independent media in Afghanistan depends on it. While the violence directed at media makers is productive in generating debates, it does not bode well for the future of Afghanistan if it continues to increase without any real legal enforcement measures.

Although the drop in the number of incidents of violence against journalists in figure C.1 looks hopeful, this is misleading because self-censorship is becoming more and more prevalent among media makers. Furthermore, with the overall decrease in international development aid to Afghanistan, including substantial decreases in the USAID allotment, which supports Internews, which in turn supports Nai, local media watchdog groups like Nai, which record and research such incidents, are struggling to remain open and maintain their activities to protect journalists. Thus the 2016 drop in the number of incidents of violence in figure C.1 also reflects this issue.

Over the last decade, censorship has taken a Foucauldian turn to self-discipline as a means of appeasing the hegemonic powers of a few power elites. An example of self-censorship is the case of Nilofar Habibi, who was an up-and-coming star on a local television station in the city of Herat. After being repeatedly threatened and then cut and stabbed twice by unknown assailants, Habibi was hospitalized. Subsequently she stopped working, putting an end to her promising journalism career and dreams. She said she is choosing her life over TV (Burch 2008). Not wanting to become another female media martyr like Shaima Rezayee, Shakiba Sanga Amaj, and Zakia Zaki before her, Habibi heeded the seriousness of the situation. Another example of self-censorship that was brought to my attention by media professionals and audiences was the case of Ahmad Saeedi, a high-profile journalist, television commentator, and Kabul University professor (Moslih 2016). He had built a reputation as an astute and fearless purveyor of the truth who did not engage in *quowm baazi* and always spoke truth to power on behalf of the public. He was particularly known for his criticism of the Karzai and Ghani administrations as well as the US War on Terror. In November 2015 a gunman shot him twice in the face; he barely survived this assassination attempt. Since then he has become much more timid and cautious with his television political commentary and analysis. People I spoke to continue to admire and respect him despite the noticeable shift in his commentary. They empathically understood why he does not report with the same vigor.

Once the venues for mass communication and mediation are controlled and censored by direct force or fear and intimidation, cultural debates cease to be in the service of the public. The question then is how much longer will the media remain a viable institution reflective of the peoples' voices, if the threat of internal and external *zoor awarah* or *zoor mundah* goes unchallenged and crimes committed against media professionals go unpunished? What will happen to the lively, though volatile, debates currently fostered by the media? Will the public service and developmental programs disappear entirely? What new models of media, if any, will emerge?

Finally, despite its risks and limitations, I want to consider the viability and necessity of a continued presence of development aid in Afghanistan as a counterbalance to the rise of insecurity and violence. If international aid and funding are contingent solely on military presence and expenditure, then this reinforces the common sentiment among Afghans that the Americans are in the country only for their own long-term strategic interests, war profiteering, and to exploit natural resources. Peace and democracy, including rebuilding the media and public sphere, then, are just rhetoric. Surprisingly, at least the media development model of a much grander national reconstruction project, long a source of critique from the Left, is proving successful in Afghanistan. This is contingent, of course, on the input and agency of local producers within media institutions, which are in turn contingent on those same producers being protected and valued. Of course, Afghanistan cannot indefinitely be dependent on foreign development aid. However, at this current juncture, when the United States has escalated its seemingly endless war in Afghanistan and the public perception of the US presence has shifted from a benevolent partner to an occupying force similar to the Soviet Union, it is crucial that the development arm remain.

What will happen if the international donor community, which has subsidized so much of the current mediascape, continues to decrease its funding of development projects in Afghanistan in favor of increased military spending? Charmaine Anderson, director of Internews Afghanistan, explained to me in 2017, "The true test for Afghanistan will depend on what happens once the international community pulls out and which media outlets will be able to survive independently."[3] She continued, "USAID's Office of Transition Initiatives' goal was to set up the media in Afghanistan as an emergency measure to facilitate transition from a war environment," but it ultimately wanted the media networks to be financially independent. That office trains media professionals not only in the ethics of independent reporting but also in how to establish relationships with the market and secure advertisers and other commercial sponsors. She predicted that "in this kind of artificially inflated media market, once the development aid decreases, attrition will naturally force only those with good business models to survive and the rest of the media venues will close."[4]

Currently Tolo TV and its numerous media outlets are the most commercially viable and self-sufficient. If Tolo TV becomes a model for the future of media in Afghanistan, will the remaining television stations, in order to survive and compete, follow suit and provide more programming that appeals to wide audiences? Will Tolo TV itself be forced to reduce its in-depth news coverage, political satire shows, and other public service programming? If a commercial model prevails, will less-entertaining programs that focus on elevating dialogue by providing much-needed information and education, such as *Challenge* and *One Plus One* (Negaah TV), *The Truth* (ATN), *The Mask*, *Target*, and *Special Talk* (1TV), *Question and Search* (Tolo TV), and *Enlighten* and *Open Jirga* (RTA), disappear and programs that appeal to base desires become the main attraction? Will the public sphere degenerate from in-depth coverage and debate to sensationalism and overt signifiers of progress, such as women without veils singing and dancing? If, on the other hand, religious and tribal warlords become the victors in the War on Terror, a return to a Taliban-like media blackout might occur, with their Sharia Radio once again the only media outlet.

With more suicide bombs, attacks, and killings of civilians by official forces and unofficial groups of Afghans and foreigners, cases of rampant corruption and blatant disregard of the law by Afghans and foreigners, and a litany of other disasters associated with failed, war-torn countries, everyone agrees that the situation in Afghanistan is becoming more dire. Yet the media is often extolled as the one "candle that burns in the darkness."[5] Of course, the media generally and television more specifically have also been described as "addictive like opium" and "uncontrollable like Satan" by their opponents.

In development circles and in political science terminology, Afghanistan is frequently described as a "failed," "broken," "fragmented," or "collapsed" nation (Ghani and Lockhart 2008; B. Rubin 2002), terms that have replaced the earlier classifications of "late state formation," "the rentier state," and "third world despotism" (B. Rubin 2002). Such terms continue the pervasive rhetoric of "failure" in Western discourse and thereby gloss over progressive historical and present-day achievements of nations like Afghanistan (Abu-Lughod 2006; Crews 2015; Gregorian [1969] 2013; Nawid 2000; Shahrani 2018; T. Mitchell 1991, 2002b). At the same time, it cannot be denied that after over four decades of guerrilla warfare and international militarization, Afghanistan has lost its previous state, civil, and governmental infrastructural capacities. Decades of ethnic, religious, and gender violence have left an almost indelible mark of disunity and fractured any sense of a cohesive society. Within this context, the media world of television in Afghanistan offers glimpses of possibility—of the alternative modernity that might in the end shape an Afghan national imaginary in which Afghan citizens feel they have a stake beyond their local loyalties and against foreigners. The media sector has given Afghans previews of other nations, cultures, and possibilities of being.

At this critical juncture in the tangled history of US-Afghan relations, when war and instability continue to plague the region, the US-led international community must renew its commitments to support nation-building and development projects, especially the media. Mending of the broken and collapsed nation that is Afghanistan—or, to use the official language, "nation-building" and "reconstruction"—can happen only via a mass venue for healing and purging, remembering and forgetting, debating and imagining. For that, there is no better—or worse—medium than television.

Ethnic Groups in Afghanistan according to Source

	Library of Congress[1]	World Factbook[2]	Williams[3]	Barfield[4]	Rubin[5]	Dupree[6]
Pashtun[7]	42%	42%	40%	40%	7 million	6.5 million (spells it Pushtun)
Tajik	27%	27%	25–30% (7–8 million)	30%	3.5 million	3.5 million
Hazara	9%	9%	8–10% (2–3 million)	15%	1.5 million	870,000
Uzbek	9%	9%	10–12%	10% (includes Turkmen)	1.3 million	1 million (spells it Uzbak)
Aimak	4%	4%	.5 million	.5 million (spells it Aimaq)	800,000 (spells it Aimaq)	800,000 (spells it Aimaq)
Turkman	3%	3%	.5–1 million	Included in Uzbek	300,000	125,000 (spells it Turkoman)
Baluch	2%	2%	100,000–200,000 (spells it Baluchis)	Included in other[8]	100,000 (spells it Baluch)	100,000 (spells it Baluch or Baluchi)
Other (does not include major groups)[9]	[10]	4%		3%		
Nooristani			100,000	Included in other	100,000	100,000
Pashai			.5 million	Included in other		

	Library of Congress[1]	World Factbook[2]	Williams[3]	Barfield[4]	Rubin[5]	Dupree[6]
Qizilbash			100,000 (spells it Kizil Bashis)	Included in other		Unsure[11]
Kyrgyz			2,000	Included in other		>1,000
Pamiris			Numbers unknown[12]	Included in other		>1,000
Farsiwan (Parsiwan or Parsiban)					600,000	600,000
Brahui					100,000	200,000
Jat Guji			Numbers unknown (spells it Jats)			Does not specify[13]
Arab			>100,000	Included in other		Does not specify
Kochis	1.5 million					
Jugis and Jats				Included in other		
Moghol						>1,000
Kohistani						Does not specify
Gujar						Does not specify
Hindu						20,000
Sikh						20,000
Jewish						>1,000
Total Population	32.7 million	30,419,928 (July 2012 est.)	Does not specify	Does not specify	Does not specify	Does not specify

1. *Country Profile: Afghanistan.* 2008. Library of Congress: Federal Research Division, August. http://lcweb2.loc.gov/frd/cs/profiles/Afghanistan.pdf.

2. "South Asia: Afghanistan." 2012. *The World Factbook.* CIA. Page last updated August 27, 2012. https://www.cia.gov/library/publications/the-world-factbook/geos/af.html.

3. Brian Glyn Williams. 2012. *Afghanistan Declassified: A Guide to America's Longest War.* Philadelphia: University of Pennsylvania Press. 16–46.

4. Thomas Barfield. 2010. *Afghanistan: A Cultural and Political History.* Princeton: Princeton University Press. 24–31.

5. Barnett R. Rubin. 2002. *The Fragmentation of Afghanistan: State Formation and Collapse in the International System.* 2nd ed. New Haven: Yale University Press. 26.

6. Louis Dupree. 1973. *Afghanistan.* Princeton: Princeton University Press. 59–64. Data was derived from *Kabul Times Annual* (1949) and author's own estimates of data (1949–68).

7. Bold = major ethnic groups (all sources include these groups).

8. Included in other = source confirmed the particular ethnic group but grouped it as "other" for population estimates.

9. Italics = two or more sources include these groups.

10. Blank cell = source did not specify the particular ethnic group.

11. Unsure = source was not certain about the population estimate for the particular ethnic group.

12. Numbers unknown = source claimed that no one knew population estimates for the particular ethnic group.

13. Does not specify = source included the ethnic group but did not specify any population estimate or did not specify the total population.

Television Stations and Affiliations in Afghanistan

Name of TV network	Full name of owner	Owner's background	Type of support	Location
1TV	Fahim Hashimy	Hazara minister of MCIT/ businessman	Commercial-based; international donor–based	Wazir Akbar Khan, Kabul
3 Sport	Shafiqullah Salim Poya	Tajik politician (ran for parliamentary election 2019)	Commercial-based	Karte 3, Kabul
7TV	Barry Salaam	Tajik businessman/ journalist/civil society activist	Commercial-based; international donor–based	Kolola Pushta, Kabul
Afghan	Mohammad Homayun Afghanzai Ahmed Shah Afghanzai	Pashtun businessman	Commercial-based; international donor–based	Macroyan, Kabul
Arezo/Arzo	Kamal Nabizada Atta Muhammad Nur	Tajik businessman Tajik leader/former governor of Balkh Province	Commercial-based; political-based	Mazar-i Sharif
Aria	Shukria Barakzai	Pashtun MP/journalist	Commercial-based; international donor–based	Wazir Akbar Khan, Kabul
Ariana Television Network	Ehsan Bayat	Bayat businessman/ owner of Afghan Wireless Communication Company	Commercial-based; international donor–based	Darulaman Street, Kabul
Ariana Television Network News	Ehsan Bayat	Bayat businessman/ owner of Afghan Wireless Communication Company	Commercial-based; international donor–based	Darulaman Street, Kabul
Ayna	Abdul Rashid Dostum	Uzbek leader/former communist general	Political-based; with support from Uzbekistan/Turkey	Charrahi Shirpoor, Kabul

Name of TV network	Full name of owner	Owner's background	Type of support	Location
Badakhshan	Ministry of Information and Culture	Multiethnic; State Broadcasting Company	Government-based; international donor-based	Faisabad, Badakhshan
Banu TV	Bashir Rustaqi	Tajik businessman	Commercial-based; international donor—based	Shar-1 Now, Kabul
Chekad	Ahmad Wali Nasiri	Tajik businessman	Commercial-based; international donor-based	Herat
Cheragh Medical	Dr. Cheragh Ali Cheragh	Bayat medical doctor	Cheragh Medical University and Hospital	Kabul
Danish	Najib Danish	Tajik journalist	Commercial-based; Danish Education Institute	Kabul, Panjsher, and Parwan
Dawat	Abdul Rasul Sayyaf Habib Rahman Sayyaf	Pashtun leaders	Religious-based; political-based; with support from Saudi Arabia	Khoshal Khan Mina, Karte Parwan, Kabul
Education	Ministry of Education	Multiethnic; Ministry of Education	Government-based; international donor-based	In front of Kabul University
Emroz	Najibullah Kabuli	Tajik former MP/businessman	Political-based; commercial-based	Khair Khana, Kabul
Esteqlal	Ahmad Ali Jibraeili	Hazara MP/religious leader	Political-based; religious-based	Herat
Hewad	Qayoom Karzai	Pashtun politician/businessman	Commercial-based	Kandahar
Jahan Noma	Muhammad Haroon Asadi	Tajik politician	Commercial-based	Karte 4, Kabul
Jawan	Sayed Habib Sadat	Hazara politician	Political-based; with support from Iran	Karte 4, Kabul
Kabul News	Abdul Karim Khurram	Pashtun former minister of culture and information	Political-based; commercial-based	Chaman Hozori, Kabul
Khurshid	General Amanullah Guzar	Tajik general/MP	Political-based; commercial-based	Kolola Pushta, Kabul
Kowsar	Sheikh Ayotullah Taghadosi	Hazara religious leader	Religious-based; political-based; with support from Iran	Dr. Mahdi Bridge, Old Ghazni Station, Pol-i Sorkh, Kabul
Lemar	Saad Mohseni	Tajik Afghan-Australian businessman	Commercial-based; international donor-based	Wazir Akbar Khan, Kabul
Maihan	Quanawizian brothers	Tajik businessmen	Commercial-based; international donor-based	Herat
Maiwand	Ali Akbar Zhowandai	Pashtun banker	Commercial-based; political-based	Mashreqi, Kabul
Mashal	Fathullah Babakarkhail	Pashtun businessman	Political-based; commercial-based	Kabul

Name of TV network	Full name of owner	Owner's background	Type of support	Location
Mehr	Abas Ebrahimzaada	Hazara businessman/MP	Commercial-based; political-based	Mazar-i Sharif
Melat	Mohammad Nasir	Tajik businessman	Commercial-based	Herat
Mitra	Atta Muhammad Nur	Tajik leader/former governor of Balkh Province	Commercial-based; political-based	Mazar-i Sharif
Negaah	Karim Khalili Alem Khalili	Hazara leader/former vice president Hazara leader	Commercial-based; political-based	Haji Nabi City, Kabul
Noor	Burhanuddin Rabbani Salahuddin Rabbani	Tajik leader/former minister of foreign affairs Tajik leader	Commercial-based; political-based	Parwan 3, Kabul
Noorin	Haji Mohammad Arif Noori	Tajik businessman	Commercial-based	Silo, 4 Street, Dehboori, Kabul
Pashto	Abdur Rahman Zahak	Pashtun businessman	Commercial-based	Kabul
Peshgam	Wahidullah Sangdel Nikmal Sangdel	Tajik politicians/businessmen	Commercial-based	Karte 3, Kabul
Radio Television Afghanistan	Ministry of Information and Culture	Multiethnic; State Broadcasting Company	Government-based; international donor-based	Headquarters in Wazir Akbar Khan, Kabul, with substations in all provinces
Rah-e-Farda	Haji Muhammad Mohaqiq	Hazara leader/MP	Religious-based; political-based; with support from Iran	Pol-i Sorkh, Karte 3/Karte 4, Kabul
Rahnaward	Abas Ebrahimzaada	Hazara businessman/MP	Commercial-based; political-based	Mazar-i Sharif
Saba	Cooperative	Multiethnic; media/civil society activists	Commercial-based; international donor-based	In front of Dawat University, Khoshhal Khan Mina, Karte 3, Kabul
Saqi	Tariq Nabi	Tajik-Pashtun chancellor of Herat University	Commercial-based; international donor-based	Herat
Sepehr	Dr. Najib Sepehr	Tajik businessman	Commercial-based; international donor-based	Dehboori, Kabul
Shamshad	Fazal Karim Fazal	Pashtun businessman	Commercial-based; international donor-based	Behind Chaman Hozoori, Macroyan, Kabul
Tamadon	Jawad Mohseni and Sheikh Asif Mohseni	Pashtun Shiite religious leaders	Religious-based; political-based; with support from Iran and Saudi Arabia	Darulaman Street, Karte 4, Kabul
Taraqi	Nasir Mojaddedi	Pashtun businessman	Commercial-based; political-based	Sultan Ghias Uddin Ghouri Rd, Herat, Afghanistan
Tolo	Saad Mohseni	Tajik Afghan-Australian businessman	Commercial-based; international donor-based	Wazir Akbar Khan, Kabul

Name of TV network	Full name of owner	Owner's background	Type of support	Location
Tolo News	Saad Mohseni	Tajik Afghan-Australian businessman	Commercial-based; international donor-based	Wazir Akbar Khan, Kabul
Watan	Abdul Majid Muqri	Pashtun politician	Commercial-based	12 Square, Karte 3, Kabul
Watandar	Internews	Multiethnic; Media Development Agency	International donor-based	Shar-i Now, Kabul
Wolesi Jirga	Afghan Parliament	Multiethnic; Afghan Parliament	Government-based; international donor-based	Darulaman Street, Kabul
Zan	Hamid Samar	Tajik businessman	Commercial-based; international donor-based	Ansari Square, Kabul
Zhwandoon	Ismail Yoon	Pashtun politician/journalist	Commercial-based; political-based; with support from Pakistan	Taimani, Kabul

APPENDIX C

Media Funders

Agency	Recipients	Project/purpose	Amount	Date of funding	Source
Department of Defense	Ministry of Interior for television broadcasting in Afghanistan		$531,786	2012–13	SIGAR 2016a, p. 15
	Military communications budget in 2010		$100 million	2010	Cary 2012, p. 26
	Combined Afghanistan and Iraq military media budget in 2011		$180 million	2011	Cary 2012, p. 26
	US Army 2016 budget allocation for Information Operations in Afghanistan		$49.4 million	2016	Cary 2015, p. 4
Department of State	US embassy in Kabul, Public Affairs Section	Afghan Media and Rule of Law development	$83 million	2010–15	SIGAR 2016a, p. 4
		Various media projects (includes funding for Tolo TV's police serial *Eagle Four*)	$183 million	2010 (over the course of 18 months)	Cary 2012, p. 26
	Sesame Workshop	Production of the first season (and additional seasons) of *Sesame Street* in Afghanistan and radio programs	$8.6 million	2010–16	SIGAR 2017, p. 30
	Afghanistan Media Production and Outreach Program		$4.5 million	2011–15	SIGAR 2016b, p. 45

Agency	Recipients	Project/purpose	Amount	Date of funding	Source
USAID	Office of Transition Initiatives	Media development and training	$23 million	2002–3	Cary 2012, pp. 4, 24–25
	Office of Democracy and Governance	Media development and training	$20 million	2006–9	Cary 2012, pp. 4, 24–25
	Counterpart International Inc.	Afghan Civic Engagement Program	$70 million	2013–18	USAID 2019
	Afghan Media Development and Empowerment Project (AMDEP)	Bids awarded to Internews	$22 million, expanded to $32 million	2010–13	Cary 2012, p. 27; SIGAR 2015b, p. 2
	AMDEP Subgrants	Welfare Association for the Development of Afghanistan	$3.7 million	2010–13	SIGAR 2011, pp. 108–9
		Pajwok Afghan News	$418,050	2010–13	SIGAR 2011, pp. 108–9
		Nai	$2.7 million	2010–13	SIGAR 2011, pp. 108–9
		Lhassa Consulting (Altai)	$350,000	2010–13	SIGAR 2011, pp. 108–9
	Rasana		$9 million	2017–20	SIGAR 2017, p. 133
	Cetena Group		$7.2 million (modified three times)	2010–12	SIGAR 2015a, p. 34
	USAID ICT Programs	To increase ICT capacity	$44.5 million	2011–16	SIGAR 2016a, p. 6
	Moby Group	Start-up funds for Arman Radio and Tolo TV	$2.7 million*	2005 (start of funding)	Cary 2012, p. 4
	Internews		$1.45 million initial start-up funds, increased to $7.8 million by 2006	2003 (start of funding)	Cary 2012, p. 5; Sigal and McArthur 2006, p. 9

*Various sources have this number listed with unexplained differences, ranging from $10,000 to $100,000.

Notes

Introduction

1. NATO disbanded the International Security Assistance Force (ISAF) in 2014 and created its successor, Resolute Support Mission (RSM), in 2015 with a slightly different mission.

2. The Northwest Frontier Province (NWFP) also encompasses areas known in Pakistan as the Federally Administered Tribal Areas (FATA) and Khyber Pakhtunkhwa (KP).

3. Please see appendix A, Ethnic Groups in Afghanistan, for the details of Afghanistan's ethnic composition.

4. The Shura-i Ulama in exile, called Shura-i Itihaad Islami, tried to block my father from opening the school and took him to its Shura court on charges of anti-Islamic activity, claiming he was an agent of the Soviet-backed Afghan Communist Party, but he prevailed by securing enough votes from progressive mullahs to start the school.

5. I have compiled a table of the fifty active television channels along with details about them. Please see appendix B, Television Stations and Affiliations, for information about them.

6. One reason Afghans can access many television stations for free is because Afghan televisions broadcast in Ultra High Frequency (UHF), which allows for far more channels to operate. The other reason is that, to their credit, most Afghan governments, unlike those of many other countries, have not constrained the technological aspects of television broadcasting. Both during the 1970s and in the post-9/11 era, they have worked with technologically advanced countries to solicit the latest technologies of television transmission and reception that they could afford. As television scholar William Boddy has shown, in

the US, due to the corporatized and monopolistic nature of the media industry, television broadcasting was initially located in the Very High Frequency (VHF) portion of the electromagnetic spectrum, which could only support twelve channels, thus limiting free competition. A decade after television's inception in the US, the Federal Communication Commission (FCC) in conjunction with television corporations and manufacturers very slowly began to enable UHF competition. Yet at the same time, they chipped away at the free-viewing option, forcing all Americans to pay for cable or satellite television (1992).

7. Please see https://www.internetworldstats.com/stats3.htm (modified March 26, 2020).

8. In August of 2014, then vice president of Afghanistan and owner of Negaah TV, Karim Khalili officially inaugurated the transition to digital television transmission at a ceremony in Kabul's Serena Hotel. However, due to the high cost of upgrading, many stations have still not transitioned or have only partially transitioned. Furthermore, contrary to popular understanding, digital television is also terrestrial (land based) and uses radio waves like analog television except with more advanced receivers and transmitters.

9. The documentary is available at https://store.der.org/postcards-from-tora-bora -p523.aspx (published 2020), and its website is http://www.postcardsfromtorabora.com/ (published 2007).

10. For the Second Take film program, see http://mazefilm.de/wp-content/uploads/ 2019/02/SECOND-TAKE_Filmprogramm.pdf (accessed March 26, 2020).

11. After translating and transcribing my 109 formal interviews, which were all recorded on a combination of audio and video, I used the qualitative research software Atlas.ti to code some of the transcriptions. To determine what to code for I cast a wide net using terms and themes from my field notes, which included my interview notes. I combed through my three field note notebooks and extracted 117 emerging themes, patterns, and connections I noticed. In order to reduce this large number to a more manageable subset of themes, I coded a representative sample of twenty-one interviews on Atlas.ti. From that experiment I was able to quantitatively distinguish between central and secondary themes. Then I chose the most frequently recurring themes and used them to manually color-code my interview transcriptions the old-fashioned way. Due to space and time constraints, I only present and quote a fraction of my total interviews in this book. Nonetheless, all of these formal interviews along with other informal interviews, interactions, and personal communications served as critical background for contextualizing my research and fortifying my conclusions.

12. As is the case in contemporary ethnography and qualitative research, telecommunications are frequently used to expand the reach of location-specific fieldwork. Building on my in-person interviews, I have used internet and mobile technologies to remain in touch and in dialogue with many of the people I met during my fieldwork trips. These technologically mediated follow-up interviews were conducted via video conferencing, e-mailing, texting, and mobile calling. The exact method depended on the speed and connectivity of technologies accessible to my interviewees, which further depended on their socioeconomic status and location.

13. My analysis of television programming including different genres, programs, episodes, and series was premised on my interviews. Since my goal was to gauge the popularity of different types of programming and determine in what ways programming met or did not meet the needs of Afghans, I foregrounded my reception interviews. Whereas content analysis typically involves recording and quantitatively coding the instances that particular topics appear in media texts, my media analysis was led by people's prompts in terms of what programs to study and what to look for. In this respect my method is more in line with textual and discourse analysis, which takes a more holistic approach.

14. Given that my site of research is a volatile war zone and affected by warlordism, I gave all the people I interviewed the option of anonymity in any publications resulting from my research. Most of the participants, however, readily gave me permission to use either their name or name and title. After all, most of my research subjects are media professionals and public figures. Their names often appear in the bylines or credits of the media they produce and they frequently give expert interviews on topics similar to those addressed in my book in the local and foreign press as well as in conferences and government proceedings. Yet in a number of interviews, especially with lower-level media makers and other vulnerable people or when I believed extra sensitive information was being shared with me, I made the decision to avoid potentially endangering those individuals by not disclosing their identities.

Chapter 1. Legitimizing Modernization

1. Completed in 2010 and funded by the Asian Development Bank, one stretches from Termiz, Uzbekistan, to the airport in Mazar-i Sharif, and the other railway, funded by Turkmenistan, links Serhetabat, Turkmenistan, with Toorghundi and has reportedly been halted due to security threats posed by the Taliban.

2. *Mahaly* literally means belonging to or of a specific place, especially in reference to the customs, folklore, culture, and traditions from the countryside and villages. However, more generally it is translated as indigenous or native to a local community or nation.

3. MENASA is the acronym the United Nations designated to represent over thirty countries across the Middle East, North Africa, and South Asia

4. For more information on postcolonial responses to Western modernity and how subaltern studies scholars have conceptualized these moments and theorized indigenous and alternative modernities, and critiques of them, please see Lila Abu-Lughod's edited volume, R*emaking Women: Feminism and Modernity in the Middle East* (1998), Dipesh Chakrabarty's, "The Difference-Deferral of Colonial Modernity: Public Debates on Domesticity in British Bengal," (1994), Néstor García Canclini's, *Hybrid Cultures: Strategies for Entering and Leaving Modernity* (1995), and Timothy Mitchell's edited volume, *Questions of Modernity* (2000).

5. Mitchell primarily wrote his article in order to redress the false and dangerous binaries that Benjamin Barber presents in his book *Jihad vs. McWorld* (1996), which is premised on Samuel Huntington's even more simplistic and problematic notion of cultural and

national difference in his book *The Clash of Civilizations and the Remaking of World Order* (1996).

6. Queen Soraya was part of the prominent Tarzi family, well known for their *roshan fikr* or enlightened and progressive work. Her father was the intellectual Mahmud Tarsi, known as the "father of Afghan media." The Tarzis lived in exile in modern-day Turkey for about twenty years. The British-backed King Abdul Rahman Khan had expelled them because he feared their modernist and nationalist views. The Tarzis returned in 1901 to Afghanistan at the invitation of Amanullah's father, King Habibullah Khan.

7. Sims-Williams, in her article "The Afghan Newspaper *Siraj al-Akhbar*," explains that Afghanistan's first newspaper was *Shams al-Nahar*, and she also states that the first issue of *Siraj al-Akhbar* was published on January 11, 1906 (1980, 118). Senzil Nawid in her article "The State, the Clergy, and British Imperial Policy in Afghanistan during the 19th and Early 20th Centuries" concurs with this information (1997, 598), while Vartan Gregorian in his article "Mahmud Tarzi and *Siraj-ol-Akhbar*" explains that *Siraj al-Akhbar* was Afghanistan's first newspaper and first published in October 1911 (1967, 345). Regardless of the discrepancies, the India Office Libraries has an almost complete file of *Siraj al-Akhbar*, from the period of October 24, 1911, to October 22, 1918.

8. Individually, Louis and Nancy Dupree wrote many well-researched and groundbreaking books on Afghanistan, with topics ranging from anthropology and archaeology to tourism and cultures. I first met the Duprees when I was a child and my family were refugees in Peshawar, Pakistan. I then came to know Nancy Dupree while conducting research during my post-9/11 trips to Afghanistan. She was in her eighties at that time but continued to be fierce, feisty, and driven by her unrelenting intellectual commitment to produce, preserve, and share knowledge on Afghanistan. She was actively involved in running and setting up multiple educational and cultural institutions. I had the opportunity to formally interview her on three occasions.

9. Interview with Nancy Dupree, June 9, 2009.

Chapter 2. Imperialism, Globalization, and Development

1. Please see the SIGAR graph of US development money allocations in the next chapter (figure 3.1).

2. For more information on the Splice In and Second Take film festivals as well as their corresponding projects, see http://mazefilm.de/projects/splice-in-second-take/ (published 2018).

3. For more information on Ateliers Varan's documentary training workshops, programs, and mentorship, see http://www.ateliersvaran.com/en/dans-le-monde-atelier/workshop-afghanistan (accessed April 29, 2020).

4. For more information, see the Nai fact sheet on the USAID website: https://www.usaid.gov/news-information/fact-sheets/nai-supporting-open-media-afghanistan (last updated May 7, 2019).

5. See the BBC Media Action website for more information on their mission: https://www.bbc.co.uk/mediaaction/about (accessed April 28, 2020).

6. To learn more about BBC Media Action's projects in Afghanistan, see its "Afghanistan country profile" at https://www.bbc.com/news/world-south-asia-12011352 (last modified January 31, 2018).

7. At BBC Persian TV I interviewed journalist Najieh Ghulami in October of 2009. Later in the same month Ghulami's place of residence in Kabul, the Serena Hotel, which is popular with diplomats and journalists was targeted and hit in a Taliban rocket attack. At BBC World Service I interviewed the journalist and academic Dr. Dawood Azami in January of 2014. At BBC Media Action I initially spoke with Shirazuddin Siddiqi, the country director for Afghanistan in August of 2008 and then again in February of 2018 via Skype.

8. See the UNESCO website for more information on its sponsorship of the Voice of Afghan Women: http://www.unesco.org/new/en/communication-and-information/resources/news-and-in-focus-articles/all-news/news/afghan_women_get_tv_frequency/ (published April 26, 2005).

9. Interview with Jamila Mujahed, December 2009.

10. At the Killid Group I interviewed Melek Zimmer-Zahine and her husband, Shahir Zahine, who are the founders of the Killid Group in December 2009. I also interviewed the managing director, Najiba Ayubi, in October 2009. At Pajhwok Afghan News I interviewed director Danish Karokhel once in November 2009 and then again in February 2014. I also interviewed three reporters at Pajhwok who also work as freelancers for different television stations.

11. At UNAMA I jointly interviewed Dominic Medley and Nilob Barekzai from their Strategic Communication Unit in January of 2010. I also spoke with the UNAMA spokesperson Aleem Siddique. I am grateful for their generosity in sharing their insights and resources.

12. For more on US media development projects in Israel/Palestine, also see Tawil-Souri (2012) and Aouragh (2011).

Chapter 3. Afghan Television Production

1. Ramazan Bashardost, former presidential candidate and current parliamentarian, first coined the phrase. He is one of the few members of Parliament who have not been involved or implicated in the numerous corruption scandals that have plagued other MPs.

2. Constitution of Afghanistan, https://www.aihrc.org.af/media/files/Laws/afghan_constituion(1).pdf (accessed May 3, 2020).

3. The deputy director of the Ministry of Information and Culture, Din Mohammad Mubariz Rashidi, whom I interviewed in February of 2014, is an advocate of freedom of the press.

4. At the South Asian Free Media Association I interviewed its president, Ehsanullah Arianzai, and the president of the women's division, Delafroz Zerak, in January 2014.

5. For a list of television stations and their ethnic affiliations and funding sources, among other pertinent information, see appendix B, Television Stations and Affiliations in Afghanistan.

6. For the latest SIGAR figures on US expenditures, see https://www.sigar.mil/quarterlyreports/fundingtables/index.aspx?SSR=6&SubSSR=25&WP=Funding%20Tables (published March 31, 2020).

7. The USAID offices are located in the Green Zone of Kabul near the US embassy. There I interviewed the senior development outreach and communication officer, twice. I also interviewed five other USAID personnel.

8. Interview with Sekandar Saleh, September 2009.

9. According to some of Tolo's employees who did not want to be identified, the Mohsenis are Sayyids. "Sayyid" is an honorific or title used to refer to descendants of the Prophet Muhammad and therefore implies Arab ancestry. However, tracing Sayyid ancestry is complicated in Afghanistan. Afghan ruling elites have invited Sayyids to come to Afghanistan during different time periods. Some Sayyids are relative newcomers, having moved to Afghanistan more recently, as in the last two centuries. Other Sayyids trace their lineage, or origin of arrival in Afghanistan, to centuries ago, even as far back as the Arab conquest of the region in the seventh century. As a result they have intermarried with indigenous Afghan ethnic populations. Hence, although Sayyid designates a religio-ethnic category, it is just as complicated as the other ethnicities.

10. At ATN I observed many of its departments, including voice-over, graphics and design, and news. I also had the opportunity to speak informally and formally with many of ATN's behind-the-scenes workers as well as its on-air hosts, presenters, and personalities. I especially want to thank chief of operations Habib Durani and news director Abdul Qadir Mirzai for allowing me to fully explore ATN.

11. See Independent Elections Commission, http://www.iec.org.af/en/elections/2009-elections/2009-elections-regulations (accessed April 30, 2020).

12. At Radio Television Afghanistan (RTA), I want to especially thank commissioner Jalani Shams and senior media and communication adviser Malek Shafi'i for their time and for sharing documents related to RTA's mission and operations.

13. RTA also has a vast archive from the 1980s when it was under the Soviet-backed Afghan government, but those pictures are not displayed. They exist only in the archives.

14. Interview, Kabul, December 2009.

15. At Emroz I interviewed the owner, Najibullah Kabuli, in September 2009 as well the station manager, Fahim Kohdamani, in January 2010. At Tamadon I interviewed two people I have decided not to name in February 2010.

16. Germany, France, and the European Union are particularly active in their efforts to rebuild all sectors of Afghan civil society.

17. Interview with Noor TV production manager, July 2009.

18. Interview with Alem Khalili, September 2009.

19. The Sherpur land grab and building boom was particularly controversial as it involved the Kabul police forcefully removing and injuring destitute war-displaced Afghans and bulldozing their makeshift homes that they had built on a large swath of public land in the heart of Kabul's affluent international district, where embassies, the UN, and large NGOs have their headquarters located. The directive for this ruthless exertion of power over the powerless came from the then defense minister and vice president of Afghani-

stan Mohammad Qasim Fahim. During the jihad, Marshall Fahim, as he was colloquially called, was a mujahedeen commander and second-in-command to the Tajik leader Ahmad Shah Massoud. After the 9/11 attacks and the assassination of Massoud, Fahim lead the US-backed Northern Alliance to oust the Taliban, thus heightening his status as a war hero. The irony of a NATO-backed Afghan war commander displacing internal Afghan war refugees in the diplomatic district of Kabul under the watchful gaze of powerful international and transnational human rights organization was not lost on journalists and the media.

20. Interview with Fazal Karim Fazal, November 2009.

21. In addition to interviewing Sanjar Sohail in September 2009, at Saba TV I also interviewed production manager Zainab Nadery in October 2009.

22. At Noorin TV I interviewed *Talak*'s director, Osman Aqrab Sargardan, and Noorin's station and news manager, Abdul Hamid Noorzad, in February 2010.

23. Shirazuddin Siddiqi, Afghanistan's BBC Media Action country director and creator of *Open Jirga*, also confirmed this trend via Skype in February of 2018.

Chapter 4. Producers and Production

1. For example, in their influential works *Orality and Literacy* (Ong 1982) and *The Gutenburg Galaxy* (McLuhan 1962), Walter Ong and Marshall McLuhan, whose works influenced one another, make the argument that print and literate cultures are inherently rational and therefore have democratic tendencies, whereas oral cultures and television cultures have the opposite effect. McLuhan coined the terms the "global village" and "re-tribalizing" of society by television. These now famous McLuhanisms have since been co-opted to mean many things, but he intended them as a warning that broadcast technologies have the ability to create provincial and tribal-minded people rather than transcending parochial mindsets and embracing a cosmopolitan worldview.

2. This is not the case with Shiites, as expressions of crying and martyrdom are a central part of their piety.

3. In addition to interviewing Sepehr and Mohammadi in December 2009 shortly after the incident, I also interviewed director of programming Ahmad Saeed Ghafoury.

Chapter 5. Reaching Vulnerable and Dangerous Populations

1. All quotes from Fazal are from my interview with him in November 2009.

2. Fazal imparted this information to me in our interview.

3. See appendix A, Ethnic Groups in Afghanistan.

4. I had several conversations with Felix Kuehn in which he shared this information with me in Kabul in September and November of 2009 in between his fieldwork trips to Kandahar and also followed up by e-mail in 2012.

5. This was relayed on the news on a number of television stations.

6. Interview with Husn Banu Ghazanfar, January 2010.

7. RTA, because it is the national broadcasting company, is financially reliant on the government. Thus it tends to be more restrictive in some of its policies, whereas the pri-

vate and pseudo-private stations that operate on advertising revenue, donor support, or other sources have more freedom.

8. Interview with Rahimullah Samandar, January 2010.

9. This information was imparted to me in a series of e-mail correspondences in October 2011 by Madeline Earp, senior researcher, and Bob Dietz, program coordinator, of Committee to Protect Journalists' Asia bureau.

10. Interview with Samia Mirzad by telephone, June 2019.

11. Interview with Roya Sadat, September 2009.

12. Interview with Fazal Karim Fazal, November 2009.

13. This was reported on various television stations.

14. Havana Marking made the statement during a panel on which we both served, "Television, Religion, and Gender in the Afghan Culture Wars," New York University Abu Dhabi Lecture Series, "Digital Religion: Knowledge, Politics, and Practice." The video of the entire presentation and audience discussion is available online: https://www.youtube .com/watch?v=0-2gPTuj5pI (accessed May 2, 2020).

15. Ismail Khan also has a track record of muzzling freedom of speech in Herat by threatening, detaining, and beating journalists (Reporters Without Borders 2016).

16. Interview with Negaah TV's program director, March 2010.

17. This line of thinking perpetuates the colonial teleological project of modernity and its "civilizing mission." The assumption is that the future of the third world will be the present of the first world. Therefore, since the West is ahead, the past of the first world offers clues for the development of the third world. In this equation, the past of the third world then becomes irrelevant. It is an undesirable, premodern past associated with archaic systems and tradition-based structures such as tribalism, religiosity, and the like.

18. I interviewed Zara Sepher and the producer of her program, Maryam Kasra, together in February 2010.

19. Interview with Farahnaz Forotan via a series of e-mail correspondences from January to February 2020.

20. To learn more about people's perceptions and practices of *baad* exchange, see the Asia Foundation survey, https://asiafoundation.org/publication/afghanistan-2016-survey -afghan-people/ (accessed May 2, 2020).

21. See the Afghan Independent Human Rights Commission (AIHRC), http://www.aihrc .org.af/ (accessed May 2, 2020).

22. Again, see the website of the Afghan Independent Human Rights Commission (AIHRC).

Chapter 6. Reception and Audiences

1. *Zoor awarah* or *zoor mundah*, which can be translated as "strongmen" or "thugs," are new words in the Afghan lexicon, born out of the nation's turbulent recent history and troubled present. They are umbrella terms used ubiquitously to describe ruthless, powerful people, well-known warlords and lesser known "mini-warlords," who brutally exercise violence without worry of retribution.

2. Interview with Sanjar Sohail, September 2009.

3. Interview with Nader Nadery, November 2009.

4. Malalai Joya's speech can be found on YouTube; see https://www.youtube.com/watch?v=iLC1KBrwbck.

5. Interview with Diana Saqeb, June 2009.

6. Interview with Kabuli schoolteacher, February 2010.

7. Interview with Fazal Karim Fazal, November 2009.

8. Latin American telenovelas have also recently started airing on Afghan television stations, but their entrance was after my audience research; hence I cannot hypothesize about their relative popularity.

9. Constitution of Afghanistan, p. 3 https://www.aihrc.org.af/media/files/Laws/afghan_constituion(1).pdf (accessed May 3, 2020). In addition to the previously mentioned interviews at ATN, Tolo, Noor, and Emroz, I also interviewed key personnel at Rah-e-Farda, including its production manager, Gholam Abbas Agah, in October 2009.

10. A very popular Indian serial, *Kyunki Saas Bhi Kabhi Bahu Thi*, is referred to simply as *Tulsi* in Afghanistan. Tulsi is the kind-hearted daughter-in-law and wife of the protagonist Mir.

11. Interview with an expatriate UN worker, May 2009.

12. Interview with a judge, June 2009.

13. Interview with Fahim Kohdamani, January 2010.

14. I conducted these interviews gauging the popularity of Indian serials in comparison to Iranian ones at two different women's social and professional events hosted by the Ministry of Women's Affairs in Kabul in January and February 2010.

15. The quotes in this paragraph are from the same events mentioned in the previous note.

16. I conducted these audience interviews informally during a dinner party in Kabul in March 2010.

17. I interviewed Saba Sahar in March of 2009 and then again in February of 2014. On August 25, 2020, she was shot by unknown gunmen while traveling to work in her car.

18. Interview with a mobile phone vendor, February 2010.

Conclusion

1. It was this issue of the independence of media that caused Habermas to switch to the grim side of media theory and proclaim that corporate ownership has led to a new form of feudalism or "refeudalization" by causing fake "publicness" in the West.

2. The Internews-supported Nai website is currently discontinued. "Violence against Journalists in Afghanistan," https://nai.org.af/data/ (site discontinued; last accessed April 2016).

3. Interview with Charmaine Anderson, January 2014.

4. Interview Charmaine Anderson, December 2009.

5. Ramazan Bashardost, former presidential candidate and current parliamentarian, first coined the phrase "the media is the candle that burns in the darkness" and spoke about this in our interview, Kabul, September 2009.

References

Abrahamian, Ervand. 2008. *A History of Modern Iran*. Cambridge, UK: Cambridge University Press.

———. 2013. *The Coup: 1953, the CIA, and the Roots of Modern U.S.-Iranian Relations*. New York: New Press.

Abu-Lughod, Lila, ed. 1998. *Remaking Women: Feminism and Modernity in the Middle East*. Princeton: Princeton University Press.

———. 2002. "Do Muslim Women Really Need Saving? Anthropological Reflections on Cultural Relativism and Its Others." *American Anthropologist* 104 (3): 783–90.

———. 2004. *Dramas of Nationhood: The Politics of Television in Egypt*. Chicago: University of Chicago Press.

———. 2006. "Writing against Culture." In *Feminist Anthropology: A Reader*, edited by Ellen Lewin, 153–69. Oxford: Wiley-Blackwell.

Adamec, Ludwig W. 1974. *Afghanistan's Foreign Affairs to the Mid-Twentieth Century: Relations with the USSR, Germany, and Britain*. Tucson: University of Arizona Press.

———. 2005. *Historical Dictionary of Afghan Wars, Revolutions, and Insurgencies*. Lanham, MD: Scarecrow Press.

Adinabay, Esfandiar. 2013. *Changing Media and Politics in Tajikistan*. Reuters Institute Fellow's paper. Oxford, UK: Reuters Institute for the Study of Journalism. Accessed June 15, 2019. https://reutersinstitute.politics.ox.ac.uk/our-research/changing-media -and-politics-tajikistan.

Ahmed, Sara, Claudia Castañeda, and Anne-Marie Fortie, eds. 2004. *Uprootings/Regroundings: Questions of Home and Migration*. London: Berg.

Alexander, Anne, and Miriyam Aouragh. 2014. "Egypt's Unfinished Revolution: The Role of the Media Revisited." *International Journal of Communication* 8: 890–915.

Ali, Mohammed. 1933. *Progressive Afghanistan.* Lahore, Pakistan: Punjab Educational Electric Press.

Altai Consulting. 2010. *Afghan Media in 2010: Synthesis Report.* October 13. http://www .altaiconsulting.com/docs/media/2010/Afghan%20Media%20in%202010.pdf. Site discontinued.

Anderson, Benedict. 2006. *Imagined Communities: Reflections of the Origin and Spread of Nationalism.* New ed. New York: Verso.

Ang, Ien. 1985. *Watching "Dallas": Soap Opera and the Melodramatic Imagination.* New ed. London: Routledge.

———. 2006. *Living Room Wars: Rethinking Media Audiences for a Postmodern World.* London: Routledge.

Ansari, Ahmad. 2020. *Tragedy and Triumph: An Afghan Immigrant's Journey to America.* Independently published.

Ansary, Tamim. 2003. *West of Kabul, East of New York: An Afghan American Story.* New York: Picador.

Aouragh, Miriyam. 2011. *Palestine Online: Transnationalism, the Internet and the Construction of Identity.* London: I. B. Tauris.

Aouragh, Miriyam, and Paula Chakravartty. 2016. "Infrastructures of Empire: Towards a Critical Geopolitics of Media and Information Studies." *Media, Culture, and Society* 38 (4): 559–75.

Appadurai, Arjun. 1990. "Disjuncture and Difference in the Global Cultural Economy." *Theory, Culture and Society* 7 (2–3): 295–310.

———. 1996a. "Disjuncture and Difference in the Global Cultural Economy." In *Modernity at Large: Cultural Dimensions of Globalization,* 27–47. Minneapolis: University of Minnesota Press.

———. 1996b. *Modernity at Large: Cultural Dimensions of Globalization.* Minneapolis: University of Minnesota Press.

———. 1996c. "Global Ethnoscapes: Notes and Queries for a Transnational Anthropology." In *Modernity at Large: Cultural Dimensions of Globalization,* 48–65. Minneapolis: University of Minnesota Press.

———. 2006. *Fear of Small Numbers: An Essay on the Geography of Anger.* Durham: Duke University Press Books.

Arbabzadah, Nushin. 2013. "We Waited for My Uncle for 35 Years. Now I Finally Know What Happened." *Guardian,* September 19. https://www.theguardian.com/commentisfree/2013/sep/19/afghanistan-unresolved-grief.

Armbrust, Walter. 2000. *Mass Mediations: New Approaches to Popular Culture in the Middle East and Beyond.* Berkeley: University of California Press.

Asad, Talal. 1993. *Genealogies of Religion: Discipline and Reasons of Power in Christianity and Islam.* Baltimore: Johns Hopkins University Press.

———. 2003. *Formations of the Secular: Christianity, Islam, Modernity*. Stanford: Stanford University Press.

The Asia Foundation. 2011. *Afghanistan in 2011: A Survey of the Afghan People*. https://asiafoundation.org/resources/pdfs/TAF2011AGSurvey.pdf.

The Associated Press. 2008. "Afghanistan: TV Host Detained." *New York Times*, July 30. https://www.nytimes.com/2008/07/30/world/asia/30brief-TVHOSTDETAIN_BRF.html.

Auletta, Ken. 2010. "The Networker: Afghanistan's First Media Mogul." *New Yorker*, July 5. http://www.newyorker.com/reporting/2010/07/05/100705fa_fact_auletta.

Bagdikian, Ben H. 2004. *The New Media Monopoly*. New York: Beacon Hill Press.

Barber, Benjamin R. 1996. *Jihad vs. McWorld*. New York: Ballantine Books.

Barfield, Thomas. 2010. *Afghanistan: A Cultural and Political History*. Princeton: Princeton University Press.

Barker, M. J. 2008. "Democracy or Polyarchy? US-Funded Media Developments in Afghanistan and Iraq Post 9/11." *Media, Culture, and Society* 30 (1): 109–30. http://citeseerx.ist.psu.edu/viewdoc/download?doi=10.1.1.1000.709&rep=rep1&type=pdf.

BBC Media Action. 2017. "History and Links to the BBC." Accessed April 22, 2020. http://www.bbc.co.uk/mediaaction/about/history.

BBC News. 2017. "Afghan Television Channel Shamshad TV Back on Air after Attack." *BBC*, November 7. https://www.bbc.com/news/world-asia-41898011.

Bishara, Amahl. 2006. "Local Hands, International News: Palestinian Journalists and the International Media." *Ethnography* 7 (2): 19–46.

Blumer, Herbert. (1933) 2004. "Conclusion—from *Movies and Conducts*." In *Mass Communication and American Social Thought: Key Texts, 1919–1968*, edited by John Durham Peters and Peter Simonson, 91–96. Lanham, MD: Rowman and Littlefield.

Boddy, William. 1992. *Fifties Television: The Industry and Its Critics*. Urbana: University of Illinois Press.

Boone, Jon. 2011. "The Financial Scandal That Broke Afghanistan's Kabul Bank." *Guardian*, June 16. https://www.theguardian.com/world/2011/jun/16/kabul-bank-afghanistan-financial-scandal.

Bose, Purnima. 2020. *Intervention Narratives: Afghanistan, the United States, and the Global War on Terror*. New Brunswick: Rutgers University Press.

Boyd-Barrett, Oliver. 1977. "Media Imperialism: Towards an International Framework for the Analysis of Media Systems." In *Mass Communication and Society*, edited by James Curran, Michael Gurevitch, and Janet Woollacott, 116–35. London: Edward Arnold.

———. 1998. "Media Imperialism Reformulated." In *Electronic Empires: Global Media and Local Resistance*, edited by Daya Kishan Thussu, 157–76. London: Edward Arnold.

———, ed. 2007. *Communications Media, Globalization, and Empire*. Bloomington: Indiana University Press.

Burch, Jonathon. 2008. "Stabbed Afghan Woman Journalist Fears for Future." *Reuters*, May 28. https://www.reuters.com/article/us-afghan-journalist/stabbed-afghan-woman-journalist-fears-for-future-idUSISL33555020080528.

Burdick, John. 1992. "Rethinking the Study of Social Movements: The Case of Christian Based Communities in Urban Brazil." In *Making of Social Movements in Latin America: Identity, Strategy and Democracy*, edited by Arturo Escobar and Sonia Alvarez, 171–85. Boulder: Westview Press.

Calhoun, Craig. 1992. *Habermas and the Public Sphere*. Cambridge, MA: MIT Press.

Cary, Peter. 2012. *An Explosion of News: The State of Media in Afghanistan*. Washington, DC: CIMA. Accessed May 13, 2020. https://www.cima.ned.org/wp-content/uploads/2015/02/CIMA-Afghanistan%20-%2003–01–12.pdf.

———. 2015. *The Pentagon and Independent Media—an Update*. Washington, DC: CIMA. Accessed May 13, 2020. https://www.cima.ned.org/wp-content/uploads/2015/11/CIMA-The-Pentagon-and-Independent-Media-Update.pdf.

Chakrabarty, Dipesh. 1994. "The Difference-Deferral of Colonial Modernity: Public Debates on Domesticity in British Bengal." In *Subaltern Studies VIII: Essays in Honour of Ranajit Guha*, edited by David Arnold and David Hardiman, 50-88. New Delhi: Oxford University Press India.

Chakravartty, Paula. 2019. "The Media, 'Race' and the Infrastructure of Empire." In *Media and Society*, edited by James Curran and David Hesmondhalgh, 242–62. New York: New York University Press.

Chakravartty, Paula, and Yuezhi Zhao, eds. 2008. "Introduction: Toward a Transcultural Political Economy of Global Communications." In *Global Communications: Toward a Transcultural Political Economy*. Lanham, MD: Rowman and Littlefield.

Chatterjee, Partha. 1997. "Our Modernity." In *South-South Exchange Programme for Research on the History of Development and the Council for the Development of Social Science Research in Africa*, 1–20. Selangor, Malaysia: Vinlin Press.

Chiovenda, Andrea. 2019. *Crafting Masculine Selves: Culture, War, and Psychodynamics in Afghanistan*. Oxford: Oxford University Press.

Clinton, Hillary Rodham. 2011. "Remarks at the Bonn Conference Center." Speech. December 5, Bonn, Germany. https://2009–2017.state.gov/secretary/20092013clinton/rm/2011/12/178267.htm.

Cloud, Dana L. 2006. "'To Veil the Threat of Terror': Afghan Women and the Clash of Civilizations in the Imagery of the U.S. War on Terrorism." *Quarterly Journal of Speech* 90 (3): 285–306.

Coburn, Noah. 2011. *Bazaar Politics: Power and Pottery in an Afghan Market Town*. Stanford: Stanford University Press.

Coburn, Noah, and Anna Larson. 2014. *Derailing Democracy in Afghanistan: Elections in an Unstable Political Landscape*. New York: Columbia University Press.

Committee to Protect Journalists (CPJ). 2019. "Getting Away with Murder." Committee to Protect Journalists, October 29. https://cpj.org/reports/2019/10/getting-away-with-murder-killed-justice.php.

Cordesman, Anthony H. 2012. "The US Cost of the Afghan War: FY2002–FY2013: Cost in Military Operating Expenditures and Aid, for Prospects in 'Transition.'" *Washington,*

DC: *Center for Strategic and International Studies, May 15, 2012*. Accessed June 15, 2019. https://www.csis.org/analysis/us-cost-afghan-war-fy2002-fy2013.

Corner, John. 1999. *Critical Ideas in Television Studies*. London: Oxford University Press.

Crews, Robert. 2015. *Afghan Modern: The History of a Global Nation*. Cambridge, MA: Harvard University Press.

Crews, Robert, and Wazhmah Osman. Forthcoming. *Afghanistan: A Very Short Introduction*. Oxford: Oxford University Press.

Croteau, David R., and William D. Hoynes. 2003. *Media/Society: Industries, Images, and Audiences*. 3rd ed. Thousand Oaks: Pine Forge Press.

Curran, James, and David Hesmondhalgh. 2019. *Media and Society*. 6th ed. London: Bloomsbury Academic.

Darling-Wolf, Fabienne. 2008. "Getting Over Our 'Illusion d'Optique': From Globalization to Mondialisation (Through French Rap)." *Communication Theory* 18:187–209.

Das, Veena. 1995. "What Kind of Object Is It?" In *Worlds Apart: Modernity through the Prism of the Local*, edited by Daniel Miller, 169–89. London: Routledge.

Dewey, John. 1927. *The Public and Its Problems*. New York: H. Holt.

Dorfman, Ariel, and Armand Mattelart. 1975. *How to Read Donald Duck: Imperialist Ideology in the Disney Comic*. New York: International General.

Dornfeld, Barry. 1998. *Producing Public Television, Producing Public Culture*. Princeton: Princeton University Press.

Dupree, Louis. 1973. *Afghanistan*. Princeton: Princeton University Press.

Dupree, Nancy H. 1977. *An Historical Guide to Afghanistan*. Kabul: Afghan Air Authority, Afghan Tourist Organization.

———. 1984. "Revolutionary Rhetoric and Afghan Women." In *Revolutions and Rebellions in Afghanistan: Anthropological Perspectives*, edited by M. Nazif Shahrani and Robert L. Canfield, 306–40. Berkeley: Institute of International Studies, University of California.

———. 1988. "Demographic Reporting on Afghan Refugees in Pakistan." *Modern Asian Studies* 22: 845–65.

———. 1996. "Museum under Siege." *Archaeology* 49 (2): 42–51.

———. 2002. "Cultural Heritage and National Identity in Afghanistan." *Third World Quarterly* 23 (5): 977–89.

Eck, Diana L. 1998. *Darsan: Seeing the Divine Image in India*. 3rd ed. New York: Columbia University Press.

Edelman, Marc. 2001. "Social Movements: Changing Paradigms and Forms of Politics." *Annual Review of Anthropology* 30: 285–317.

Edwards, David B. 1993. "Summoning Muslims: Print, Politics, and Religious Ideology in Afghanistan." *Journal of Asian Studies* 53 (3): 609–28.

———. 1995. "Print Islam: Media and Religious Revolution in Afghanistan." *Anthropological Quarterly* 68 (3): 171–84.

———. 2002. *Before Taliban: Genealogies of the Afghan Jihad*. Berkeley: University of California Press.

Emadi, Hafizullah. 2005. *Culture and Customs of Afghanistan (Culture and Customs of Asia)*. Westport, CT: Greenwood Press.

Escobar, Arturo. 1992. "Culture, Practice, and Politics: Anthropology and the Study of Social Movements." *Critique of Anthropology* 12 (4): 395–431.

Evans, Christine Elaine. 2016. *Between Truth and Time: A History of Soviet Central Television*. New Haven: Yale University Press.

Fahmy, Khaled. 2005. "Modernizing Cairo: A Revisionist Account." In *Making Cairo Medieval*, edited by Nezar AlSayyad, Irene A. Bierman, and Nasser Rabbat, 173–201. Lanham, MD: Lexington Books.

———. 2009. *Mehmed Ali: From Ottoman Governor to Ruler of Egypt*. London: Oneworld Publications.

Fiske, John. 1988. *Television Culture*. New ed. London: Routledge.

Foucault, Michel. 1977. *Discipline and Punish: The Birth of the Prison*. Translated by Alan Sheridan. New York: Vintage Books.

———. 1980. *Power/Knowledge: Selected Interviews and Other Writings, 1972–1977*. New York: Pantheon.

Foucault, Michel. 1988. *History of Sexuality, Vol. 3: The Care of the Self*. Translated by Robert Hurley. New York: Vintage Books.

Foucault, Michel. 2007. *Security, Territory, Population: Lectures at the Collège de France, 1977–1978*. Translated by Graham Burchell. New York: Picador.

Fraenkel, Eran, Emrys Schoemaker, and Sheldon Himelfarb. 2010. *Afghanistan Media Assessment: Opportunities and Challenges for Peacebuilding*. Washington, DC: United States Institutes of Peace. Accessed May 2, 2020. https://www.usip.org/sites/default/files/PW68_Afghanistan_Media_Assessment.pdf.

Freedom House. 2008. *Afghanistan Country Report 2008*. http://www.freedomhouse.org/template.cfm?page=22&year=2008&country =7336. Site discontinued.

Freeman, Carla. 2001. "Is Local:Global as Feminine:Masculine? Rethinking the Gender of Globalization." *Signs* 26 (4): 1007–37.

Friedman, Susan Stanford. 1998. *Mappings: Feminism and the Cultural Geographies of Encounter*. Princeton: Princeton University Press.

Ganti, Tejaswini. 2004. *Bollywood: A Guidebook to Popular Hindi Cinema*. London: Routledge.

———. 2012. *Producing Bollywood: Inside the Contemporary Hindi Film Industry*. Durham: Duke University Press.

Gaonkar, Dilip P., ed. 2001. *Alternative Modernities*. Durham: Duke University Press.

García Canclini, Néstor. 1995. *Hybrid Cultures: Strategies for Entering and Leaving Modernity*. Translated by Christopher L. Chiappari and Silvia L. López. Minneapolis: University of Minnesota Press.

Ghani, Ashraf, and Clare Lockhart. 2008. *Fixing Failed States: A Framework for Rebuilding a Fractured World*. London: Oxford University Press.

Ginsburg, Faye D. 1991. "Indigenous Media: Faustian Contract or Global Village?" *Cultural Anthropology* 6 (1): 92–112.

———. 1998. *Contested Lives: The Abortion Debate in an American Community*. Updated ed. Berkeley: University of California Press.

Ginsburg, Faye D., Lila Abu-Lughod, and Brian Larkin, eds. 2002. *Media Worlds: Anthropology on New Terrain*. Berkeley: University of California Press.

Ginsburg, Faye D., and Rayna Rapp. 1999. "Fetal Reflections: Confessions of Two Feminist Anthropologists as Mutual Informants." In *The Fetal Subjects: Feminist Positions*, edited by Lynn Morgan and Meredith Michaels, 279–95. Philadelphia: University of Pennsylvania Press.

Göle, Nilüfer, and Ludwig Ammann. 2006. *Islam in Public: Turkey, Iran and Europe*. Istanbul: Istanbul Bilgi University Press.

Graham, Stephen. 2002. "'Clean Territory': Urbicide in the West Bank." *openDemocracy*, August 6. https://www.opendemocracy.net/en/article_241jsp/.

Grant, Bruce. 2009. *The Captive and the Gift: Cultural Histories of Sovereignty in Russia and the Caucasus*. Culture and Society after Socialism. Ithaca: Cornell University Press.

Gregorian, Vartan. 1967. "Mahmud Tarzi and *Saraj-ol-Akhbar*: Ideology of Nationalism and Modernization in Afghanistan." *Middle East Journal* 21 (3): 345–68.

———. (1969) 2013. *The Emergence of Modern Afghanistan: Politics of Reform and Modernization, 1880–1946*. Stanford: Stanford University Press.

Grewal, Inderpal, and Caren Kaplan. 1994. *Scattered Hegemonies: Postmodernity and Transnational Feminist Practices*. Minneapolis: University of Minnesota Press.

Haber, Marc, Daniel E. Platt, Maziar Ashrafian Bonab, Sonia C. Youhanna, David F. Soria-Hernanz, Begoña Martínez-Cruz, Bouchra Douaihy, et al. 2012. "Afghanistan's Ethnic Groups Share a Y-chromosomal Heritage Structured by Historical Events." *PloS one* 7 (3): e34288. https://doi.org/10.1371/journal.pone.0034288.

Habermas, Jürgen. (1962) 1991. *The Structural Transformation of the Public Sphere: An Inquiry into a Category of Bourgeois Society*. Cambridge, MA: MIT Press.

———. 1991. "The Public Sphere: An Encyclopedia Article." In *Rethinking Popular Culture: Contemporary Perspectives in Cultural Studies*, edited by C. Mukerji and M. Schudson, 398–404. Berkeley: University of California Press.

Habermas, Jürgen, Sara Lennox, and Frank Lennox. 1974. "The Public Sphere: An Encyclopedia Article (1964)." *New German Critique*, no. 3: 49–55.

Hall, Stuart. 1997. *Representation: Cultural Representations and Signifying Practices*. London: SAGE.

———. 2006. "Encoding/Decoding." In *Media and Cultural Studies: KeyWorks*, edited by Meenakshi Gigi Durham and Douglas M. Kellner. Malden: Blackwell.

Hirschkind, Charles, and Saba Mahmood. 2002. "Feminism, the Taliban, and Politics of Counter-Insurgency." *Anthropological Quarterly* 75 (2): 339–54.

Hodgetts, Darrin, Christopher Sonn, Cate Curtis, Linda Nikora, and Neil Drew. 2010. *Social Psychology and Everyday Life*. London: Red Globe Press.

Horkheimer, Max, and Theodor W. Adorno. (1944) 2002. *Dialectic of Enlightenment*. Stanford: Stanford University Press.

Human Rights Watch. 2006. "Afghanistan: Justice for War Criminals Essential to Peace." Human Rights Watch, December 12. https://www.hrw.org/news/2006/12/12/afghanistan-justice-war-criminals-essential-peace#.

———. 2008. "Country Summary: Afghanistan." Accessed May 2, 2020. https://www.hrw.org/sites/default/files/related_material/afghanistan_0.pdf.

Huntington, Samuel P. 1996. *The Clash of Civilizations and the Remaking of World Order.* New York: Simon and Schuster.

Independent Election Commission (IEC) of Afghanistan Media Commission. 2014. "Media Monitoring Project Afghanistan First Weekly Narrative Report, 16–23 February 2014." Accessed May 2, 2020. http://www.iec.org.af/pdf/mediacommission/reports/mmpa_weekly_report_23-02-2014_eng.pdf.

Inskeep, Steve. 2010. "Ahmad Zahir: The Voice of the Golden Years." *NPR*, February 1. https://www.npr.org/templates/story/story.php?storyId=123137188.

Internet World Stats. 2020. "Usage and Population Stats." Accessed May 2, 2020. https://www.internetworldstats.com/stats3.htm.

Kakar, Mohammed Hasan. 1995. *Afghanistan: The Soviet Invasion and the Afghan Response, 1979–1982.* Berkeley: University of California Press.

Kalinovsky, Artemy M. 2018. *Laboratory of Socialist Development: Cold War Politics and Decolonization in Soviet Tajikistan.* Ithaca: Cornell University Press.

Katz, Cindi. 2001. "On the Grounds of Globalization: A Topography for Feminist Political Engagement." *Signs* 26 (4): 1213–34.

Katz, Elihu, and Paul Lazarsfeld. 2005. *Personal Influence: The Part Played by People in the Flow of Mass Communications.* New York: Transaction.

Khalidi, Rashid. 2013. *Brokers of Deceit: How the U.S. Has Undermined Peace in the Middle East.* Boston: Beacon Press.

Khitab, Muhammad Hasan. 2014. "14 Media Outlets Fined for Law Violation." Pajhwok Afghan News, April 23. http://beta.pajhwok.com/en/2014/04/23/14-media-outlets-fined-law-violation.

The Killid Group. 2016. "Silenced by Security Threats." The Killid Group, August 1. http://tkg.af/english/2016/08/01/silenced-by-security-threats/.

Kordunsky, Anna. 2011. "Foreign Aid Sustains Fragile Afghan Media." Writing about War: Columbia SIPA Student Journalism, February 25. http://thanassiscambanis.com/sipa/2011/02/foreign-aid-sustains-fragile-afghan-media/.

Kraidy, Marwan M. 2002. "Globalization of Culture through the Media." In *Encyclopedia of Communication and Information,* edited by J. R. Schement, 359–63. New York: Macmillan Reference USA. http://repository.upenn.edu/asc_papers/325.

———. 2005. *Hybridity, or the Cultural Logic of Globalization.* Philadelphia: Temple University Press.

———. 2010. *Reality Television and Arab Politics: Contention in Public Life (Communication, Society, and Politics).* Cambridge: Cambridge University Press.

Kraidy, Marwan M., and Joe F. Khalil. 2009. *Arab Television Industries.* London: Palgrave Macmillan.

Larkin, Brian. 2008. *Signal and Noise: Media, Infrastructure, and Urban Culture in Nigeria*. Durham: Duke University Press.

Lasswell, Harold. 1927. "The Theory of Political Propaganda." *American Political Science Review* 21 (3): 627–31.

Latour, Bruno. 2004. "Why Has Critique Run Out of Steam? From Matters of Fact to Matters of Concern." *Critical Inquiry* 30 (2): 225–48.

Liebes, Tamar, and Elihu Katz. (1993) 2007. *The Export of Meaning: Cross-Cultural Readings of Dallas*. 2nd ed. Cambridge: Polity Press.

Lippmann, Walter. 1925. *The Phantom Public*. New York: Transaction Press.

Loyn, David. 2013. "Afghanistan Mourns Victims of Communist Era." BBC News, September 30. https://www.bbc.com/news/world-asia-24328640#.

MacBride, Sean. 1980. *Many Voices, One World: Communication and Society Today and Tomorrow; Towards a New More Just and More Efficient World Information and Communication Order*. London: Kogan Page.

MacDonald, Dwight. 1953. "A Theory of Mass Culture." *Diogenes* 1 (3): 1–17.

MacMunn, George F. 1977. *Afghanistan: From Darius to Amanullah*. Quetta, Pakistan: Gosha-e-Adab.

Mahmood, Saba. 2005. *Politics of Piety: The Islamic Revival and the Feminist Subject*. Princeton: Princeton University Press.

Majrooh, Parwin Ali. 1989. "Afghan Women between Marxism and Islamic Fundamentalism." *Central Asian Survey* 8 (3): 87–98. doi:10.1080/02634938908400675.

Maley, William. 1996. "Women and Public Policy in Afghanistan: A Comment." *World Development* 24 (1): 203–6.

Manchanda, Nivi. 2015. "Queering the Pashtun: Afghan Sexuality in the Homo-nationalist Imaginary." *Third World Quarterly* 36 (1): 130–46.

———. 2020. *Imagining Afghanistan: The History and Politics of Imperial Knowledge*. Cambridge: Cambridge University Press.

Mandel, Ruth. 2002. "A Marshall Plan of the Mind: The Political Economy of Kazakh Soap Opera." In *Media Worlds: Anthropology of New Terrain*, edited by Faye D. Ginsburg, Lila Abu-Lughod, and Brian Larkin, 211–28. Berkeley: University of California Press.

Mankekar, Purnima. 1999. *Screening Culture, Viewing Politics: An Ethnography of Television, Womanhood, and Nation in Postcolonial India*. Durham: Duke University Press.

Mashal, Mujib. 2011. "Gained by Blood, Threatened by a Declaration." *Al Jazeera*, June 14. https://www.aljazeera.com/indepth/features/2011/06/201161392394129.html.

Mauss, Marcel. 1954. *The Gift: The Form and Reason of Exchange in Archaic Societies*. Abingdon, UK: Routledge.

Mbembe, Joseph-Achille. 2003. "Necropolitics." Translated by Libby Meintjes. *Public Culture* 15 (1): 11–40.

McCarthy, Anna. 2010. *The Citizen Machine: Governing by Television in 1950s America*. New York: New Press.

McChesney, Robert. 2004. *The Problem of the Media: U.S. Communication Politics in the Twenty-First Century*. New York: Monthly Review Press.

McLuhan, Marshall. 1952. "Technology and Political Change." *International Journal* 7: 189–95.

———. 1962. *The Gutenberg Galaxy: The Making of Typographic Man*. Toronto: University of Toronto Press.

———. 1969. "The Playboy Interview: Marshall McLuhan." *Playboy Magazine*. Accessed May 2, 2020. http://www.nomads.usp.br/leuphana/mcluhan_the_playboy_interview.pdf.

McLuhan, Marshall, and Quentin Fiore. 1967. *The Medium Is the Message*. New York: Bantam.

McQuail, Denis. 1994. *Mass Communication Theory: An Introduction*. 3rd ed. London: SAGE.

Mendrinos, Jim, and Frank Santopadre. 2004. "The Women of Afghanistan, beneath the Burka: Burkaliscious!" *Jest Magazine* 6 (3).

Michaels, Eric, Marcia Langton, and Dick Hebdige. 1994. *Bad Aboriginal Art: Tradition, Media, and Technological Horizons*. Minneapolis: University of Minnesota Press.

Mills, C. Wright. 1956. *The Power Elite*. New York: Oxford University Press.

Mills, Margaret A. 1991. *Rhetorics and Politics in Afghan Traditional Storytelling*. Philadelphia: University of Pennsylvania Press.

Minow, Newton M. 1961. "Television and the Public Interest." Speech delivered by FCC chairman at convention of the National Association of Broadcasters, May 9.

Mitchell, Timothy, ed. 2000. *Questions of Modernity*. Minneapolis: University of Minnesota Press.

———. 1991. *Colonising Egypt*. Berkeley: University of California Press.

———. 2002a. "McJihad: Islam in the US Global Order." *Social Text* 70 (4): 1–18.

———. 2002b. *Rule of Experts: Egypt, Techno-politics, Modernity*. Berkeley: University of California Press.

Mitchell, W. J. T. 2006. *What Do Pictures Want? The Lives and Loves of Images*. Chicago: University of Chicago Press.

Mohanty, Chandra Talpade. 2003. *Feminism without Borders: Decolonizing Theory, Practicing Solidarity*. Durham: Duke University Press.

Morley, David. 1992. *Television, Audiences and Cultural Studies*. London: Routledge.

Morris, Nancy. 2003. "A Comparative Analysis of the Diffusion and Participatory Models in Development Communication." *Communication Theory* 13 (2): 225–48.

Moslih, Hashmat. 2016. "Q&A: The High Price of Freedom of Speech in Afghanistan." *Al Jazeera*, January 7. https://www.aljazeera.com/indepth/features/2016/01/qa-high-price-freedom-speech-afghanistan-160107143833358.html.

Murphy, Patrick D., and Marwan M. Kraidy. 2003. "International Communication, Ethnography, and the Challenge of Globalization." *Communication Theory* 13 (3): 304–23.

Murray, Susan. 2005. *Hitch Your Antenna to the Stars: Early Television and Broadcast Stardom*. London: Routledge.

———. 2018. *Bright Signals: A History of Color Television*. Durham: Duke University Press.

———. 2019. "The Politics of Reality Television." In *Media and Society*, 6th ed., edited by James Curran and David Hesmondhalgh, 263–80. London: Bloomsbury Academic.

Myre, Greg. 2017. "The 'Butcher of Kabul' Is Welcomed Back in Kabul." *NPR*, May 4. https://www.npr.org/sections/parallels/2017/05/04/526866525/the-butcher-of-kabul-is-welcomed-back-in-kabul.

Nai. "Violence against Journalists in Afghanistan." https://nai.org.af/data/. Site discontinued.

Nash, June, ed. 2004. *Social Movements: An Anthropological Reader*. Malden, MA: Blackwell.

Nathan, Joanna. 2012. "Land Grab in Sherpur: Monuments to Powerlessness, Impunity, and Inaction." *Middle East Institute*, April 19. https://www.mei.edu/publications/land-grab-sherpur-monuments-powerlessness-impunity-and-inaction.

Nawa, Fariba. 2006. "Afghanistan, Inc. A CorpWatch Investigative Report." CorpWatch, October 6. https://www.corpwatch.org/sites/default/files/Afghanistan%20Inc.pdf.

Nawid, Senzil K. 1997. "The State, the Clergy, and British Imperial Policy in Afghanistan during the 19th and Early 20th Centuries." *International Journal of Middle East Studies* 29 (4): 581–605.

———. 2000. *Religious Response to Social Change in Afghanistan, 1919–29: King Aman-Allah and the Afghan Ulama*. Costa Mesa, CA: Mazda.

———. 2007. "Afghan Women under Marxism." In *From Patriarchy to Empowerment: Women's Participation, Movements, and Rights in the Middle East, North Africa, and South Asia*, edited by Valentine M. Moghadam, 58–72. Syracuse: Syracuse University Press.

———. 2009. "Tarzi and the Emergence of Afghan Nationalism: Formation of a Nationalist Ideology." Accessed May 2, 2020. https://www.bu.edu/aias/nawid_article.pdf.

Nazar, Zarif, and Charles Recknagel. 2010. "Controversial Madrasah Builds Iran's Influence in Kabul." RadioFreeEurope RadioLiberty, November 6. https://www.rferl.org/a/Controversial_Madrasah_Builds_Irans_Influence_In_Kabul/2212566.html.

Newcomb, Horace. 2006. *Television: The Critical View*. 7th ed. London: Oxford University Press.

Newell, Richard S. 1972. *The Politics of Afghanistan*. Ithaca: Cornell University Press.

Nordland, Rod. 2013. "Old Atrocities, Now Official, Galvanize Afghanistan." *New York Times*, September 30. https://www.nytimes.com/2013/10/01/world/middleeast/release-of-decades-old-death-lists-stirs-anger-and-grief-in-afghanistan.html.

Nordland, Rod, and Alissa J. Rubin. 2012. "Taliban Captives Dispute U.S. View on Afghanistan War." *New York Times*, February 1. https://www.nytimes.com/2012/02/02/world/asia/nato-plays-down-report-of-collaboration-between-taliban-and-pakistan.html.

Nunan, Timothy. 2016. *Humanitarian Invasion: Global Development in Cold War Afghanistan*. Cambridge: Cambridge University Press.

Ong, Walter J. 1982. *Orality and Literacy: The Technologizing of the Word*. London: Routledge.

Oren, Tasha. 2004. *Demon in the Box: Jews, Arabs, Politics, and Culture in the Making of
Israeli Television*. Newark: Rutgers University Press.

Osman, Wazhmah. 2005. "Contentious Births: Modernity and Gender Rights in Afghanistan." Master's thesis, New York University.

———. 2010a. "Afghanistan: Vultures in the 'Graveyard of Empires.'" *The Women's International Perspective*, January 25. http://thewip.net/arts-culture/feature-articles/
afghanistan-vultures-in-the-graveyard-of-empires/.

———. 2010b. "Another 5 Years of Karzai: An Afghan-American Perspective from Kabul."
The Women's International Perspective, January 7. http://thewip.net/regions/middle
-east/afghanistan/another-5-years-of-karzai-an-afghan-american-perspective-from
-kabul/.

———. 2010c. "Violence Breeds Violence: 'Afghanistan without Bombs and Burqas.'"
The Women's International Perspective, March 1. http://thewip.net/regions/middle
-east/afghanistan/violence-breeds-violence-afghanistan-without-bombs-and-burqas/.

———. 2011. "'Trashy Tastes' and Permeable Borders: Indian and Iranian Soap Operas on
Afghan Television." In *Soap Operas and Telenovelas in the Digital Age*, edited by Diana
I. Rios and Mari Castañeda, 237–56. New York: Peter Lang.

———. 2012. "Between a Rock and a Cave: The Uneven Development of the Afghan Public Sphere." In *Engaging Afghanistan*, edited by S. Balaghi and M. D. Kennedy. Provi-
dence: Brown University, The Watson Institute for International and Public Affairs.
https://www.engagingafghanistan.org/wp-content/uploads/2012/10/OsmanPublic
Sphere-2.pdf. Site discontinued.

———. 2012/2013. "Thinking outside the Box: Television and the Afghan Culture Wars."
PhD diss., New York University. Ann Arbor: Proquest LLC.

———. 2014a. "On Media, Social Movements, and Uprisings: Lessons from Afghanistan, Its Neighbors, and Beyond." *Signs: Journal of Women in Culture and Society* 39
(4): 874–87.

———. 2014b. "US Exports Its Warped Democracy to Afghanistan." *Al Jazeera America*, July 14. http://america.aljazeera.com/opinions/2014/7/afghanelectionsusmedia
abdullahabdullahashrafghani.html.

———. 2017. "Jamming the Simulacrum: On Drones, Virtual Reality, and Real Wars."
In *Culture Jamming: Activism and the Art of Cultural Resistance*, edited by M. Fink and
M. DeLaure, 348–64. New York: New York University Press.

———. 2018. "Brought to You by Foreigners, Warlords, and Local Activists: TV and the
Afghan Culture Wars." In *Modern Afghanistan: The Impact of 40 Years of War*, edited by
M. N. Shahrani, 149–76. Bloomington: Indiana University Press.

———. 2019a. "Between the White House and the Kremlin: A Comparative Analysis of
Afghan and Tajik Media." *International Journal of Communication* 13: 619–41. https://
ijoc.org/index.php/ijoc/article/view/7576/2551.

———. 2019b. "Media and Imperialism in the Global Village: A Case Study of Four Malalais." In *Global Digital Cultures: Perspectives from South Asia,* edited by A. Punathambekar and S. Mohan, 280–300. Ann Arbor: University of Michigan Press.

———. 2019c. "Racialized Agents and Villains of the Security State: How African Americans Are Interpellated against Muslims and Muslim Americans." *Asian Diasporic Visual Cultures and the Americas* 5 (1–2): 155–82.

Parks, Lisa. 2005. *Cultures in Orbit: Satellites and the Televisual.* Durham: Duke University Press.

Pinney, Christopher. 2004. *Photos of the Gods: The Printed Image and Political Struggle in India.* London: Oxford University Press.

Pool, Ithiel de Sola. 1979. "Direct Broadcast Satellites and the Integrity of National Cultures." In *National Sovereignty and International Communication,* edited by K. Nordenstreng and H. Schiller, 145. Norwood, NJ: Ablex.

Poullada, Leon B. 1973. *Reform and Rebellion in Afghanistan, 1919–1929: King Amanullah's Failure to Modernize a Tribal Society.* Ithaca: Cornell University Press.

Puar, Jasbir K. 2007. *Terrorist Assemblages: Homonationalism in Queer Times.* Durham: Duke University Press.

Qassem, Ahmad Shayeq. 2007. "Afghanistan–Pakistan Relations: Border Controversies as Counter-Terrorist Impediments." *Australian Journal of International Affairs* 61 (1): 65–80.

Radway, Janice A. 1991. *Reading the Romance: Women, Patriarchy, and Popular Literature.* 2nd ed. Chapel Hill: University of North Carolina Press.

Rajagopal, Arvind. 2001. *Politics after Television: Religious Nationalism and the Reshaping of the Indian Public.* London: Cambridge University Press.

Ramadan, Tariq. 2012. "Made to Order Uprisings." In *Islam and the Arab Awakening,* 6–22. Oxford: Oxford University Press.

Rashid, Ahmed. 2001. *Taliban: Militant Islam, Oil and Fundamentalism in Central Asia.* New Haven: Yale University Press.

Reporters Without Borders (RSF). 2015. "2015: Another Turn of the Screw in the Post-Soviet Region." rsf.org. Accessed May 2, 2020. https://rsf.org/en/2015-another-turn-screw -post-soviet-region.

———. 2016. "Radio Free Afghanistan Journalist Flees Herat." Accessed July 17, 2020. https://rsf.org/en/news/radio-free-afghanistan-journalist-flees-herat.

———. 2016. *Round-Up 2016 of Journalists Killed Worldwide.* rsf.org. Accessed May 2, 2020. https://rsf.org/sites/default/files/rsf_2016-part_2-en.pdf.

———. 2018. "Worldwide Round-Up of Journalists Killed, Detained, Held Hostage, or Missing in 2018." rsf.org. Accessed May 2, 2020. https://rsf.org/sites/default/files/ worldwilde_round-up.pdf.

———. 2019. "2019 World Press Freedom Index." rsf.org. Accessed May 2, 2020. https:// rsf.org/en/ranking/2019.

Risen, James. 2010. "U.S. Identifies Vast Mineral Riches in Afghanistan." *The New York Times,* June 13. https://www.nytimes.com/2010/06/14/world/asia/14minerals.html.

Robbins, Bruce. 1993. *The Phantom Public Sphere.* Minneapolis: University of Minnesota Press.

Rohde, David, and Carlotta Gall. 2004. "The U.S. Has a Favorite in Afghanistan. That's a Problem." *New York Times,* September 26. https://www.nytimes.com/2004/09/26/weekinreview/the-us-has-a-favorite-in-afghanistan-thats-a-problem.html.

Rollberg, Peter. 2014. "Media Democratization in Russia and Eurasia." *Demokratizatsiya* 22 (2): 175–77.

Roth-Ey, Kristin. 2011. *Moscow Prime Time: How the Soviet Union Built the Media Empire That Lost the Cultural Cold War.* Ithaca: Cornell University Press.

Rubin, Barnett R. 2002. *The Fragmentation of Afghanistan: State Formation and Collapse in the International System.* 2nd ed. New Haven: Yale University Press.

Rubin, Elizabeth. 2010. "Studio Kabul." *New York Times,* October 21. http://www.nytimes.com/2010/10/24/magazine/24SoapOpera-t.html?pagewanted=all.

Said, Edward. 2004. *Humanism and Democratic Criticism.* Columbia Themes in Philosophy. New York: Columbia University Press.

Saikal, Amin, A. G. Ravan Farhadi, and Kirill Nourzhanov. 2012. *Modern Afghanistan: A History of Struggle and Survival.* London: Bloomsbury.

Salamandra, Christa. 2004. *A New Old Damascus: Authenticity and Distinction in Urban Syria.* Bloomington: Indiana University Press.

———. 2008. "Creative Compromise: Syrian Television Makers between Secularism and Islamism." *Contemporary Islam* 2 (3): 177–89.

Schiller, Dan. 2000. *Digital Capitalism: Networking the Global Market System.* Cambridge, MA: MIT Press.

———. 2014. *Digital Depression: Information Technology and Economic Crisis.* Urbana: University of Illinois Press.

Schiller, Herbert I. 1976. *Communication and Cultural Domination.* White Plains, NY: International Arts and Sciences.

———. 1989. *Culture, Inc.: The Corporate Takeover of Public Expression.* New York: Oxford University Press.

———. 1991. "Not Yet the Post-imperialist Era." *Critical Studies in Media Communication* 8 (1): 13–28.

———. 2004. "TV Overseas: The U.S. Hard Sell." In *Mass Communication and American Social Thought: Key Texts, 1919–1968,* edited by John Durham Peters and Peter Simonson, 480–84. Lanham, MD: Rowman and Littlefield.

Schiller, Naomi. 2018. *Channeling the State: Community Media and Popular Politics in Venezuela.* Durham: Duke University Press.

Schudson, Michael. 1998. *The Good Citizen: A History of American Civic Life.* New York: Free Press.

———. 1999. "Good Citizens and Bad History: Today's Political Ideals in Historical Perspective." Paper presented at conference on the Transformation of Civic Life, Nashville, TN, November 12–13.

Scott, Joan Wallach. 2002. "Feminist Reverberations." *Differences: A Journal of Feminist Cultural Studies* 13 (3): 1–23.

———. 2010. *The Politics of the Veil*. Princeton: Princeton University Press.

Shah, Hemant. 2012. *The Production of Modernization: Daniel Lerner, Mass Media, and the Passing of Traditional Society*. Philadelphia: Temple University Press.

Shahrani, M. Nazif Mohib, ed. 2018. *Modern Afghanistan: The Impact of 40 Years of War*. Bloomington: Indiana University Press.

Shahrani, M. Nazif, and Robert L. Canfield, eds. 1984. *Revolutions and Rebellions in Afghanistan: Anthropological Perspectives*. Berkeley: Institute of International Studies, University of California.

Shalizi, Hamid. 2008. "Afghan Reporter Detained after Criticizing Government." *Reuters*, July 29. https://www.reuters.com/article/us-afghan-journalist/afghan-reporter-detained -after-criticizing-government-idUSISL19260220080729.

Shohat, Ella. 1989. *Israeli Cinema: East/West and the Politics of Representation*. Austin: University of Texas Press.

———. 2001. *Talking Visions: Multicultural Feminism in a Transnational Age*. Cambridge, MA: MIT Press.

Shohat, Ella, and Robert Stam. 1994. *Unthinking Eurocentrism: Multiculturalism and the Media*. London: Routledge.

Sienkiewicz, Matt. 2016. *The Other Air Force: U.S. Efforts to Reshape Middle Eastern Media since 9/11*. New Brunswick: Rutgers University Press.

Sifton, John. 2005. "Blood-Stained Hands: Past Atrocities in Kabul and Afghanistan's Legacy of Impunity." *Human Rights Watch*, July 7. https://www.hrw.org/report/ 2005/07/06/blood-stained-hands/past-atrocities-kabul-and-afghanistans-legacy -impunity.

Sigal, Ivan, and Jan McArthur. 2006. "Final Report: Building Independent Media in Afghanistan." Internews. Accessed May 13, 2020. http://pdf.usaid.gov/pdf_docs/ PDACI368.pdf.

Sims-Williams, Ursula. 1980. "The Afghan Newspaper *Siraj al-Akhbar*." *Bulletin (British Society for Middle Eastern Studies)* 7 (2): 118–22.

Skuse, Andrew. 2002. "Radio, Politics and Trust in Afghanistan: A Social History of Broadcasting." *International Communication Gazette* 64 (3): 267–79. doi: 10.1177/ 1748048502064003O401.

Skuse, Andrew, Marie Gillespie, and Gerry Power, eds. 2011. *Drama for Development: Cultural Translation and Social Change*. London: SAGE.

Smith, Graeme. 2011. "Many in Kandahar Fear Looming Disaster as Canada Withdraws." *Globe and Mail*, July 9. http://www.theglobeandmail.com/news/world/many-in-kandahar -fear-looming-disaster-as-canada-withdraws/article5 86642/.

Special Inspector General for Afghanistan Reconstruction (SIGAR). 2011. *April 30, 2011:*

Quarterly Report to the United States Congress. Accessed May 13, 2020. https://www.sigar
.mil/pdf/quarterlyreports/2011–04–30qr.pdf.

———. 2015a. *January 30, 2015: Quarterly Report to the United States Congress.* Accessed
May 13, 2020. https://www.sigar.mil/pdf/quarterlyreports/2015–01–30qr.pdf.

———. 2015b. *USAID's Afghanistan Media Development and Empowerment Project: Audit
of Costs Incurred by Internews Network.* SIGAR 15–64 Financial Audit. Accessed May
13, 2020. https://www.sigar.mil/pdf/audits/Financial_Audits/SIGAR-15–64-FA.pdf.

———. 2016a. *Afghanistan's Information and Communications Technology Sector: U.S.
Agencies Obligated over $2.6 Billion to the Sector, but the Full Scope of U.S. Efforts Is Un-
known.* SIGAR 16–46 Audit Report. Accessed May 2, 2020. https://www.sigar.mil/
pdf/audits/SIGAR-16–46-AR.pdf.

———. 2016b. *October 30, 2016: Quarterly Report to the United States Congress.* Accessed
May 13, 2020. https://www.sigar.mil/pdf/quarterlyreports/2016–10–30qr.pdf.

———. 2017. *July 30, 2017: Quarterly Report to the United States Congress.* Accessed May
13, 2020. https://www.sigar.mil/pdf/quarterlyreports/2017–07–30qr.pdf.

———. 2018. *Promoting Gender Equity in National Priority Programs (Promote): USAID
Needs to Assess This $216 Million Program's Achievements and the Afghan Government's
Ability to Sustain Them.* SIGAR 18–69 Audit Report. Accessed May 2, 2020. https://
www.sigar.mil/pdf/audits/SIGAR-18–69-AR.pdf.

Spigel, Lynn. 1992. *Make Room for TV: Television and the Family Ideal in Postwar America.*
Chicago: University of Chicago Press.

Sreberny, Annabelle, and Gholam Khiabany. 2010. *Blogistan: The Internet and Politics in
Iran.* London: I. B. Tauris.

Sreberny-Mohammadi, Annabelle. 1997. "The Many Cultural Faces of Imperialism." In
*Beyond Cultural Imperialism: Globalization, Communication and the New International
Order,* edited by P. Golding and P. Harris, 49–68. London: SAGE.

Sreberny-Mohammadi, Annabelle, and Ali Mohammadi. 1994. *Small Media, Big Revolution: Communication, Culture, and the Iranian Revolution.* Minneapolis: University of
Minnesota Press.

Stankiewicz, Damien. 2017. "Nationalism without Borders: Contradictory Politics at a
Transborder European Media Organization." *American Ethnologist* 44 (4): 670–83.

Stanley, Alessandra. 2012. "Veiled Anchors, Koranic Contests and Racy Romance." *New
York Times,* August 19. http://www.nytimes.com/2012/08/20/arts/television/arab-tv
-nagi-atallahs-gang-tartil-night-owl.html.

Strick van Linschoten, Alex, and Felix Kuehn. 2012. *An Enemy We Created: The Myth of
the Taliban-Al Qaeda Merger in Afghanistan.* Oxford: Oxford University Press.

Stronski, Paul. 2010. *Tashkent: Forging a Soviet City, 1930–1966.* Pittsburgh: University of
Pittsburgh Press.

Synovitz, Ron. 2005. "Afghanistan: Private Kabul Station Offers Country's Answer To
MTV." Radio Free Europe/Radio Liberty. June 13. https://www.rferl.org/a/1057497
.html

Tapper, Nancy. 1977. "Pashtun Nomad women in Afghanistan." *Asian Affairs* 8 (2): 163–70.

————. 1991. *Bartered Brides: Politics, Gender and Marriage in an Afghan Tribal Society.* London: Cambridge University Press.

Tapper, Nancy, and Richard Tapper. 1982. "Marriage Preferences and Ethnic Relations among Durrani Pashtuns of Afghan Turkestan." *Folk* 24: 155–77.

Tapper, Richard, and Nancy Tapper. 1992/1993. "Marriage, Honour and Responsibility: Islamic and Local Models in the Mediterranean and the Middle East." *Cambridge Anthropology* 16 (2): 3–21.

Tawil-Souri, Helga. 2012. "Digital Occupation: Gaza's High-Tech Enclosure." *Journal of Palestine Studies* 41 (2): 27–43.

Tomlinson, John. 1995. "Homogenisation and Globalisation." *History of European Ideas* 20 (4–6): 891–97.

————. 2002. *Cultural Imperialism: A Critical Introduction.* London: Continuum.

————. 2004. "Cultural Imperialism." In *The Globalization Reader,* edited by Frank J. Lechner and John Boli, 303–11. 2nd ed. Cambridge, MA: Harvard University Press.

UK Border Agency. 2008. *Country of Origin Information Report: Afghanistan.* Accessed May 2, 2020. https://www.statewatch.org/news/2009/mar/afghanistan-ukba-c-of-origin-report.pdf.

UK Parliament. 1999. "Minutes of Evidence Memorandum Submitted by the BBC World Service." In *Select Committee on Foreign Affairs.* London: Committee Publications. https://publications.parliament.uk/pa/cm199899/cmselect/cmfa/815/9101206.htm. Site discontinued.

United Nations Development Programme (UNDP). 2009. *Human Development Report 2009: Overcoming Barriers: Human Mobility and Development.* New York: Palgrave Macmillan. Accessed May 2, 2020. http://hdr.undp.org/sites/default/files/reports/269/hdr_2009_en_complete.pdf.

United Nations Office on Drugs and Crime (UNODC). 2010. "Corruption Widespread in Afghanistan, UNODC Survey Says." United Nations, January 19. https://www.unodc.org/unodc/en/frontpage/2010/January/corruption-widespread-in-afghanistan-unodc-survey-says.html?ref=enews190110.

United Press International (UPI). "U.N. Report on Poverty in Afghanistan." March 31, 2010, Accessed April 22, 2020. https://www.upi.com/Top_News/World-News/2010/03/31/UN-report-on-poverty-in-Afghanistan/38721270011610.

United States Government Accountability Office (GAO). 2011. *Iraq and Afghanistan: DOD, State, and USAID Cannot Fully Account for Contracts, Assistance Instruments, and Associated Personnel.* GAO.gov. Accessed May 13, 2020. https://www.gao.gov/new.items/d11886.pdf.

USAID. 2019. "Afghan Civic Engagement Program (ACEP) Overview." USAID.gov. Updated May 7, 2019. https://www.usaid.gov/news-information/fact-sheets/afghan-civic-engagement-program-acep-counterpart.

Walsh, Elizabeth. 2017. "Afghan Women Write New Narratives about Themselves, with Courage." *PassBlue: Independent Coverage of the UN,* October 24. https://www.passblue

.com/2017/10/24/afghan-women-write-new-narratives-about-themselves-with
-courage/.

Whitlock, Craig. 2020. "Afghan War Plagued by 'Mendacity' and Lies, Inspector General Tells Congress." *Washington Post*, January 15. https://www.washingtonpost.com/investigations/afghan-war-plagued-by-mendacity-and-lies-inspector-general-tells-congress/2020/01/15/c65d0d46-37b5-11ea-bf30-ad313e4ec754_story.html.

WikiLeaks. 2010. "CIA Report into Shoring Up Afghan War Support in Western Europe, 11 Mar 2010." WikiLeaks. Accessed May 2, 2020. https://wikileaks.org/wiki/CIA_report_into_shoring_up_Afghan_war_support_in Western_Europe,_11_Mar_2010.

Wild, Nicolas. 2018. *Kabul Disco: How I Managed Not to Be Abducted in Afghanistan*. Los Angeles: Humanoids, Inc.

Wilkins, Karin G. 2000. *Redeveloping Communication for Social Change: Theory, Practice, and Power*. Lanham, MD: Rowman and Littlefield.

———. 2010. "Considering 'Traditional Society' in the Middle East: Learning Lerner All Over Again." *Journal of Middle East Media* 6 (1): 62–76.

Wilkins, Karin, and Jody Waters. 2000. "Current Discourse on New Technologies in Development Communication." *Media Development* 47 (1): 57–60.

Williams, Raymond. (1974) 2003. *Television: Technology and Cultural Form*. 3rd ed. London: Routledge.

Wortham, Erica C. 2000. "News from the Mountains: Redefining the Televisual Borders of Oaxaca." *World Studio Sphere* 5 (1): 32–33.

Yesil, Bilge. 2015. "Transnationalization of Turkish Dramas: Exploring the Convergence of Local and Global Market Imperatives." *Global Media and Communication* 11 (1): 43–60.

———. 2016. *Media in New Turkey: The Origins of an Authoritarian Neoliberal State*. Champaign: University of Illinois Press.

Young, Iris Marion. 2003. "The Logic of Masculinist Protection: Reflections on the Current Security State." *Signs: Journal of Women in Culture and Society* 29 (1): 1–25.

Index

WAZHMAH OSMAN is a filmmaker and assistant professor in the Klein College of Media and Communication at Temple University. She is the codirector of the critically acclaimed documentary *Postcards from Tora Bora* and the coauthor of *Afghanistan: A Very Short Introduction*.

THE GEOPOLITICS OF INFORMATION

The University of Illinois Press
is a founding member of the
Association of University Presses.

University of Illinois Press
1325 South Oak Street
Champaign, IL 61820-6903
www.press.uillinois.edu